The Expositor's Bible
The First Epistle To
The Corinthians

By

Marcus Dods

Double9
BOOKS

The Expositor's Bible
The First Epistle To The Corinthians
by Marcus Dods

ISBN: 978-93-61157-12-7

Published by

DOUBLE 9 BOOKS

2/13-B, Ansari Road
Daryaganj, New Delhi – 110002
info@double9books.com
www.double9books.com
Tel. 011-40042856

This book is under public domain

ABOUT THE AUTHOR

Marcus Dods was a Scottish divine and controversial biblical scholar. He was a minister for the Free Church of Scotland. He was Principal of New College, Edinburgh. He was born in Belford, Northumberland, the youngest son of Rev Marcus Dods, a Church of Scotland clergyman, and his wife, Sarah Pallister. He attended Edinburgh Academy before studying divinity at Edinburgh University, where he graduated in 1854 and received his licence in 1858. He had a terrible probationary period, being turned down by 23 congregations. In 1864, he was appointed preacher of Renfield Free Church in Glasgow, where he served for 25 years. He joined the United Free Church of Scotland when it was formed in 1900, and was chosen Moderator of its General Assembly in 1902. He declined the appointment, citing that "he cannot see his way to undertake the duties". It was expected that as a neutral moderator, he would be unable to convey his views on certain doctrinal issues that were to be examined. In later life, he lived with his children and grandchildren in a massive Georgian townhouse at 23 Great King Street in Edinburgh's Second New Town.

CONTENTS

I
INTRODUCTION

Corinth was the first Gentile city in which Paul spent any considerable time. It afforded him the opportunities he sought as a preacher of Christ. Lying as it did on the famous Isthmus which connected Northern and Southern Greece, and defended by an almost impregnable citadel, it became a place of great political importance. Its position gave it also commercial advantages. Many traders bringing goods from Asia to Italy preferred to unlade at Cenchrea and carry their bales across the narrow neck of land rather than risk the dangers of doubling Cape Malea. So commonly was this done that arrangements were made for carrying the smaller ships themselves across the Isthmus on rollers; and shortly after Paul's visit Nero cut the first turf of an intended, but never finished, canal to connect the two seas.

Becoming by its situation and importance the head of the Achaian League, it bore the brunt of the conqueror's onslaught and was completely destroyed by the Roman general Mummius in the year 146 B.C. For a hundred years it lay in ruins, peopled by few but relic-hunters, who groped among the demolished temples for bits of sculpture or Corinthian brass. The all-discerning eye of Julius Cæsar, however could not overlook the excellence of the site; and accordingly he sent a colony of Roman freedmen, the most industrious of the metropolitan population, to rebuild and replenish the city. Hence the names of Corinthians mentioned in the New Testament are mainly such as betoken a Roman and servile origin, such as Gaius, Fortunatus, Justus, Crispus, Quartus, Achaicus. Under these auspices Corinth speedily regained something of its former beauty, all its former wealth, and apparently more than its original size. But the old profligacy was also to some extent revived; and in Paul's day "to live as they do at Corinth" was the equivalent for living in luxury and licentiousness. Sailors from all parts with a little money to spend, merchants eager to compensate for the privations of a voyage, refugees and adventurers of all kinds, were continually passing through the city, introducing foreign customs and confounding moral distinctions. Too plainly are the innate vices of the Corinthians reflected in this Epistle. On the stage the Corinthian was usually represented drunk, and Paul found that this characteristic vice was allowed to follow his converts even to the communion table. In the letter there are also discernible some reminiscences of what Paul had seen in the Isthmian and gladiatorial contests. He had noted, too, as he walked through Corinth, how the fire of the Roman army had consumed the meaner houses of wood, hay, stubble, but had left standing, though charred, the precious marbles.

Nowhere do we see so clearly as in this Epistle the multifarious and delicate work required of one on whom lay the care of all the Churches. A host of difficult questions poured in upon him: questions regarding conduct, questions of casuistry, questions about the ordering of public worship and social intercourse, as well as questions which struck to the very root of the Christian faith. Are we to dine with our heathen relatives? May we intermarry with those who are not yet Christian? may we marry at all? Can slaves continue in the service of heathen masters? What relation does the Communion hold to our ordinary meals? Is the man who speaks with tongues a superior kind of Christian, and must the prophet who speaks with the Spirit be allowed to interrupt other speakers? Paul in a previous letter had instructed the Corinthians on some of these points, but they had misunderstood him; and he now takes up their difficulties point by point, and finally disposes of them. Had nothing been required but the solution of practical difficulties, Paul's part had not been so delicate to play. But even through their request for advice there shone the ineradicable Greek vices of vanity, restless intellectualism, litigiousness, and sensuality. They even seemed to be on the perilous brink of glorying in a spurious liberality which could condone vices condemned by the heathen. In these circumstances the calmness and patience with which Paul pronounces on their entanglements are striking. But even more striking are the boundless intellectual vigour, the practical sagacity, the ready application to life, of the profoundest Christian principles. In reading the Epistle, one is amazed at the brevity and yet completeness with which intricate practical problems are discussed, the unerring firmness with which, through all plausible sophistry and fallacious scruples, the radical principle is laid hold of, and the sharp finality with which it is expressed. Nor is there any lack in the Epistle of the warm, rapid, and stirring eloquence which is associated with the name of Paul. It was a happy circumstance for the future of Christianity that in those early days, when there were almost as many wild suggestions and foolish opinions as there were converts, there should have been in the Church this one clear, practical judgment, this pure embodiment of the wisdom of Christianity.

It is in this Epistle we get the clearest view of the actual difficulties encountered by Christianity in a heathen community. We here see the religion of Christ confronted by the culture, and the vices, and the various social arrangements of paganism; we see the ferment and turmoil its introduction occasioned, the changes it wrought in daily life and common customs, the difficulty men honestly experienced in comprehending what their new principles required; we see how the higher aims and views of Christianity sifted the social customs of the ancient world, now allowing and now rejecting; and, above all, we see the principles on which we ourselves must proceed in solving the social and ecclesiastical difficulties that embarrass ourselves. It is in this Epistle, in short, that we see the Apostle of the Gentiles in his proper and peculiar element, exhibiting the applicability of the religion of Christ to the Gentile world and its power, not to satisfy merely the aspirations of devout Jews, but to scatter the darkness and quicken the dead soul of the pagan world.

Paul's experience in Corinth is full of significance. On arriving at Corinth, he went, as usual, to the synagogue; and when his message was rejected by the Jews, he betook himself to the Gentiles. Next door to the synagogue, in the house of a convert called Justus, the Christian congregation was founded; and, to the annoyance of the Jews, one of the rulers of the synagogue, Crispus by name, attached himself to it. The Jewish irritation and envy smouldered until a new governor came from Rome, and then it found vent. This new governor was one of the most popular men of his time, the brother of Nero's tutor, the well-known Seneca. He was himself so markedly the representative of "sweetness and light" that he was commonly spoken of as "the sweet Gallio." The Jews in Corinth evidently fancied that a man of this character would be facile and would desire to make favour with all parties in his new province. They accordingly appealed to him, but were met with a prompt and decided rebuff. Their new governor assured them he had no jurisdiction over such questions. As soon as he hears it is not a matter in which the property or persons of his lieges is implicated he bids his lictors clear the court. The rabble that always gathers round a courthouse, seeing a Jew ignominiously dismissed, set upon him and beat him under the very eye of the judge, the beginning of that furious, unreasoning, brutal outrage which has pursued the Jews in all countries of Christendom.

Gallio has become the synonym for religious indifference. We call the easy-going, good-natured man who meets all your religious appeals with a shrug of the shoulders or a genial, bantering answer a Gallio. This is perhaps a little hard upon Gallio, who no doubt attended to his own religion in much the same spirit as his friends. When the narrative says that "he cared for none of those things," it means that he gave no heed to what seemed a common street brawl. It is rather the haughtiness of the Roman proconsul than the indifference of the man of the world that appears in his conduct. These squabbles among Jews about matters of their law were not affairs he could stoop to investigate or was by his office required to investigate.

And yet it is not Gallio's proconsulship of Achaia nor his relationship to Roman celebrities that has made his name familiar to the modern world, but his connection with these wretched Jews that appeared before his small chair that morning. In Paul's little, insignificant, worn figure it was not to be expected he should see anything so remarkable as to stimulate inquiry; he could not have comprehended that the chief connection in which his name would afterwards appear would be in connection with Paul; and yet had he but known, had he but interested himself in what evidently so deeply interested his new subjects, how different might his own history have become, and how different, too, the history of Christianity. But filled with a Roman's disdain for questions of which the sword could not cut the knot, and with a Roman's reluctance to implicate himself with anything which was not sufficiently of this world to be adjusted by Roman law, he cleared his court and called the next case. The "sweet Gallio," patient and affable to every other kind of complainant, had nothing but disdain and undisguised repugnance for these Eastern dreamers. The Roman, who could sympathize with almost every nationality and find room for all men in the wide lap of the empire, made himself detested in the East by his harsh contempt for mysticism and religion, and was met by a disdain deeper than his own.

"The brooding East with awe beheld
Her impious younger world;
The Roman tempest swelled and swelled,
And on her head was hurled:

The East bowed low before the blast
In patient, deep disdain;
She let the legions thunder past,
And plunged in thought again."

Now in the Englishman there is much that closely resembles the Roman character. There is the same ability for practical achievement, the same capacity for conquest and for making much of conquered peoples, the same reverence for law, the same faculty for dealing with the world and the human race as it actually is! the same relish for and mastery of the present system of things. But along with these qualities there go in both races their natural defects: a tendency to forget the ideal and the unseen in the seen and the actual; to measure all things by material standards; to be more deeply impressed with the conquests of the sword than with those of the Spirit, and with the gains that are counted in coin rather than with those that are seen in character; and to be far more intensely interested in whatever concerns politics than in anything that concerns religion. So pronounced is this materialistic, or at any rate worldly, tendency in this country, that it has been formulated into a system for the conduct of life, under the name of secularism. And so popular has this system become, especially among working-men, that the chief promoter of it believes that his adherents may be numbered by hundreds of thousands.

The essential idea of secularism is "that precedence should be given to the duties of this life over those which pertain to another life," the reason being that this life is the first in certainty, and should therefore be the first in importance. Mr. Holyoake carefully states his position in these words: "We do not say that every man ought to give an *exclusive* attention to this world, because that would be to commit the old sin of dogmatism, and exclude the possibility of another world and of walking by different light from that by which alone we are able to walk. But as our *knowledge* is confined to this life, and testimony, and conjecture, and probability are all that can be set forth with respect to another life, we think we are justified in giving *precedence* to the duties of this state and of attaching primary importance to the morality of man to man." This statement has the merit of being undogmatic, but it is in consequence proportionately vague. If a man is not to give *exclusive* attention to this world, how much attention is he to give to another? Would Mr. Holyoake think the amount of attention most Christians give to the other world excessive? If so, the attention he thinks suitable must be limited indeed.

But if this theoretical statement, framed in view of the exigencies of controversy, be scarcely intelligible, the position of the practical secularist is perfectly intelligible. He says to himself, I have occupations and duties now that require all my strength; and if there is another world, the best preparation for it I can have is to do thoroughly and with all my strength the duties now pressing upon me. Most of us have felt the attraction of this position. It has a sound of candid, manly common-sense, and appeals to the English character in us, to our esteem for what is practical. Besides, it is perfectly true that the best preparation for any future world is to do thoroughly well the duties of our present state. But the whole question remains, What *are* the duties of the present state? These can not be determined unless we come to some decision as to the truth or untruth of Christianity. If there is a God, it is not merely in the future, but now, that we have duties to Him, that all our duties are tinged with the idea of His presence and of our relation to Him. It is absurd to defer all consideration of God to a future world; God is as much in this world as in any: and if so, our whole life, in every part of it, must be, not a secular, but a godly, life—a life we live well and can only live well when we live it in fellowship with Him. The mind that can divide life into duties of the present and duties that concern the future entirely misapprehends the teaching of Christianity, and misconceives what life is.

If a man does not know whether there is a God, then he cannot know what his present duties are, neither can he do these duties as he ought. He may do them better than I can; but he does not do them as well as he himself could were he owning the presence and accepting the gracious, sanctifying influences of the Divine Spirit.

To the help of secularism comes also in our case another influence, which told with Gallio. Even the gentle and affable Gallio felt annoyed that so squalid a case should be among the first that came before him in Achaia. He had left Rome with the good wishes of the Imperial Court, had made a triumphal procession of several weeks to Corinth, had been installed there with all the pomp that Roman officials, military and civil, could devise; he had been met and acknowledged by the authorities, had sworn in his new officers, had caused his tesselated pavement to be laid and his chair of state set down: and as if in mockery of all this ceremony and display of power came this pitiful squabble from the synagogue, a matter of which not a man of standing in his court knew or cared anything, a matter in which Jews and slaves alone were interested. Christianity has always found its warmest supporters in the lower strata of society. It has not always been quite respectable. And here again Englishmen are like Romans: they are strongly influenced by what is respectable, by what has position and standing in the world. If Christianity were zealously promoted by princes, and leading officials, and distinguished professors and writers of genius, how much easier would it be to accept it; but its most zealous promoters are so commonly men of no education, men with odd names, men whose grammar and pronunciation put them beyond the pale of good society, men whose methods are rough and whose views are unphilosophical and crude. As in Corinth, so now, not many wise, not many mighty, not many noble, are called; and we must beware therefore of shrinking, as Gallio did, from what is essentially the most powerful agent for good in the world because it is so often found with vulgar and repulsive adjuncts. The earthen vessels, as Paul reminds us, the pots of coarsest clay, chipped and crusted with coarse contact with the world, may yet hold treasure of priceless value.

It is always a question how far we should endeavour to become all things to all men, to win the wise of this world by presenting Christianity as a philosophy, and to win the well-born and cultured by presenting it in the dress of an attractive style. Paul as he left Athens, where he had met with so little success, was apparently exercised with this same question. He had tried to meet the Athenians on their own ground, showing his familiarity with their writers; but he seems to think that at Corinth another method may be more successful, and, as he tells them, "I determined to know nothing among you save Jesus Christ and Him crucified." It was, he says, with much fear and trembling he adopted this course; he was weak and dispirited at the time, at any rate; and it is plain that his resolve to abandon all such appeals as might tell with rhetoricians cost him an effort and made a deep impression upon him. He himself saw so clearly the foolishness of the Cross; he knew so well what a field for mockery was presented to the Greek mind by the preaching of salvation through a crucified person. He was very conscious of the poor appearance he made as a speaker among these fluent Greeks, whose ears were as cultivated as musicians', and whose sense of beauty, trained by seeing their picked young men contend in the games, received a shock from "his weak and contemptible bodily presence," as they called it. Yet, all things considered, he made up his mind that he would trust his success to the simple statement of facts. He would preach "Christ and Him crucified." He would tell them what Jesus had been and done. He felt jealous of anything which might attract men to his preaching save the Cross of Christ. And he was more successful in Corinth than he had been elsewhere. In that profligate city he was obliged to stay eighteen months, because the work so grew under his hand.

And so it has ever been since. As matter of fact, it is not Christ's teaching, but His death, which has kindled the enthusiasm and the devotion of men. It is this which has conquered and won them, and delivered them from the bondage of self, and set them in a larger world. It is when we believe that this Person has loved us with a love stronger than death that we become His. It is when we can use Paul's words "who loved me and gave Himself for me" that we feel, as Paul felt, the constraining power of this love. It is this that forms between the soul and Christ that secret tie which has been the strength and happiness of so many lives. If our own life is neither strong nor happy, it is because we are not admitting the love of Christ, and are striving to live independently of Him who is our Life. Christ is the perennial fountain of love, of hopefulness, of true spiritual life. In Him there is enough to purify, and brighten, and sustain all human life. Brought into contact with the intellectualism and the vice of Corinth, the love of Christ proved its reality and its overcoming strength; and when we bring it into contact with ourselves, burdened, and perplexed, and tempted as we are, we find that still it is the power of God unto salvation.

THE CHURCH IN CORINTH

"Paul, called to be an apostle of Jesus Christ through the will of God, and Sosthenes our brother, unto the church of God which is at Corinth, to them that are sanctified in Christ Jesus, called to be saints, with all that in every place call upon the name of Jesus Christ our Lord, both their's and our's: Grace be unto you, and peace, from God our Father, and from the Lord Jesus Christ. I thank my God always on your behalf, for the grace of God which is given you by Jesus Christ; that in everything ye are enriched by him, in all utterance, and in all knowledge: even as the testimony of Christ was confirmed in you: so that ye come behind in no gift; waiting for the coming of our Lord Jesus Christ: who shall also confirm you unto the end, that ye may be blameless in the day of our Lord Jesus Christ. God is faithful, by whom ye were called unto the fellowship of His Son Jesus Christ our Lord."—1 Cor. i. 2-9.

II
THE CHURCH IN CORINTH

In the year 58 A.D., when Paul wrote this Epistle, Corinth was a city with a mixed population, and conspicuous for the turbulence and immorality commonly found in seaports frequented by traders and seamen from all parts of the world. Paul had received letters from some of the Christians in Corinth which disclosed a state of matters in the Church far from desirable. He had also more particular accounts from some members of Chloe's household who were visiting Ephesus, and who told him how sadly disturbed the little community of Christians was by party spirit and scandals in life and worship.

In the letter itself the designation of the writer and of those addressed first claims our attention.

The writer identifies himself as "Paul, an Apostle of Jesus Christ by call, through the will of God." An Apostle is one sent, as Christ was sent by the Father. "As the Father sent Me, even so send I you." It was therefore an office no one could take to himself, nor was it the promotion resulting from previous service. To the apostleship the sole entrance was through the call of Christ; and in virtue of this call Paul became, as he says, an Apostle. And it is this which explains one of the most prominent of his characteristics: the singular combination of humility and authority, of self-depreciation and self-assertion. He is filled with a sense of his own unworthiness; he is "less than the least of the Apostles," "not worthy to be called an Apostle." On the other hand, he never hesitates to command the Churches, to rebuke the foremost man in the Church, to assert his claim to be listened to as the ambassador of Christ.

This extraordinary humility and equally remarkable boldness and authority had one common root in his perception that it was through Christ's call and by God's will he was an Apostle. The work of going to all the busiest parts of the world and proclaiming Christ was to his mind far too great a work for him to aspire to at his own instance. He could never have aspired to such a position as this gave him. But God called him to it; and, with this authority at his back, he feared nothing, neither hardship nor defeat.

And this is for us all the true and eternal source of humility and confidence. Let a man feel sure that he is called of God to do what he is doing, let him be fully persuaded in his own mind that the course he follows is God's will for him, and he will press on undauntedly, even though opposed. It is altogether a new strength with which a man is inspired when he is made conscious that God calls him to do this or that, when behind conscience or the plain requirements of human affairs and circumstances the presence of the living God makes itself felt. Well may we exclaim, with one who had to stand alone and follow a solitary path, conscious only of God's approval, and sustained by that consciousness against the disapproval of all, "Oh that we could take that simple view of things as to feel that the one thing which lies before us is to please God! What gain is it to please the world, to please the great, nay even to please those whom we love, compared with this? What gain is it to be applauded, admired, courted, followed, compared with this one aim of not being disobedient to a heavenly vision?"

In addressing the Church at Corinth, Paul unites with himself a Christian called Sosthenes. This was the name of the chief ruler of the synagogue at Corinth who was beaten by the Greeks in Gallio's court, and it is not impossible that it was he who was now with Paul in Ephesus. If so, this would account for his being associated with Paul in writing to Corinth. What share in the letter Sosthenes actually had it is impossible to say. He may have written it to Paul's dictation; he may have suggested here and there a point to be touched upon. Certainly Paul's easy assumption of a friend as joint writer of the letter sufficiently shows that he had no such stiff and formal idea of inspiration as we have. Apparently he did not stay to inquire whether Sosthenes was qualified to be the author of a canonical book; but knowing the authoritative position he had held among the Jews of Corinth, he naturally conjoins his name with his own in addressing the new Christian community.

The persons to whom this letter is addressed are identified as "the Church of God which is at Corinth." With them are joined in character, if not as recipients of this letter, "all that in every place call upon the name of Jesus Christ our Lord." And therefore we should perhaps not be far wrong if we were to gather from this that Paul would have defined the Church as the company of all those persons who "call upon the name of Jesus Christ." Calling upon the name of any one implies trust in him; and those who call upon the name of Jesus Christ are those who look up to Christ as their supreme Lord, able to supply all their need. It is this belief in one Lord which brings men together as a Christian Church.

But at once we are confronted with the difficulty that many persons who call upon the name of the Lord do so with no inward conviction of their need, and consequently with no real dependence upon Christ or allegiance to Him. In other words, the apparent Church is not the real Church. Hence the distinction between the Church visible, which consists of all who nominally or outwardly belong to the Christian community, and the Church invisible, which consists of those who inwardly and really are the subjects and people of Christ. Much confusion of thought is avoided by keeping in mind this obvious distinction. In the Epistles of Paul it is sometimes the ideal, invisible Church which is addressed or spoken of; sometimes it is the actual, visible Church, imperfect, stained with unsightly blots, calling for rebuke and correction. Where the visible Church is, and of whom composed, we can always say; its members can be counted, its property estimated, its history written. But of the invisible Church no man can fully write the history, or name the members, or appraise its properties, gifts, and services.

From the earliest times it has been customary to say that the true Church must be one, holy, catholic, and apostolic. That is true if the Church invisible be meant. The true body of Christ, the company of persons who in all countries and ages have called upon Christ and served Him, do form one, holy, catholic, and apostolic Church. But it is not true of the Church visible and disastrous consequences have at various times followed the attempt to ascertain by the application of these notes which actual visible Church has the best claim to be considered the true Church.

Without concerning himself explicitly to describe the distinguishing features of the true Church, Paul here gives us four notes which must always be found[1]: —

1. Consecration. The Church is composed of "them that have been sanctified in Christ Jesus."

2. Holiness: "called to be saints."

3. Universality: "all that in every place call on the name," etc.

4. Unity: "both their Lord and ours."

1. The true Church is, first of all, composed of consecrated people. The word "sanctify" bears here a somewhat different meaning from that which we commonly attach to it. It means rather that which is set apart or destined to holy uses than that which has been made holy. It is in this meaning the word is used by our Lord when He says, "For your sakes I sanctify"—or set apart—"Myself." The Church by its very existence is a body of men and women set apart for a holy use. The New Testament word for Church, *ecclesia*, means a society "called out" from among other men. It exists not for common purposes, but to witness for God and for Christ, to maintain before the eyes and in all the common ways and works of men the ideal

life realized in Christ and the presence and holiness of God. It becomes those who form the Church to meet God's purpose in calling them out of the world and to consider themselves as devoted and set apart to attain that purpose. Their destination is no longer that of the world; and a spirit set upon the attainment of the joys and advantages the world gives is wholly out of place in them.

2. More particularly those who compose the Church are called to be "saints." Holiness is the unmistakable characteristic of the true Church. The glory of God, inseparable from His essence, is His holiness, His eternally willing and doing only what is the very best. To think of God as doing wrong is blasphemy. Were God even once to do other than the best and right, the loving and just thing, He would cease to be God. It is the task of the Church to exhibit in human life and character this holiness of God's. Those whom God calls into His Church, He calls to be, above all else, holy.

The Church of Corinth was in some danger of forgetting this. One of its members in particular had been guilty of a scandalous breach even of the heathen code of morals; and of him Paul uncompromisingly says, "Put away from among yourselves that wicked person." Even with sinners of a less flagrant sort, no communion was to be held. "If any man that is called a brother"—that is, claiming to be a Christian—"be a fornicator, or covetous, or an idolater, or a railer, or a drunkard, or an extortioner, with such a one you must not even eat." No doubt there is risk and difficulty in administering this law. The graver hidden sin may be overlooked, the more obvious and venial transgression be punished. But the duty of the Church to maintain its sanctity is undeniable, and those who act for the Church must do their best in spite of all difficulty and risk.

The prime duty, however, lies with the members, not with the rulers, in the Church. Those whose function it is to watch over the purity of the Church would be saved from all doubtful action were the individual members alive to the necessity of holy living. This, they should bear in mind, is the very object of the Church's existence and of their being in it.

3. Thirdly, it is ever to be borne in mind that the true Church of Christ is to be found, not in one country nor in one age, not in this or that Church, whether it assume the title of "Catholic" or pride itself on being national, but is composed of "all that in every place call upon the name of our Lord Jesus Christ." Happily the time is gone by when with any show of reason any one Church can claim to be catholic on the ground of its being coextensive with Christendom. It is true that Cardinal Newman, one of the most striking figures and probably the greatest Churchman of our own generation, attached himself to the Church of Rome on this very ground:

that it possessed this note of catholicity. To his eye, accustomed to survey the fortunes and growth of Christ's Church during the early and mediæval centuries, it seemed that the Church of Rome alone had any reasonable claim to be considered the Church catholic. But he was betrayed, as others have been, by confounding the Church visible with the Church invisible. No one visible Church can claim to be the Church catholic. Catholicity is not a matter of more or less; it cannot be determined by a majority. No Church which does not claim to contain the whole of Christ's people without exception can claim to be catholic. Probably there are some who accept this alternative, and do not see it to be absurd to claim for any one existing Church that it is coextensive with the Church of Christ.

4. The fourth note of the Church here implied is its unity. The Lord of all the Churches is one Lord; in this allegiance they centre, and by it are held together in a true unity. Plainly this note can belong only to the Church invisible, and not to that multifarious collection of incoherent fragments known as the visible Church. It is indeed doubtful whether a visible unity is desirable. Considering what human nature is and how liable men are to be overawed and imposed upon by what is large, it is probably quite as conducive to the spiritual well-being of the Church that she is broken up into parts. Outward divisions into national Churches and Churches under different forms of government and holding various creeds would sink into insignificance, and be no more bewailed than the division of an army into regiments, were there the real unity which springs from true allegiance to the common Lord and zeal for the common cause rather than for the interests of our own particular Church. When the generous rivalry exhibited by some of our regiments in battle passes into envy, unity is destroyed; and indeed the attitude sometimes assumed towards sister-Churches is rather that of hostile armies than of rival regiments striving which can do most honour to the common flag. One of the hopeful signs of our times is that this is generally understood. Christian people are beginning to see how much more important are those points on which the whole Church is agreed than those often obscure or trivial points which split the Church into sects. Churches are beginning to own with some sincerity that there are Christian gifts and graces in all Churches, and that no one Church comprises all the excellences of Christendom. And the only outward unity that is worth having is that which springs from inward unity, from a genuine respect and regard for all who own the same Lord and spend themselves in His service.

Paul, with his usual courtesy and instinctive tact, introduces what he has to say with a hearty acknowledgment of the distinctive excellences of the Corinthian Church: "I thank my God always on your behalf, for the grace of God which is given you in Christ Jesus, that in everything ye have been enriched in Him, in all utterance and in all knowledge, even as the testimony of Christ was confirmed in you." Paul was one of those large-natured men who rejoice more in the prosperity of others than in any private good fortune. The envious soul is glad when things go no better with others than with himself, but the generous and unselfish are lifted out of their own woes by their sympathy with the happy. Paul's joy—and it was no mean or shallow joy—was to see the testimony he had borne to Christ's goodness and power confirmed by the new energies and capacities which were developed in those who believed his testimony. The gifts which the Christians in Corinth exhibited made it manifest that the Divine presence and power proclaimed by Paul were real. His testimony regarding the risen but unseen Lord was confirmed by the fact that those who believed this testimony and called upon the name of the Lord received gifts not previously enjoyed by them. Further argument regarding the actual and present power of the unseen Lord was needless in Corinth. And in our day it is the new life of believers which most strongly confirms the testimony regarding the risen Christ. Every one who attaches himself to the Church either damages or aids the cause of Christ, propagates either belief or unbelief. In the Corinthians Paul's testimony regarding Christ was confirmed by their reception of the rare gifts of utterance and knowledge. It is indeed somewhat ominous that the incorruptible honesty of Paul can only acknowledge their possession of "gifts," not of those fine Christian graces which distinguished the Thessalonians and others of his converts. But the grace of God must always adjust itself to the nature of the recipient; it fulfils itself by means of the material which nature furnishes: The Greek nature was at all times lacking in seriousness, and had attained little moral robustness; but for many centuries it had been trained to admire and excel in intellectual and oratorical displays. The natural gifts of the Greek race were quickened and directed by grace. Their intellectual inquisitiveness and apprehensiveness enabled them to throw light on the grounds and results of the Christian facts; and their fluent and flexible speech formed a new wealth and a more worthy employment in their endeavours to formulate Christian truth and exhibit Christian experience. Each race has its own contribution to make to complete and full-grown Christian manhood. Each race has its own gifts; and only when grace has developed all these gifts in a Christian direction can we actually see the fitness of Christianity for all men and the wealth of the nature and work of Christ, which can appeal to and best develop all.

Paul thanked God for their gift of utterance. Perhaps had he lived now, within sound of an utterance dizzying and ceaseless as the roar of Niagara, he might have had a word to say in praise of silence. There is more than a risk nowadays that talk take the place of thought on the one hand and of action on the other. But it could not fail to occur to Paul that this Greek utterance, with the instrument it had in the Greek language, was a great gift to the Church. In no other language could he have found such adequate, intelligible, and beautiful expression for the new ideas to which Christianity gave birth. And in this new gift of utterance among the Corinthians he may have seen promise of a rapid and effective propagation of the Gospel. For indeed there are few more valuable gifts the Church can receive than utterance. Legitimately may we hope for the Church when she so apprehends her own wealth in Christ as to be stirred to invite all the world to share with her, when through all her members she feels the pressure of thoughts that demand utterance, or when there arise in her even one or two persons with the rare faculty of swaying large audiences, and touching the common human heart, and lodging in the public mind some germinant ideas. New epochs in the Church's life are made by the men who speak, not to satisfy the expectation of an audience, but because they are driven by an inward compelling force, not because they are called upon to say something, but because they have that in them which they must say.

But utterance is well backed by knowledge. Not always has it been remembered that Paul recognises knowledge as a gift of God. Often, on the contrary, has the determination to satisfy the intellect with Christian truth been reprehended as idle and even wicked. To the Corinthians the Christian revelation was new, and inquiring minds, could not but endeavour to harmonize the various facts it conveyed. This attempt to understand Christianity was approved. The exercise of the human reason upon Divine things was encouraged. The faith which accepted testimony was a gift of God, but so also was the knowledge which sought to recommend the contents of this testimony to the human mind.

But however rich in endowments the Corinthians were, they could not but feel, in common with all other men, that no endowment can lift us above the necessity of conflict with sin or put us beyond the hazard which that conflict entails. In point of fact, richly endowed men are often most exposed to temptation, and feel more keenly than others the real hazard of human life. Paul therefore concludes this brief introduction by assigning the reason of his assurance that they will be blameless in the day of Christ; and that reason is that God is in the matter: "God is faithful, by whom ye were called unto the fellowship of His Son Jesus Christ our Lord." God calls us with a purpose in view, and is faithful to that purpose. He calls us to the fellowship of Christ that we may learn of Him and become suitable agents to carry out the whole will of Christ. To fear that, notwithstanding our hearty desire to become of Christ's mind and notwithstanding all our efforts to enter more deeply into His fellowship, we shall yet fail, is to reflect upon God as either insincere in His call or inconstant. The gifts and calling of God are without repentance. They are not revoked on further consideration. God's invitation comes to us, and is not withdrawn, even though it is not met with the hearty acceptance it deserves. All our obstinacy in sin, all our blindness to our true advantage, all our lack of anything like generous self-devotion, all our frivolity, and folly, and worldliness, are understood before the call is given. By calling us into the fellowship of His Son God guarantees to us the possibility of our entering into that fellowship and of becoming fit for it.

Let us then revive our hopes and renew our belief in the worth of life by remembering that we are called to the fellowship of Jesus Christ. This is satisfying; all else that calls us in life is defective and incomplete. Without this fellowship with what is holy and eternal, all we find in life seems trivial or is embittered to us by the fear of loss. In worldly pursuits there is excitement; but when the fire burns out, and the cold ashes remain, chill and blank desolation is the portion of the man whose all has been the world. We cannot reasonably and deliberately choose the world; we may be carried away by greed, or carnality, or earthliness to seek its pleasures, but our reason and our better nature cannot approve the choice. Still less does our reason approve that what we cannot deliberately choose we should yet allow ourselves to be governed by and actually join in fellowship of the closest kind. Believe in God's call, listen to it, strive to maintain yourself in the fellowship of Christ, and every year will tell you that God, who has called you, is faithful and is bringing you nearer and nearer to what is stable, happy, and satisfying.

THE FACTIONS

"Now I beseech you, brethren, by the name of our Lord Jesus Christ, that ye all speak the same thing, and that there be no divisions among you; but that ye be perfectly joined together in the same mind and in the same judgment. For it hath been declared unto me of you, my brethren, by them which are of the house of Chloe, that there are contentions among you. Now this I say, that every one of you saith, I am of Paul; and I of Apollos; and I of Cephas; and I of Christ. Is Christ divided? was Paul crucified for you? or were ye baptized in the name of Paul? I thank God that I baptized none of you, but Crispus and Gaius; lest any should say that I had baptized in mine own name. And I baptized also the household of Stephanas: besides, I know not whether I baptized any other." —1 Cor. i. 10-16.

III
THE FACTIONS

The first section of this Epistle, extending from the tenth verse of the first chapter to the end of the fourth chapter, is occupied with an endeavour to quench the factious spirit which had shown itself in the Corinthian Church. Paul, with his accustomed frankness, tells the Corinthians from whom he had received information regarding them. Some members of the household of Chloe who were then in Ephesus were his informants. Chloe was evidently a woman well known in Corinth, and probably was resident there, although it has with some reason been remarked that it "is more in harmony with St. Paul's discretion to suppose that she was an Ephesian known to the Corinthians, whose people had been in Corinth and returned to Ephesus."[2] The danger of this factious spirit, which in subsequent ages has so grievously weakened the Church and hindered her work, seemed to Paul so urgent that he abruptly adjured them to unity of sentiment and of confession by that name which was at once "the bond of union and the most holy name by which they could be entreated." Before speaking of the important topics he wished to discuss, he must first of all give them to understand that he does not write to a party, but seeks to win the ear of a whole and united Church.

The parties in the Corinthian Church had not as yet outwardly separated from one another. The members were known as belonging to this or that party, but they worshipped together and had not as yet renounced one another's communion. They differed in doctrine, but their faith in one Lord held them together.

Of these parties Paul names four. There were first of all those who held by Paul himself and the aspect of the Gospel he had presented. They owed to him their own salvation; and having experienced the efficacy of his gospel, they could not believe that there was any other efficacious mode of presenting Christ to men. And gradually they became more concerned to uphold Paul's authority than to help the cause of Christ. They probably fell into the mistake to which all mere partisans are liable, and became more Pauline than Paul himself, magnifying his peculiarities and attaching importance to casual sayings and private practices of his which were in themselves indifferent. There was apparently some danger that they might become more Pauline than Christian, should allow their indebtedness to Paul to obscure their debt to Christ, and should so pride themselves in the teacher as to neglect the thing taught.

There was a second party, grouped round Apollos. This learned and eloquent Alexandrian had come to Corinth after Paul left, and what Paul had planted he so successfully watered that many seemed to owe everything to him. Until he came and fitted the Gospel into their previous knowledge, and showed them its relations to other faiths, and opened up to them its ethical wealth and bearing on life, they had been unable to make full use of Paul's teaching. He had sown the seed in their minds; they had owned the truth of his statements and accepted them; but until they heard Apollos they could not lay hold on the truth with sufficient definiteness, and could not boldly act upon it. The teaching of Apollos was not opposed to Paul's, but supplementary of it. At the end of this letter Paul tells the Corinthians that he had asked Apollos to revisit them, but Apollos had refused, and refused very probably because he was aware that a party had been formed in his name, and that his presence in Corinth would only foster and increase it. It is obvious therefore that there was no jealousy between Paul and Apollos themselves, whatever rivalry might exist among their followers.

The third party gloried in the name of Cephas; that is, Peter, the Apostle of the circumcision. It is possible that Peter had been in Corinth, but it is not necessary to suppose so. His name was used in opposition to Paul's as representing the original group of Apostles who had companied with the Lord in His lifetime, and who adhered to the observance of the Jewish law. How far the party of Cephas in Corinth indulged in disparagement of Paul's authority we cannot exactly say. There are indications, however, in the Epistle that they cited against him even his self-denial, arguing that he did not dare either to ask the Church to maintain him or to marry, as Peter had done, because he felt that his claim to be an Apostle was insecure. It may be imagined how painful it must have been for a high-minded man like Paul to be compelled to defend himself against such accusations, and with what mingled indignation and shame he must have written the words, "Have we not power to lead about a sister, a wife, as well as other Apostles, and as the brethren of the Lord and Cephas? Or I only and Barnabas, have not we power to forbear working?" This party then had in it more dangerous elements than the party of Apollos. Extreme Judaizers would find among its members a soil prepared for their apparently conservative and orthodox but really obstructive and pernicious teaching.

Of the fourth party, which named itself "of Christ," we learn more in the Second Epistle than in the First. From a striking and powerful outburst in that Epistle (2 Cor. x. 7-xii. 18), it would appear that the Christ party was formed and led by men who prided themselves on their Hebrew descent (xi. 22), and on having learned their Christianity, not from Paul, Apollos, or Cephas, but from Christ Himself (1 Cor. i. 12; 2 Cor. x. 7). These men came to Corinth with letters of commendation (2 Cor. iii. 1), probably from Palestine, as they had known Jesus, but not from the Apostles in Jerusalem, for they separated themselves from the Petrine party in Corinth. They claimed to be apostles of Christ (2 Cor. xi. 13) and "ministers of righteousness" (xi. 15); but as they taught "another Jesus," "another spirit," "another gospel" (xi. 4), Paul does not hesitate to denounce them as false apostles and ironically to hold them up as "out-and-out apostles." As yet, however, at the date of the First Epistle, they had either not so plainly shown their true colours, or Paul was not aware of all the evil they were doing.

The Apostle hears of these four parties with dismay. What then would he think of the state of the Church now? There was as yet in Corinth no schism, no secession, no outward disruption of the Church; and indeed Paul does not seem to contemplate as possible that which in our day is the normal condition: a Church broken up into little sections, each of which worships by itself, and looks upon the rest with some distrust or contempt. It did not as yet appear possible that the members of the one body of Christ should refuse to worship their common Lord in fellowship with one another and in one place. The evils attaching to such a condition of things may no doubt be unduly magnified; but we are probably more inclined to overlook than to magnify the mischief done by disunion in the Church. The Church was intended to be the grand uniter of the race. Within its pale all kinds of men were to be gathered. Distinctions were to be obliterated; differences were to be forgotten; the deepest thoughts and interests of all men were to be recognised as common; there was to be neither Jew nor Gentile, Greek nor barbarian, bond nor free. But instead of uniting men otherwise alienated, the Church has alienated neighbours and friends; and men who will do business together, who will dine together, will not worship together. Thus the Church has lost a large part of her strength. Had the kingdom of Christ been visibly one, it would have been supreme and without a rival in the world. Had there been union where there has been division, the rule and influence of Christ would have so far surpassed every other influence that peace and truth, right and justice, godliness and mercy, would have everywhere reigned. But instead of this the strength of the Church has been frittered away in civil strife and party warfare, her ablest men have spent themselves in controversy, and through division her influence has become insignificant. The world looks on and laughs while it sees the Church divided against itself and wrangling over petty differences while it ought to be assailing vice, ungodliness, and ignorance. And yet schism is thought no sin; and that which the Reformers shuddered at and shrank from, that secession which they feared to make even from a Church so corrupt as that of Rome then was, every petty ecclesiastic now presumes to initiate.

Now that the Church is broken into pieces, perhaps the first step towards a restoration of true unity is to recognise that there may be real union without unity of external organization. In other words, it is quite possible that Churches which have individually a separate corporate existence—say the Presbyterian, Independent, and Episcopalian Churches—may be one in the New Testament sense. The human race is one; but this unity admits of numberless varieties and diversities in appearance, in colour, in language, and of endless subordinate divisions into races, tribes, and nations. So the Church may be truly one, one in the sense intended by our Lord, one in the *unity of the Spirit* and the bond of peace, though there continue to be various divisions and sects. It may very well be argued that, constituted as human nature is, the Church, like every other society or institution, will be the better of a competing, if not an opposing, rival; that schism, divisions, sects, are necessary evils; that truth will be more thoroughly investigated, discipline more diligently and justly maintained, useful activities more vigorously engaged in, if there be rival Churches than if there be one. And it is certainly true that, so far as man can foresee, there is no possibility, not to say prospect, of the Church of Christ becoming one vast visible organization. Oneness in that sense is prevented by the very same obstacles that hinder all States and governments on earth from being merged into one great kingdom. But as amidst all diversities of government and customs it is the duty of States to remember and maintain their common brotherhood and abstain from tyranny, oppression, and war, so it is the duty of Churches, however separate in creed or form of government, to maintain and exhibit their unity. If the sects of the Church will frankly and cordially recognise one another as parts of the same whole, if they will exhibit their relationship by combining in good works, by an interchange of ecclesiastical civilities, by aiding one another when aid is needed, this is, I conceive, real union. Certainly Churches which see it to be their duty to maintain a separate existence ought to be equally careful to maintain a real unity with all other Churches.

Again, it is to be borne in mind that there may be real union without unity in creed. As Churches may be truly one though, for the sake of convenience or of some conscientious scruple, they maintain a separate existence, so the unity required in the New Testament is not uniformity of belief in respect to all articles of faith. This uniformity is desirable; it is desirable that all men know the truth. Paul here and elsewhere entreats his readers to endeavour to agree and be of one mind. It is quite true that the Church has gained much by difference of opinion. It is true that were all men to be agreed there might be a danger of truth becoming lifeless and forgotten for want of the stimulus it derives from assault, and discussion, and cross-questioning. It is undoubtedly the fact that doctrine has been ascertained and developed precisely in proportion and in answer to the errors and mistakes of heretics; and were all assault and opposition even now to cease, there might be some danger of a lifeless treatment of truth ensuing. And yet no one can desire that men be in error; no one can wish heresies to multiply that the Church may be stimulated. A visitation of cholera may result in cleanliness and carefulness, but no one desires that cholera may come. Opposition in Parliament is an acknowledged service to the country, yet each party desires that its sentiments become universal. So, too, notwithstanding every good result which may flow from diversity of opinion regarding Divine truth, agreement and unanimity are what all should aim at. We may even see reason to believe that men will never all think alike; we may think that it is not in the nature of things that men of diverse natural disposition, diverse experience and upbringing, should think the same thing; if it is true, as a great thinker has said, that "our system of thought is very often only the history of our heart," then the effort to bring men to precise uniformity of thought is hopeless: and yet this effort must be made. No man who believes he has found the truth can forbear disseminating it to the utmost of his ability. If his favourite views are opposed in conversation, he does what he can to convince and make converts of his antagonists. There is truth, there is a right and a wrong, and it is not all the same whether we know the truth or are in error; and doctrine is simply truth expressed: and though the whole truth may not be expressed, yet even this partial expression of it may be much safer and nearer what we ought to believe than some current denial of the truth. Paul wishes people to believe certain things, not as if then they would be fully enlightened, but because so far they will be enlightened and so far defended against error.

But the question remains, What truths are to be made terms of communion? Is schism or secession ever justifiable on the ground that error is taught in the Church?

This is a question most difficult to answer. The Church of Christ is formed of those who are trusting to Him as the power of God unto salvation. He is in communion with all who thus trust Him, whether their knowledge be great or small; and we cannot refuse to communicate with those with whom He is in communion. And it may very reasonably be questioned whether any part of the Church has a right to identify herself with a creed which past experience proves that the whole Church will never adopt, and which therefore necessarily makes her schismatic and sectarian. As manifestoes or didactic summaries of truth, confessions of faith may be very useful. Systematic knowledge is at all times desirable; and as a backbone to which all the knowledge we acquire may be attached a catechism or confession of faith is part of the necessary equipment of a Church. But no doctrinal error which does not subvert personal faith in Christ should be allowed to separate Churches. Theology must not be made more of than Christianity. We cannot pay too much attention to doctrine or too earnestly contend for the faith; we cannot too anxiously seek to have and to disseminate clear views of truth: but if we make our clear views a reason for quarrelling with other Christians and a bar to our fellowship with them, we forget that Christ is more than doctrine and charity better than knowledge.

Paul certainly was contemplating Christ, and not a creed, as the principle and centre of the Church's unity, when he exclaimed, "Is Christ divided?" The indivisible unity of Christ Himself is in Paul's mind the sufficient argument for the unity of the Church. If you can divide the one Christ, and if one Church can live on one part, another on another, then you may have several Churches; but if there be one Christ indivisible, then is there but one Church indivisible. In all Christians and in all Churches the one Christ is the life of each. And it is monstrous that those who are vitally united to one Person and quickened by one Spirit should in no way recognise their unity.

It is with something akin to horror that Paul goes on to ask, "Was Paul crucified for you?" He implies that only on the death of Christ can the Church be founded. If those who prided themselves on being followers of Paul were in danger of exalting him into the place of Christ, they were forfeiting their salvation, and had no right to be in the Church at all. Take away the death of Christ and the personal connection of the believer with the crucified Redeemer, and you take away the Church.

From this casual expression of Paul we see his habitual attitude towards Christ; and more distinctly than from any laboured exposition do we gather that in his mind the pre-eminence of Christ was unique, and that this pre-eminence was based upon His crucifixion. Paul understood, and was never slow to affirm, the indebtedness of the young Christian Churches to himself: he was their father, and without him they would not have existed. But he was not their saviour, the foundation on which they were built. Not for one moment did he suppose that he could occupy towards men the position Christ occupied. That position was unique, altogether distinct from the position he occupied. No one could share with Christ in being the Head of the Church and the Saviour of the body. Paul did not think of Christ as of one among many, as of the best among many who had done well. He did not think of Him as the best among renowned and useful teachers, as one who had added to what previous teachers had been building. He thought of

His work as so transcending and distinct from the work of other men that it was with a kind of horror he saw that there was even a possibility of some confounding his own apostolic work with the work of Christ. He fervently thanks God that he had not even baptized many persons at Corinth, lest it should be supposed he had baptized them into his own name, and so implied, as baptism implies, that men were to acknowledge him as their leader and head. Had the chief part of Christ's work been its lesson in self-sacrifice, might not Paul's life have very well rivalled it, and might not those who had themselves seen the life of Paul and felt the power of his goodness have been forgiven if they felt more indebted to him than to the more remote Jesus?

The ever-recurring disposition then to reduce the work of Christ to the level of comparison with the work done for the race by other men must take account of this expression which reveals to us Paul's thought about it. Certainly Paul understands that between his work and the work of Christ an impassable gulf is fixed. Paul was wholly devoted to his fellow-men, had suffered and was prepared again to suffer any hardships and outrage in their cause, but it seemed to him monstrous that any person should confound the influence of his work with that of Christ's. And that which gave Christ this special place and claim was His crucifixion. We miss what Paul found in the work of Christ so long as we look more to His life than to His death. Paul does not say, Was Paul your teacher in religion, and did he lead your thoughts to God? did Paul by his life show you the beauty of self-sacrifice and holiness? but "Was Paul crucified for you?" It was Christ's death for His people which gave Him the unique claim on their allegiance and devotedness. The Church is founded on the Cross.

It was not, however, the mere fact of His dying which gave Christ this place, and which claims the regard and trust of all men. Paul had really given his life for men; he had been more than once taken up for dead, having by the truth he taught provoked the hatred of the Jews, even as Jesus had done. But even this did not bring him into rivalry with the unapproachable Redeemer. Paul knew that in Christ's death there was a significance his own could never have. It was not only human self-sacrifice that was there manifested, but Divine self-sacrifice. It was as God's Representative Christ died as truly as He died as man's Representative. This Paul could not do. In Christ's death there was what there could be in none other: a sacrifice for the sins of men and an atonement for these sins. Through this death sinners find a way back to God and assurance of salvation. There was a work accomplished by it which the purest of men could not help Him in, but must himself depend upon and receive the benefit of. Christ by His death is marked off from all men, He being the Redeemer, they the redeemed.

This exceptional, unique work then—what have we made of it? Paul, probably on the whole the most richly endowed man, morally and intellectually, the world has seen, found his true life and his true self in the work of this other Person. It was in Christ Paul first learned how great a thing human life is, and it was through Christ and His work Paul first came into fellowship with the true God. This greatest of men owed everything to Christ, and was so inwardly convinced of this that, heart and soul, he yielded himself to Christ, and gloried in serving Him. How is it with us? Does the work of Christ actually yield to us those grand results it yielded to Paul? Or is the greatest reality in this human world of ours wholly resultless so far as we are concerned? It filled Paul's mind, his heart, his life; it left him nothing else to desire: this man, formed on the noblest and largest type, found room in Christ alone for the fullest development and exercise of his powers. Is it not plain that if we neglect the connection with Christ which Paul found so fruitful, we are doing ourselves the greatest injustice and preferring a narrow prison-house to liberty and life?

THE FOOLISHNESS OF PREACHING

"For Christ sent me not to baptize, but to preach the gospel: not with wisdom of words, lest the cross of Christ should be made of none effect. For the preaching of the cross is to them that perish foolishness; but unto us which are saved it is the power of God. For it is written, I will destroy the wisdom of the wise, and will bring to nothing the understanding of the prudent. Where is the wise? where is the scribe? where is the disputer of this world? hath not God made foolish the wisdom of this world? For after that in the wisdom of God the world by wisdom knew not God, it pleased God by the foolishness of preaching to save them that believe. For the Jews require a sign, and the Greeks seek after wisdom: but we preach Christ crucified, unto the Jews a stumblingblock, and unto the Greeks foolishness; but unto them which are called, both Jews and Greeks, Christ the power of God, and the wisdom of God. Because the foolishness of God is wiser than men; and the weakness of God is stronger than men. For ye see your calling, brethren, how that not many wise men after the flesh, not many mighty, not many noble, are called: but God hath chosen the foolish things of the world to confound the wise; and God hath chosen the weak things of the world to confound the things which are mighty; and base things of the world, and things which are despised, hath God chosen, yea, and things which are not, to bring to nought things that are: that no flesh should glory in His presence. But of Him are ye in Christ Jesus, who of God is made unto us wisdom, and righteousness, and sanctification, and redemption: that, according as it is written, He that glorieth, let him glory in the Lord."

"And I, brethren, when I came to you, came not with excellency of speech or of wisdom, declaring unto you the testimony of God. For I determined not to know any thing among you, save Jesus Christ, and Him crucified. And I was with you in weakness, and in fear, and in much trembling. And my speech and my preaching was not with enticing words of man's wisdom, but in demonstration of the spirit and of power: that your faith should not stand in the wisdom of men, but in the power of God."—1 Cor. i. 17-ii. 5.

IV
THE FOOLISHNESS OF PREACHING

In the preceding section of this Epistle Paul introduced the subject which was prominent in his thoughts as he wrote: the divided state of the Corinthian Church. He adjured the rival parties by the name of Christ to hold together, to discard party names and combine in one confession. He reminded them that Christ is indivisible, and that the Church which is founded on Christ must also be one. He shows them how impossible it is for any one but Christ to be the Church's foundation, and thanks God that he had given no pretext to any one to suppose that he had sought to found a party. Had he even baptized the converts to Christianity, there might have been persons foolish enough to whisper that he had baptized in his own name and had intended to found a Pauline, not a Christian, community. But providentially he had baptized very few, and had confined himself to preaching the Gospel, which he considered to be the proper work to which Christ had "*sent*" him; that is to say, for which he held an Apostle's commission and authority. But as he thus repudiates the idea that he had given any countenance to the founding of a Pauline party, it occurs to him that some may say, Yes, it is true enough, he did not baptize; but his preaching may more effectually have won partisans than even baptizing them into his own name could have done. And so Paul goes on to show that his preaching was not that of a demagogue or party-leader, but was a bare statement of fact, garnished and set off by absolutely nothing which could divert attention from the fact either to the speaker or to his style. Hence this digression on the foolishness of preaching.

In this section of the Epistle then it is Paul's purpose to explain to the Corinthians (1) the style of preaching he had adopted while with them and (2) why he had adopted this style.

I. His time in Corinth, he assures them, had been spent, not in propagating a philosophy or system of truth peculiar to himself, and which might have been identified with his name, but in presenting the Cross of Christ and making the plainest statements of fact regarding Christ's death. In approaching the Corinthians, Paul had necessarily weighed in his own mind the comparative merits of various modes of presenting the Gospel. In common with all men who are about to address an audience, he took into consideration the aptitudes, peculiarities, and expectations of his audience, that he might so frame his arguments, statements, and appeals as to be most likely to carry his point. The Corinthians, as Paul well knew, were especially open to the attractions of rhetoric and philosophical discussion. A new philosophy clothed in elegant language was likely to secure a number of disciples. And it was quite in Paul's power to present the Gospel as a philosophy. He might have spoken to the Corinthians in large and impressive language of the destiny of man, of the unity of the race, and of the ideal man in Christ. He might have based all he had to teach them on some of the accepted dicta or theories of their own philosophers. He might have propounded some new arguments for immortality or the existence of a personal God, and have shown how congruous the Gospel is to these great truths. He might, like some subsequent teachers, have emphasized some particular aspect of Divine truth, and have so identified his teaching with this one side of Christianity as to found a school or sect known by his name. But he deliberately rejected this method of introducing the Gospel, and "determined not to know anything among them save Jesus Christ and Him crucified." He stripped his mind bare, as it were, of all his knowledge and thinking, and came among them as an ignorant man who had only facts to tell.

Paul then in this instance deliberately trusted to the bare statement of facts, and not to any theory about these facts. This is a most important distinction, and to be kept in view by all preachers, whether they feel called by their circumstances to adopt Paul's method or not. In preaching to audiences with whom the facts are familiar, it is perfectly justifiable to draw inferences from them and to theorize about them for the instruction and edification of Christian people, Paul himself spoke "wisdom among them that were perfect." But what is to be noted is that for doing the work proper to the Gospel, for making men Christians, it is not theory or explanation, but fact, that is effective. It is the presentation of Christ as He is presented in the written Gospels, the narrative of His life and death without note or comment, theory or inference, argument or appeal, which stands in the first rank of efficiency as a means of evangelizing the world. Paul, ever moderate, does not denounce other methods of presenting the Gospel as illegitimate; but in his circumstances the bare presentation of fact seemed the only wise method.

No doubt we may unduly press Paul's words; and probably we should do so if we gathered that he merely told his hearers how Christ had lived and died and gave them no inkling of the significance of His death. Still the least we can gather from his words is that he trusted more to facts than to any explanation of the facts, more to narration than to inference and theory. Certainly the neglect of this distinction renders a great proportion of modern preaching ineffective and futile. Preachers occupy their time in explaining how the Cross of Christ ought to influence men, whereas they ought to occupy their time in so presenting the Cross of Christ that it does influence men. They give laboured explanations of faith and elaborate instructions regarding the method and results of believing, while they should be exhibiting Christ so that faith is instinctively aroused. The actor on the stage does not instruct his audience how they should be affected by the play; he so presents to them this or that scene that they instinctively smile or find their eyes fill. Those onlookers at the Crucifixion who beat their breasts and returned to their homes with awe and remorse were not told that they should feel compunction; it was enough that they saw the Crucified. So it is always; it is the direct vision of the Cross, and not anything which is said about it, which is most effective in producing penitence and faith. And it is the business of the preacher to set Christ and Him crucified clear before the eyes of men; this being done, there will be little need of explanations of faith or inculcation of penitence. Make men see Christ, set the Crucified clear before them, and you need not tell them to repent and believe; if that sight does not make them repent, no telling of yours will make them.

The very fact that it was a Person, not a system of philosophy, that Paul proclaimed was sufficient proof that he was not anxious to become the founder of a school or the head of a party. It was to another Person, not to himself, he directed the attention and faith of his hearers. And that which permanently distinguishes Christianity from all philosophies is that it presents to men, not a system of truth to be understood, but a Person to be relied upon. Christianity is not the bringing of new truth to us so much as the bringing of a new Person to us. The manifestation of God in Christ is in harmony with all truth; but we are not required to perceive and understand that harmony, but to believe in Christ. Christianity is for all men, and not for the select, highly educated few; and it depends therefore, not on exceptional ability to see truth, but on the universal human emotions of love and trust.

II. Paul justifies his rejection of philosophy or "wisdom" and his adoption of the simpler but more difficult method of stating fact on three grounds. The first is that God's method had changed. For a time God had allowed the Greeks to seek Him by their own wisdom; now He presents Himself to them in the foolishness of the Cross (vers. 17-25). The second ground is that the wise do not universally respond to the preaching of the Cross, a fact which shows that it is not wisdom that preaching appeals to (vers. 26-31). And his third ground is that he feared lest, if he used "wisdom" in presenting the Gospel, his hearers might be only superficially attracted by his persuasiveness and not profoundly moved by the intrinsic power of the Cross (ii. 1-5).

1. His first reason is that God had changed His method. "After that in the wisdom of God the world by wisdom knew not God, it pleased God by the foolishness of preaching to save them that believe." Even the wisest of the Greeks had attained only to inadequate and indefinite views of God. Admirable and pathetic are the searchings of the noble intellects that stand in the front rank of Greek philosophy; and some of their discoveries regarding God and His ways are full of instruction. But these thoughts, cherished by a few wise and devout men, never penetrated to the people, and by their vagueness and uncertainty were incapacitated from deeply influencing any one. To pass even from Plato to the Gospel of John is really to pass from darkness to light. Plato philosophizes, and a few souls seem for a moment to see things more clearly; Peter preaches, and three thousand souls spring to life. If God was to be known by men generally, it was not through the influence of philosophy. Already philosophy had done its utmost; and so far as any popular and sanctifying knowledge of God went, philosophy might as well never have been. "The world by wisdom knew not God." No safer assertion regarding the ancient world can be made.

That which, in point of fact, has made God known is the Cross of Christ. No doubt it must have seemed foolishness and mere lunacy to summon the seeker after God away from the high and elevating speculations of Plato on the good and the eternal and to point him to the Crucified, to a human form gibbeted on a malefactor's cross, to a man that had been hanged. None knew better than Paul the infamy attaching to that cursed death, and none could more distinctly measure the surprise and stupefaction with which the Greek mind would hear the announcement that it was there God was to be seen and known. Paul understood the offence of the Cross, but he knew also its power. "The Jews require a sign, and the Greeks seek after wisdom; but we preach Christ crucified, unto the Jews a stumbling-block and unto the Greeks foolishness, but unto them which are called, both Jews and Greeks, Christ the power of God, and the wisdom of God."

As proof that God was in their midst and as a revelation of God's nature, the Jews required a sign, a demonstration of physical power. It was one of Christ's temptations to leap from a pinnacle of the Temple, for thus He would have won acceptance as the Christ. The people never ceased to clamour for a sign. They wished Him to bid a mountain be removed and cast into the sea; they wished Him to bid the sun stand still or Jordan retire to its source. They wished Him to make some demonstration of superhuman power, and so put it beyond a doubt that God was present. Even at the last it would have satisfied them had He bid the nails drop out and had He stepped down from the Cross among them. They could not understand that to remain on the Cross was the true proof of Divinity. The Cross seemed to them a confession of weakness. They sought a demonstration that the power of God was in Christ, and they were pointed to the Cross. But to them the Cross was a stumbling-block they could not get over. And yet in it was the whole power of God for the salvation of the world. All the power that dwells in God to draw men out of sin to holiness and to Himself was actually in the Cross. For the power of God that is required to draw men to Himself is not power to alter the course of rivers or change the site of mountains, but power to sympathize, to make men's sorrows His own, to sacrifice self, to give all for the needs of His creatures. To them that believe in the God there revealed, the Cross is the power of God. It is this love of God that overpowers them and makes it impossible for them to resist Him. To a God who makes Himself known to them in self-sacrifice they quickly and delightedly yield themselves.

2. As a second ground on which to rest the justification of his method of preaching Paul appeals to the constituent elements of which the Church of Corinth was actually composed. It is plain, he says, that it is not by human wisdom, nor by power, nor by anything generally esteemed among men that you hold your place in the Church. The fact is that "not many wise men after the flesh, not many mighty, not many noble, are called." If human wisdom or power held the gates of the kingdom, you yourselves would not be in it. To be esteemed, and influential, and wise is no passport to this new kingdom. It is not men who by their wisdom find out God and by their nobility of character commend themselves to Him; but it is God who chooses and calls men, and the very absence of wisdom and possessions makes men readier to listen to His call. "God hath chosen the foolish things of the world to confound the wise; and God hath chosen the weak things of the world to confound the things which are mighty, and base things of the world, and things which are despised, hath God chosen, yea, and things which are not, to bring to nought things which are; that no flesh should glory in His presence." It is all God's doing now; it is "Of Him are ye in Christ Jesus;" it is God that hath chosen you. Human wisdom had its opportunity and accomplished little; God now by the foolishness of the Cross lifts the despised, the foolish, the weak, to a far higher position than the wise and noble can attain by their might and their wisdom.

Paul thus justifies his method by its results. He uses as his weapon the foolishness of the Cross, and this foolishness of God proves itself wiser than men. It may seem a most unlikely weapon with which to accomplish great things, but it is God who uses it, and that makes the difference. Hence the emphasis throughout this passage on the agency of God. "God hath chosen" you; "Of God are ye in Christ Jesus;" "Of God He is made unto you wisdom." This method used by Paul is God's method and means of working, and therefore it succeeds. But for this reason also all ground of boasting is removed from those who are within the Christian Church. It is not their wisdom or strength, but God's work, which has given them superiority to the wise and noble of the world. "No flesh can glory in God's presence." The wise and mighty of earth cannot glory, for their wisdom and might availed nothing to bring them to God; those who are in Christ Jesus can as little glory, for it is not on account of any wisdom or might of theirs, but because of God's call and energy, they are what they are. They were of no account, poor, insignificant, outcasts, and slaves, friendless while alive and when dead not missed in any household; but God called them and gave them a new and hopeful life in Christ Jesus.

In Paul's day this argument from the general poverty and insignificance of the members of the Christian Church was readily drawn. Things are changed now; and the Church is filled with the wise, the powerful, the noble. But Paul's main proposition remains: whoever is in Christ Jesus is so, not through any wisdom or power of his own, but because God has chosen and called him. And the practical result remains. Let the Christian, while he rejoices in his position, be humble. There is something wrong with the man's Christianity who is no sooner delivered from the mire himself than he despises all who are still entangled. The self-righteous attitude assumed by some Christians, the "Look at me" air they carry with them, their unsympathetic condemnation of unbelievers, the superiority with which they frown upon amusements and gaieties, all seem to indicate that they have forgotten it is by the grace of God they are what they are. The sweetness and humble friendliness of Paul sprang from his constant sense that whatever he was he was by God's grace. He was drawn with compassion towards the most unbelieving because he was ever saying within himself, There, but for the grace of God, goes Paul. The Christian must say to himself, It is not because I am better or wiser than other men that I am a Christian; it is not because I sought God with earnestness, but because He sought me, that I am now His. The hard suspicion and hostility with which many good people view unbelievers and godless livers would thus be softened by a mixture of humble self-knowledge. The unbeliever is no doubt often to be blamed, the selfish pleasure-seeker undoubtedly lays himself open to just condemnation, but not by the man who is conscious that but for God's grace he himself would be unbelieving and sinful.

Lastly, Paul justifies his neglect of wisdom and rhetoric on the ground that had he used "enticing words of man's wisdom" the hearers might have been unduly influenced by the mere guise in which the Gospel was presented and too little influenced by the essence of it. He feared to adorn the simple tale or dress up the bare fact, lest the attention of his audience might be diverted from the substance of his message. He was resolved that their faith should not stand in the wisdom of men, but in the power of God; that is to say, that those who believed should do so, not because they saw in Christianity a philosophy which might compete with current systems, but because in the Cross of Christ they felt the whole redeeming power of God brought to bear on their own soul.

Here again things have changed since Paul's day. The assailants of Christianity have put it on its defence, and its apologists have been compelled to show that it is in harmony with the soundest philosophy. It was inevitable that this should be done. Every philosophy now has to take account of Christianity. It has shown itself to be so true to human nature, and it has shed so much light on the whole system of things and so modified the action of men and the course of civilization, that a place must be found for it in every philosophy. But to accept Christianity because it has been a powerful influence for good in the world, or because it harmonizes with the most approved philosophy, or because it is friendly to the highest development of intellect, may be legitimate indeed; but Paul considered that the only sound and trustworthy faith was produced by direct personal contact with the Cross. And this remains for ever true.

To approve of Christianity as a system and to adopt it as a faith are two different things. It is quite possible to respect Christianity as conveying to us a large amount of useful truth, while we hold ourselves aloof from the influence of the Cross. We may approve the morality which is involved in the religion of Christ, we may countenance and advocate it because we are persuaded no other force is powerful enough to diffuse a love of law and some power of self-restraint among all classes of society, we may see quite clearly that Christianity is the only religion an educated European can accept, and yet we may never have felt the power of God in the Cross of Christ. If we believe in Christianity because it approves itself to our judgment as the best solution of the problems of life, that is well; but still, if that be all that draws us to Christ, our faith stands in the wisdom of men rather than in the power of God.

In what sense then are we Christians? Have we allowed the Cross of Christ to make its peculiar impression upon us? Have we given it a chance to influence us? Have we in all seriousness of spirit considered what is presented to us in the Cross? Have we honestly laid bare our hearts to the love of Christ? Have we admitted to ourselves that it was for us He died? If so, then we must have felt the power of God in the Cross. We must have found ourselves taken captive by this love of God. God's law we may have found it possible to resist; its threatenings we may have been able to put out of our mind. The natural helps to goodness which God has given us in the family, in the world around us, in the fortunes of life, we may have found too feeble to lift us above temptation and bring us into a really high and pure life. But in the Cross we at length experience what Divine power is; we know the irresistible appeal of Divine self-sacrifice, the overcoming, regenerating pathos of the Divine desire to save us from sin and destruction, the upholding and quickening energy that flows into our being from the Divine sympathy and hopefulness in our behalf. The Cross is the actual point of contact between God and man. It is the point at which the fulness of Divine energy is actually brought to bear upon us men. To receive the whole benefit and blessing that God can now give us we need only be in true contact with the Cross: through it we become direct recipients of the holiness, the love, the power, of God. In it Christ is made to us wisdom, and righteousness, and sanctification, and redemption. In very truth all that God can do for us to set us free from sin and to restore us to Himself and happiness is done for us in the Cross; and through it we receive all that is needful, all that God's holiness requires, all that His love desires us to possess.

DIVINE WISDOM

"Howbeit we speak wisdom among them that are perfect: yet not the wisdom of this world, nor of the princes of this world, that come to nought: but we speak the wisdom of God in a mystery even the hidden wisdom, which God ordained before the world unto our glory: which none of the princes of this world knew: for had they known it, they would not have crucified the Lord of glory. But as it is written, Eye hath not seen, nor ear heard, neither have entered into the heart of man, the things which God hath prepared for them that love Him. But God hath revealed them unto us by His Spirit: for the Spirit searcheth all things, yea, the deep things of God. For what man knoweth the things of a man, save the spirit of man which is in him? even so the things of God knoweth no man, but the Spirit of God. Now we have received, not the spirit of the world, but the spirit which is of God; that we might know the things that are freely given to us of God. Which things also we speak, not in the words which man's wisdom teacheth but which the Holy Ghost teacheth; comparing spiritual things with spiritual. But the natural man receiveth not the things of the Spirit of God: for they are foolishness unto him: neither can he know them, because they are spiritually discerned. But he that is spiritual judgeth all things, yet he himself is judged of no man. For who hath known the mind of the Lord, that he may instruct him? But we have the mind of Christ."

"And I, brethren, could not speak unto you as unto spiritual, but as unto carnal, even as unto babes in Christ. I have fed you with milk, and not with meat: for hitherto ye were not able to bear it, neither yet now are ye able. For ye are yet carnal: for whereas there is among you envying, and strife, and divisions, are ye not carnal, and walk as men? For while one saith, I am of Paul; and another, I am of Apollos; we ye not carnal?" —1 Cor. ii. 6-iii. 4.

V
DIVINE WISDOM

In the preceding paragraph Paul has explained why he had proclaimed the bare facts regarding Christ and His crucifixion and trusted to the Cross itself to impress the Corinthians and lead them to God, and why he had resisted the temptation to appeal to the Corinthian taste for rhetoric and philosophy by exhibiting Christianity as a philosophy. He believed that where conversion was the object of preaching no method could compare in efficiency with the simple presentation of the Cross. But sometimes he found himself in circumstances in which conversion could not be his object. He was occasionally called, as preachers in our own day are regularly called, to preach to those who were already Christians. And he tells us that in these circumstances, speaking "among the perfect," or in presence of fairly mature Christians, he made no scruple of unfolding the "wisdom" or philosophy of Christ's truth. To expound the deeper truths revealed by Christ was useless or even hurtful to mere "babes" in Christ or to those who as yet were not even born again; but to the adolescent and to those who might lay claim to have attained some firm manhood of Christian character, he was forward to teach all he himself knew. These words, "Howbeit we speak wisdom among them that are perfect," he makes the text of the following paragraph, in which he proceeds to explain (1) what the wisdom is; (2) how he speaks it; (3) to whom he speaks it.

I. First, the wisdom which he speaks among the perfect, though eminently deserving of the name, is not on a level with human philosophies, nor is it of a similar origin. It is not just one more added to human searches after truth. The princes of this world, its men of light and leading, have had their own theories of God and man, and yet have really "come to nought." The incompetence of the men and theories that actually control human affairs is put beyond a doubt by the crucifixion of Christ. In the person of Christ the glory of God was manifested as a glory in which man was to partake; had there been diffused among men any true perception of the real nature of God, the Crucifixion would have been an impossibility. The fact that God's incarnate glory was crucified is a demonstration of the insufficiency of all previous teaching regarding God. But the wisdom taught by Paul is not just one theory more, devised by the speculative ingenuity of man; it is a disclosure made by God of knowledge unattainable by human endeavour. The three great sources of human knowledge—seeing, hearing, and thought—alike fail here. "Eye hath not seen, ear hath not heard, it has not entered into the heart of man to conceive," this wisdom. Hitherto it has been a mystery, a thing hidden; now God has Himself revealed it.

What the contents of this wisdom are, we can readily perceive from such specimens of it as Paul gives us in his Epistle to the Ephesians and elsewhere. It is a declaration of the Divine purpose towards man, or of "the things which God hath prepared for them that love Him." Paul delighted to expatiate on the far-reaching results of Christ's death, the illustrations it gives of the nature of God and of righteousness, its place as the grand moral centre, holding together and reconciling all things. He delights to show the superiority of the Gospel to the Law and to build up a philosophy of history which sheds light on the entire plan of God's training of men. The purpose of God and its fulfilment by the death of Christ he is never weary of contemplating, nor of showing how out of destitution, and disease, and war, and ignorance, and moral ruin, and what seemed a mere wreck of a world there were to be brought by this one healing element the restoration of man to God and to one another, fellowship with God and peace on earth, in short a kingdom of God among men. He clearly saw how through all that had previously happened on earth and through all that men had thought preparation had been made for the fulfilment of this gracious purpose of God. These were "the deep things of God" which caused him to see how different was the wisdom of God from the wisdom of men.

This "wisdom" which Paul taught has had a larger and more influential place in men's minds than any other system of human thought. Christendom has seen Christ through Paul's eyes. He interpreted Christianity to the world, and made men aware of what had been and was in their midst. Men of the largest faculty, such as Augustine and Luther, have been unable to find a religion in Christ until they entered His school by Paul's door. Stumbling at one or two Jewish peculiarities which attach to Paul's theology, some modern critics assure us that, "after having been for three hundred years"—and they might have said for fifteen hundred years—"the Christian doctor *par excellence*, Paul is now coming to an end of his reign." Matthew Arnold, with truer discernment, if not on sounder grounds, predicts that "the doctrine of Paul will arise out of the tomb where for centuries it has lain buried. It will edify the Church of the future. It will have the consent of happier generations, the applause of less superstitious ages. All will be too little to pay half the debt which the Church of God owes to this 'least of the Apostles, who was not fit to be called an Apostle, because he persecuted the Church of God.'"

We may find in Paul's writings arguments which, however convincing to the Jew, are not convincing to us; we may prefer his experimental and ethical to his doctrinal teaching; some estimable people can only accept him when they have purged him of his Calvinism; others shut their eyes to this or that which seems to them a blot in his writings; but the fact remains that it is to this man we owe our Christianity. It was he who disengaged from the dying body of Judaism the new-born religion and held it aloft in the eye of the world as the true heir to universal empire. It was he whose piercing intellect and keen moral discernment penetrated to the very heart of this new thing, and saw in it a force to conquer the world and to rid men of all bondage and evil of every kind. It was he who applied to the whole range of human life and duty the inexhaustible ethical force which lay in Christ, and thus lifted at one effort the heathen world to a new level of morality. He was the first to show the superiority of love to law, and to point out how God trusted to love, and to summon men to meet the trust God thus reposed in them. We cannot measure Paul's greatness, because the light he has himself shed has made it impossible for us to put ourselves back in imagination into the darkness through which he had to find his way. We can but dimly measure the strength that was required to grasp as he grasped the significance of God's manifestation in the flesh.

Paul then used two methods of teaching. In addressing those who had yet to be won to Christ, he used the foolishness of preaching, and presented to them the Cross of Christ. In addressing those who had already owned the power of the Cross and made some growth in Christian knowledge and character, he enlarged upon the significance of the Cross and the light it threw on all moral relations, on God and on man. And even in this department of his work he disclaims any desire to propagate a philosophy of his own. The system of truth he proclaims to the Christian people is not of his own devising. It is not in virtue of his own speculative ability he has discovered it. It is not one of the wisdoms of this world, having its origin in the brain of an ingenious theorist. On the contrary, it has its origin in God, and partakes therefore of the truth and stability attaching to the thoughts of God.

II. But if it be undiscoverable by man, how does Paul come to know it? To the Corinthian intelligence there seemed but these three ways of learning anything: seeing, hearing, or thinking; and if God's wisdom was attainable by none of these, how was it reached? Paul proceeds to show how he was enabled to "speak" this wisdom. He does this in vers. 10-13, in which his chief affirmations are that the Spirit of God alone knows the mind of God, that this Spirit has been given to him to reveal to him God's mind and to enable him to divulge that mind to others in suitable words.

1. The Spirit of God alone knows the mind of God and searches its deep things, just as none but the spirit of man which is in him knows the things of man. "There is in every man a life hidden from all eyes, a world of impressions, anxieties, aspirations, and struggles, of which he alone, in so far as he is a spirit—that is to say, a conscious and personal being—gives account to himself. This inner world is unknown to others, except in so far as he reveals it to them by speech."[3] And if we are baffled often and deceived regarding human character and find ourselves unable to penetrate to the "deep things" of man, to his inmost thoughts and motives, much more is it true that "the deep things" of God are wholly beyond our ken and are only known by the Spirit of God which is in Him. A vague and uncertain guess, possibly not altogether wrong, probably altogether wrong, is all we can attain to.

And still more certainly true is this of God's *purposes.* Even though you flatter yourself you know a man's nature, you cannot certainly predict his intentions. You cannot anticipate the thoughts of an able man whom you see designing a machine, or planning a building, or conceiving a literary work; you cannot say in what form a vindictive man will wreak his vengeance; nor can you penetrate through the abstracted look of the charitable and read the precise form his bounty will take. Every great work even of man comes upon us by surprise; the various inventions that facilitate business, the new poems, the new books, the new works of art, have never been conceived before. They were hidden mysteries until the originating mind disclosed them. And much more were God's intentions and His method of accomplishing inconceivable by any but Himself. What God's purpose was in creating man, what He designed to accomplish through the death of Christ, what was to be the outcome of all human life, and temptation, and struggle—these things were God's secret, known only to the Spirit of God that was in Him.

2. This Spirit, Paul declares, was given to him, and revealed to him God's purposes, "the things which are freely given to us of God." He had received "not the spirit of the world," which would have enabled him only to theorize, and speculate, and create another "wisdom of this world;" but he had received "the Spirit which is of God," and this Spirit had revealed to him "the things which God hath prepared for them that love Him."

We may think of revelation either as the act of God or as it is received by man. God reveals Himself in all He does, as man discloses his character in all he does. With God's first act therefore in the remotest past revelation began. As yet there was none to receive the knowledge of God, but God showed His nature and His purpose as soon as He began to do anything. And this revelation of Himself has continued ever since. In the world around us and the earth on which we live God reveals Himself; "the things which are made," as Paul says, "give us clearly to see and understand the invisible things of God, His unseen nature, from the creation of the world." Still more fully is God's nature revealed in man: in conscience, distinguishing between right and wrong; in the spirit craving fellowship with the Eternal. In the history of nations, and especially in the history of that nation which founded itself upon its idea of God, He revealed Himself. By guiding it, by delivering it from Egypt, by punishing it, God made Himself known to Israel. And at length in Jesus Christ God gave the fullest possible manifestation of Himself. The veil was entirely lifted, and God came as much as possible into free intercourse with His creatures. He put Himself within reach of our knowledge.

But it was not enough that God be revealed objectively in Christ; there must also be a subjective revelation within the soul of the beholder. It was not enough that God be manifested in the flesh and men be allowed to draw such inferences as they could from that manifestation; but, in addition to this, God gave His Spirit to Paul and others that they might see the full significance of that manifestation. It was quite possible for men to be witnesses of the objective revelation without understanding it. The open eye is needed as well as outward light. And Paul everywhere insists upon this: that he had received his knowledge of Divine truth *by revelation*, not by the mere exercise of his own unaided thought, but by a spiritual enlightenment through the gift of God's Spirit.

The presence of God's Spirit in any man can of course only be verified by the results. God's Spirit working in and by means of man's nature cannot be known in separation from the man's spirit and the work done in that spirit. This inward revelation which Paul refers to is accomplished by the action of the Divine Spirit on the human faculties, quickening and elevating these faculties. The revelation or new knowledge acquired by Paul was given by God, but at the same time was acquired by Paul's own faculties, so that it remained with him always, just as the knowledge we naturally acquire remains with us and can be freely used by us. An inward revelation can come to a man only in the form of impressions, convictions, thoughts arising in his own mind. Paul knew that his knowledge was a revelation of God, not by the suddenness with which it was imparted, not by supernatural appearances accompanying it, not by any sense or consciousness of another Spirit working with his own, but by the results. It is always the substance or contents of any revelation which proves its origin. Paul knew he had the mind of Christ because he found that he could understand Christ's words and work, could perfectly sympathize with His aims and look at things from Christ's point of view.

In their humility, many persons shrink from making this affirmation here made by Paul; they cannot ever unhesitatingly affirm that the Spirit of God is given them or that they have the mind of Christ. Such persons should recognise that it was the very humility of Paul which enabled him so confidently to affirm these things of himself. He knew that the knowledge of Christ's purposes he had and the sympathy with them were the evidence of God's Spirit working in him. He knew that without God's Spirit he himself could never have had these thoughts. And it is when we recognise our own insufficiency most that we are readiest to confess the presence of God's Spirit.

3. But Paul makes a further affirmation. Not only is the knowledge he has of Divine things a revelation made by God's Spirit to him, but the words in which he declares this revelation to others are taught him by the same Spirit: "which things we also speak, not in the words which man's wisdom teacheth, but which the Holy Ghost teacheth, comparing spiritual things with spiritual." The meaning of these last words is doubtful. They either mean "fitting spiritual words to spiritual truths," or "applying spiritual truths to spiritual people." The sense of the passage is not materially altered whichever meaning is adopted. Paul distinctly affirms that as his knowledge is gained by God's revealing it to him, so his utterance of this knowledge is by the inspiration of God. The spirit of the world produces its philosophies and clothes them in appropriate language. The philosophies with which the Corinthians were familiar taught how the world was made and what man's nature is, and they did so in language full of technicalities and adorned with rhetorical devices. Paul disclaimed this; both his knowledge and the form in which he taught it were dictated, not by the spirit of this world, but by the Spirit of God. The same truths which Paul declared might have been declared in better Greek than he used, and they might have been embellished with illustrative matter and references to their own authors. This style of presenting Divine truth may have been urged upon Paul by some of his Corinthian hearers as far more likely to find entrance into the Greek mind. But Paul refused to allow his style to be formed by human wisdom and the literary methods of secular authors, and thought it more suitable to proclaim spiritual truth in spiritual language and in words which were taught him by the Holy Ghost.

This statement of Paul may be construed into a guarantee of the general accuracy of his teaching; but it was not intended to be that. Paul did not express himself in this way in order to convince men of his accuracy, still less to convince them that every word he uttered was infallibly correct; what he intended was to justify his use of a certain *kind* of language and a certain *style* of teaching. The spirit of this world adopts one method of insinuating knowledge into the mind; the Spirit of God uses another method. It is the latter Paul adopts. That is what he means to say, and it is obvious that from this statement of his we can gather nothing regarding verbal inspiration or the infallibility of every word he spoke.

It might indeed seem a very simple and sound argument were we to say that Paul affirms that the words in which he embodies his teaching are taught him by the Holy Ghost, and that therefore there can be no error in them. But to interpret the words of any writer with no regard to his intention in writing them is voluntarily to blind ourselves to their true meaning. And Paul's intention in this passage is to contrast two methods of teaching, two styles of language, the worldly or secular and the spiritual, and to affirm that the style he adopted was that which the Holy Ghost taught him. An artist whose work was criticised might defend himself by saying, "I have been trained in the Impressionist school," or "I use the principles taught me by Ruskin," or "I am a pupil of this or the other great teacher;" but these replies, while quite relevant as a defence and explanation of the particular style of painting he has adopted, are not intended to identify the work of the scholar with that of the master, or to insinuate that the master is responsible for all the pupil does. Similarly Paul's reply is relevant as an explanation of his reason for refusing to use the methods of professional rhetoricians in teaching his spiritual truths. "Spiritual modes of presenting truth and an avoidance of rhetorical artifice and embellishment accord better with what I have to say." Whoever gathers from this that every individual word Paul spoke or wrote is absolutely the best does so at his own risk and without Paul's authority. Certainly it was not Paul's intention to make any such statement. And it is quite as dangerous to put too much into Paul's words as to put too little.

III. Having shown that the wisdom he teaches is spiritual, and that his method of teaching it is spiritual, he proceeds finally to show that it can be taught only to spiritual persons. "The spiritual man judgeth all things;" he can discern whether he is "among the perfect" or among the carnal, whether he may speak wisdom or must confine himself to elementary truth. But, on the other hand, he himself cannot be judged by the carnal man. It is in vain that rudimentary believers find fault with Paul's method of teaching; they cannot judge him, because they cannot understand the mind of the Lord which guides him. It would have served no purpose to teach spiritual wisdom in Corinth, for the members of that Church were as yet only babes in Christ, carnal, and not spiritual. Their carnality was proved by their factiousness. They were still governed by the passions which rule the natural man. And therefore Paul fed them with milk, and not with strong meat; with the simple and affecting Gospel of the Cross, and not with those high and far-reaching deductions from it which he divulged among prepared and sympathetic spirits.

In the distinctions of men into natural, carnal, and spiritual Paul here shows how untrammelled he was by theological technicalities, and how straight he looked at facts. He does not divide men summarily into believers and unbelievers, classing all believers as spiritual, all unbelievers as carnal. He does not unchurch all who are not spiritual. He may be disappointed that certain members of the Church are carnal and are very slow in growing up to the maturity of Christian manhood, but he does not deny such carnal persons a place in the Church. He gives them time. He does not flatter them or deceive them as to their condition. He neither counts them as perfect nor repudiates them as unregenerate. He allows they are born again; but as the babe is apparently a mere animal, exhibiting no qualities of mind or heart, but only animal instincts, and yet by care and suitable nourishment develops into adult man, so the Christian babe may as yet be carnal, with very little to differentiate him from the natural man, yet the germ of the spiritual Christian may be there, and with care and suitable nourishment will grow.

The confidence which Paul here expresses regarding his superiority to the judgment of carnal men is a superiority inseparable from knowledge in any department. Truth carries with it always a self-evidencing power, and whoever attains a clear perception of truth in any branch of knowledge is aware that it is the truth he has attained. When the mind has been long puzzling over a difficulty and at last sees the solution, it is as if the sun had risen. The mind is at once convinced.

No one had ever greater right than Paul to say, "I have the mind of Christ." Every day of his life said the same thing. He at once entered into Christ's mind and more than any other man carried it out. It was by his moral sympathy with Christ's aims that he entered so completely into the knowledge of His person and work. He lived his way into the truth. And all our best knowledge is reached in the same way. The truths we see most clearly and have deepest assurance of are those which our own experience has taught us. Spiritual truth is of a kind which only spiritual men can understand.

Spiritual men are those who can say, with Paul, "We have received, not the spirit of the world, but the Spirit which is of God, that we might know the things that are freely given to us of God." What men's eyes need especially to be opened to is the bounty of God and the consequent wealth and hopefulness of human life. Paul's wondering delight in God's grace and loving adaptation of Himself to human needs continually finds utterance in his writings. His own sense of unworthiness magnified the forgiving mercy of God. He rejoiced in a Divine love which was passing knowledge, but which he knew could be relied upon to the utmost. The vision of this love opened to his hope a vista of happiness. There is a natural joy in living that all men can understand. This life in many ways appeals to our thirst for happiness, and often it seems as if we needed nothing more. But, in one way or other, most of us learn that what is naturally presented to us in this world is not enough, indeed only brings in the long run anxiety and grief. And then it is that, by God's grace, men come to find that this life is but a small lagoon leading to, and fed by, the boundless ocean of God's love beyond. They learn that there is a hope that cannot be blighted, a joy that is uninterrupted, a fulness of life that meets and satisfies every instinct, and affection, and purpose. They begin to see the things which God hath prepared for them that love Him, the things that are freely given to us of God—"freely given," given without desert of ours, given to make us happy, given by a love that must find expression.

But to know and appreciate the things which are freely given to us of God a man must have the Spirit of God. For God's gifts are spiritual; they attach to character, to what is eternally ours. They cannot be received by those who refuse the severity of God's training and are not alive to the reality of spiritual growth, of passing from a carnal to a spiritual manhood. The path to these eternal, all-satisfying joys may be hard; Christ's path was not easy, and they who follow Him must in one form or other have their faith in the unseen tested. They must really, and not only in word, pass from dependence on this present world to dependence on God; they must somehow come to believe that underneath and in all we here see and experience lies God's unalterable, unmingled love, that ultimately it is this they have to do with, this that explains all.

How soon do men think they have exhausted the one inexhaustible, the love and resources of God; how quickly do men weary of life, and think they have seen all and known all; how ready are men to conclude that for them existence is a failure and can yield no perfect joy, while as yet they know as little of the things God has prepared for them that love Him as the new-born babe knows of the life and experiences that lie before it. You have but touched the hem of His garment; what must it be to be clasped to His heart? Happy they to whom the darkness of this world reveals the boundless distances of the starry heaven, and who find that the blows which have shattered their earthly happiness have merely broken the shell which confined their true life and have given them entrance into a world infinite and eternal.

GOD'S HUSBANDRY AND BUILDING.

"Who then is Paul, and who is Apollos, but ministers by whom ye believed, even as the Lord gave to every man? I have planted, Apollos watered; but God gave the increase. So then neither is he that planteth any thing, neither he that watereth; but God that giveth the increase. Now he that planteth and he that watereth are one: and every man shall receive his own reward according to his own labour. For we are labourers together with God: ye are God's husbandry, ye are God's building. According to the grace of God which is given unto me, as a wise masterbuilder, I have laid the foundation, and another buildeth thereon. But let every man take heed how he buildeth thereupon. For other foundation can no man lay than that is laid, which is Jesus Christ. Now if any man build upon this foundation gold, silver, precious stones, wood, hay, stubble; every man's work shall be made manifest: for the day shall declare it, because it shall be revealed by fire; and the fire shall try every man's work of what sort it is. If any man's work abide which he hath built thereupon, he shall receive a reward. If any man's work shall be burned, he shall suffer loss: but he himself shall be saved; yet so as by fire. Know ye not that ye are the temple of God, and that the Spirit of God dwelleth in you? If any man defile the temple of God, him shall God destroy; for the temple of God is holy, which temple ye are. Let no man deceive himself. If any man among you seemeth to be wise in this world, let him become a fool, that he may be wise. For the wisdom of this world is foolishness with God. For it is written, He taketh the wise in their own craftiness. And again, The Lord knoweth the thoughts of the wise, that they are vain. Therefore let no man glory in men. For all things are your's: whether Paul, or Apollos, or Cephas, or the world, or life, or death, or things present, or things to come; all are your's; and ye are Christ's; and Christ is God's."—1 Cor. iii. 5-23.

VI
GOD'S HUSBANDRY AND BUILDING

Paul, having abundantly justified his method of preaching to the Corinthians, and having shown why he contented himself with the simple presentation of the Cross, resumes his direct rebuke of their party spirit. He has told them that they were as yet unfit to hear the "wisdom" which he taught in some Churches, and the very proof of their immaturity is to be found in their partisanship. "While one saith, I am of Paul, and another, I am of Apollos, are ye not carnal? Who then is Paul, and who is Apollos, but ministers by whom ye believed?" The teachers by whose names they were proud to be known were not founders of schools nor heads of parties, who sought recognition and supremacy; they were "ministers," servants who were used by a common Lord to rouse faith, not in themselves, but in Him. Each had his own gifts and his own task. "I have planted." To me it was given to found the Church at Corinth. Apollos came after me, and helped my plant to grow. But it was God Himself who gave the vital influence requisite to make our work efficacious. Apollos and I are but one instrument in God's hand, as the man who sets the sails and he who holds the helm are one instrument used by the master of the ship, or as the mason who hews and the builder who sets the stones in their places are one instrument for the carrying out of the masterbuilder's design. "We are fellow-labourers used by God; ye are *God's* husbandry, *God's* building."

Throughout this paragraph it is this thought that Paul dwells upon: that the Church is originated and maintained, not by men, but by God. Teachers are but God's instruments; and yet, being human instruments, they have each his own responsibility, as each has his own part of the one work.

From this truth that God alone is the Giver of spiritual life and that the Church is His building several inferences may be drawn.

1. Our praise for any good we have received of a spiritual kind should be given, not solely to men, but mainly to God. The Corinthians were conscious that in receiving Christianity they had received a very great boon. They felt that gratitude was due somewhere. The new thoughts they had of God, the consciousness of Christ's eternal love, the hope of immortality, the sustaining influence of the friendship of Christ, the new world they seemed

to live in—all this made them think of those who had brought them this new happiness. But Paul was afraid lest their acknowledgment of himself and Apollos should eclipse their gratitude to God. People sometimes congratulate themselves on having adopted a good style of religion, not too sentimental, not sensational and spasmodic, not childishly external, not coldly doctrinal; they are thankful they lit upon the books they read at a critical time of their spiritual and mental growth; they can clearly trace to certain persons an influence which they know strengthened their character; and they think with gratitude and sometimes with excessive admiration of such books and persons. Paul would say to them, It is not culpable to think with gratitude of those who have been instrumental in furthering your knowledge of the truth or your Christian life; but always remember that you are God's husbandry and God's building, and that it is to Him all your praise must ultimately go.

2. It is to God we must look for all further growth. We must use the best books; we must put ourselves under influences which we know are good for us, whatever they are for others; we must conscientiously employ such means of grace as our circumstances permit; but, above all, we must ask God to give the increase. No doubt the use of the means God uses to increase our life is a silent but constant prayer; still we are not mere trees planted to wait for such influences as come to us, but have wills to choose the life these influences bring and to open our being to the living God who imparts Himself to us in and through them.

3. If we are God's husbandry and building, let us reverence God's work in ourselves. It may seem a very ricketty and insecure structure that is rising within us, a very sickly and unpromising plant; and we are tempted to mock the beginnings of good in ourselves and be disappointed at the slow progress the new man makes in us. Vexed at our small attainment, at the poor show among Christians our character makes, at the stunted appearance the plant of grace in us presents, we are tempted to trample it once for all out of sight. Grace sometimes seems to do so little for us in emergencies, and the transformation of our character seems so unutterably slow and shallow, that we are disposed to think the radical change we need can never be accomplished. But different thoughts possess us when we remember that this transformation of character is not a thing to be accomplished only by ourselves through a judicious choice and a persevering use of fit means, but is God's work. There may be little appearance or promise of good in you; but underneath the little there is lies what is infinitely great, even the purpose and love of God Himself. "Ye are God's husbandry;" therefore hope becomes you. The deliverance of the human soul from evil, its redemption to purity and nobility—this is what engages all God's care and energy.

4. For the same reason we must hope for others as for ourselves. It is the foundation of all hope to know that God has always been inclining men to righteousness and will always do so. So often we look sadly at the godlessness, and frivolity, and deep degradation and misery that abound, and feel as if the burden of lifting men to a higher condition lay all upon us; the ceaseless flow of human life into and out of the world, the hopeless conditions in which many are born, the frightful influences to which they are exposed, the extreme difficulty of winning even one man to good, the possibility that no more may be won and that the Christian stock may die out—these considerations oppress the spirit, and cause men to despair of ever seeing a kingdom of God on earth. But Paul could never despair, because he was at all times convinced that the whole energy that ceaselessly goes forth from God goes forth to accomplish good, and nothing but good, and that among the good ends God is accomplishing there is nothing for which He has sacrificed so much and at which He so determinedly aims as the restoration of men to purity, love, and goodness.

5. But the chief inference Paul draws from the truth that the Church is God's building is the grave responsibility of those who labour for God in this work. As for Paul's own part in the work, the laying of the foundation, he says that was comparatively easy. There was no chance of his making a mistake there. "Other foundation can no man lay than that is laid, which is Jesus Christ." Any teacher who professes to lay another foundation thereby gives up his claim to be a Christian teacher. If any one proceeds to lay another foundation than Christ, it is not a Christian Church he is meaning to build. He who does not proceed upon the facts of Christ's life and death, he whose instruction does not presuppose Christ as its foundation, may be useful for some purposes of life, but not as a builder of the Christian temple. He who teaches morality without ever hinting that apart from Christ it cannot be attained in its highest form may have his use, but not as a Christian teacher. He who uses the Christian pulpit for the propagation of political or socialist ideas may be a sound and useful teacher; but his proper place is the platform or the House of Commons or some such institution, and not the Christian Church. And the question at present, says Paul, is not what other institutions you may profitably found in the world, but how this institution of the Church, already founded, is to be completed. Other *foundation* no Christian teacher is proposing to lay; but on this foundation very various and questionable material is being built, in some instances gold, silver, and stones of value, in others wood, hay, stubble.

When Corinth rose from its ruins, it was no uncommon sight to see a miserable hovel reared against the marble wall of a temple or the splendid portico of some deserted palace rendered habitable by a patchwork of mud and straw. What a recent visitor saw at Luxor may be accepted as to some extent true of Corinth: "Mud hovels, mud pigeon-towers, mud yards, and a mud mosque cluster like wasps' nests in and about the ruins. Architraves sculptured with royal titles support the roofs of squalid cabins. Stately capitals peep out from the midst of sheds in which buffaloes, camels, donkeys, dogs, and human beings herd together in unsavoury fellowship." So in Corinth the huge slabs of costly and carefully chiselled stone lay stable as the rock on which they rested, but now the glory of such foundations was dishonoured by squalid superstructures. And the picture in Paul's mind's eye of the Corinthian Church vividly suggested what he had seen while walking among those heterogeneous buildings. He sees the Church rising with a strange mixture of design and material. The foundation, he knows, is the same; but on the solid marble is reared a crazy structure of second-hand and ill-adapted material, here a wall propped up with rotten planking, there a hole stopped with straw, on one side a richly decorated gateway, with gold and silver profusely wrought into its design, on the other side a clay partition or loose boarding. It grieves him to see the incongruous structure. He sees the teachers bringing, with great appearance of diligence, the merest rubbish, wood, hay, stubble, apparently unconscious of the incongruity of their material with the foundation they build upon. He sees them taken with every passing fancy—the lifeless stubble that has lost its living seed of truth, the mud of the common highway, the readiest thoughts that come to hand—and setting these in the temple wall.

What would Paul say did he now see the super-structure which eighteen hundred years have raised on the one foundation? Is any more heterogeneous structure anywhere to be seen than the Church of Christ? How obviously unworthy of the foundation is much that has been built upon it; how many teachers have laboured all their days at erecting what has already been proved a mere house of cards; and how many persons have been built into the living temple who have brought no stability or beauty to the building. How careless often have the builders been, anxious only to have quantity to show, regardless of quality, ambitious to be credited with largely extending the size of the Church apart from any consideration of the worth or worthlessness of the material added. As in any building, so in the Church, additional size is additional danger if the material be not sound.

The soundness of the material which has been built upon the foundation of Christ will, like all things else, be tested. "The day shall declare it;" that light of Christ's presence and dominance over all things, that light which shall penetrate all human things when our true life is entered on—*that* shall declare it. "The fire shall try every man's work, of what sort it is. If any man's work abide, he shall receive a reward. If any man's work be burned, he shall suffer loss; but he himself shall be saved, yet so as by fire." The Corinthians knew what a trial by fire meant. They knew how the flames had travelled over their own city, consuming all that fire could kindle on, and leaving of the slightly built houses nothing but a charred and useless timber here and there, while the massive marbles stood erect among the ruins; and the precious metals, even though molten, were prized by the conqueror. Against the fire no prayer, no appeal, prevailed. Its judgment and decisions were irreversible; wood, hay, stubble, disappeared: only what was solid and valuable remained. By such irreversible judgment are we and our work to be judged. We are to enter into a life in which the nature and character of the work we have done in this world shall bring upon it utter destruction or a rewarding and growing utility. Fire simply burns up all that will burn and leaves what will not. So shall the new life we are to pass into absolutely annihilate what is not in keeping with it, and leave only what is useful and congruous. There is no question here of admitting explanations, of adducing extenuating circumstances, of appealing to compassion, and so forth. It is a judgment, and a judgment of absolute truth, which takes things as they actually are. The work that has been well and wisely done will stand; foolish, vain, and selfish work will go. We are to pass through the fire.

Paul, with his unfailing discernment, accepts it as a very possible contingency that a Christian man may do poor work. In that case, Paul says, the man will be saved as by fire; his work shall be burned, but himself be scatheless. He shall be in the position of a man whose house has been burnt; the man is saved, but his property, all that he has slowly gathered round him and valued as the fruit of his labour, is gone. He may have received no bodily injury, but he is so stripped that he scarcely knows himself, and the whole thought and toil of his life seem to have gone for nothing. So, says Paul, shall this and that man pass into the heavenly state, hearing behind him as he barely enters the crash of all he has been building up as it falls and leaves for the result of a laborious life a ghastly, charred ruin and a cloud of dust. To have been useless, to have advanced Christ's kingdom not at all, to have spent our life building up a pretentious erection which at last falls about our ears, to come to the end and find that not one solid brick in the whole fabric is of our laying, and that the world would have been quite as well without us—this must be humiliating indeed; but it is a humiliation which all selfish, worldly, and foolishly fussy Christians are preparing for themselves. To many Christians it seems enough that they be doing *something*. If only they are decently active, it concerns them little that their work is really effecting no good, as if they were active rather for the sake of keeping themselves warm in a chilling atmosphere than to accomplish any good purpose. Work done for this world must be such as will stand inspection and actually do the thing required. Christian work should not be less, but more, thorough.

There is a degree of carelessness or malignity sometimes to be found in those who profess to be Christian teachers which Paul does not hesitate unconditionally to doom. "If any man destroy the temple of God, him shall God destroy." A teacher may in various ways incur this doom. He may in guiding some one to Christ fit him obliquely to the foundation, so that firm rest in Christ is never attained; but the man remains like a loose stone in a wall, unsettled himself and unsettling all around him. Any doctrine which turns the grace of God into licence incurs this doom. To lift stones from the mire they have been lying in and fit them into the temple is good and right, but to leave them uncleansed and unpolished is to disfigure the temple. Any teaching that does not recognise in Christianity the means of becoming holy, and encourages men to believe themselves Christians though they neither have nor wish to have the Spirit of Christ, destroys the temple.

But we are responsible as well as our teachers for the appearance we present in God's temple. The stone that is to occupy a permanent place in a building is carefully squared and beaten into its place, and its level adjusted with the utmost nicety. Would it not make a very obvious change in the appearance and in the strength of the Church if every member of it were at pains to set himself absolutely true to Christ? There is no doubt a good deal of anxiety about our relation to Christ, frequent examining and measuring of our actual position; but does not this too often merely reveal that conscience is uneasy? Some persons are prevented from resting satisfactorily on Christ because of some erroneous opinion about faith or about the manner in which the connection is formed, or some pet theory or crotchet has possessed the mind and keeps them unsettled. Some will not rest on Christ until they have such repentance as they judge sufficient; others so rest on Him that they have no repentance. Strange that men will so complicate the simplicity of Christ, who is the hand of our heavenly Father, stretched out to lift us out of our sin and draw us to Himself! If you wish God's love, accept it; if you long for holiness, take Christ as your Friend; if you see no greater joy than to serve in His great cause, do His will and follow Him.

But, alas! with some it is no misunderstanding that prevents a close connection between the soul and Christ, but some worldly purpose or some entangling and deeply cherished sin. The foundation stone is as a polished slab of marble, having its upper surface smooth as a mirror, whereas we are like stones that have been lying on the seashore, encrusted with shells and lichens, drilled with holes, grown all round and round with unsightly inequalities; and if we are to rest with entire stability on the foundation, these excrescences must be removed. Even a small one at one point is enough to prevent close adhesion. One sin consciously retained, one command or expression of Christ's will unresponded to, makes our whole connection with Him unsettled and insecure, our confessions and repentances untrue and hardening, our prayers hesitating and insincere, our love for Christ hollow, our life inconsistent, vacillating, and unprofitable.

And more must be done even after we are securely fitted into our place. Stones often look well enough when first built in, but soon lose their colour; and their surface and fine edges crumble and shale off, so that they need to be constantly looked to. So do the stones in God's temple get tarnished and discoloured by exposure. One sin after another is allowed to stain the conscience; one little corruption after another settles on the character, and eats out its fineness, and when once the fair, clean stone is no longer unsullied, we think it of little consequence to be scrupulous. Then the weather tells upon us: the ordinary atmosphere of this life, with its constant damp of worldly care and its occasional storms of loss, and disappointment, and social collisions, and domestic embroilment, eats out the heavenly temper from our character, and leaves its edges ragged; and the man becomes soured and irritable, and the surface of him, all that meets the casual eye, is rough and broken.

Above all, do not many Christian persons seem to think it enough to have attained a place in the building, and, after spending a little thought and trouble on entering the Christian life, take no step onwards during the whole remainder of their lives? But it is in God's building as in highly ornamented buildings generally. The stones are not all sculptured before they are fitted into their places; but they are built in rough-hewn, so that the building may proceed: and then at leisure the device proper to each is carved upon it. This is the manner of God's building. Long after a man has been set in the Church of Christ, God hews and carves him to the shape He designs; but we, being not dead, but living, stones, have it in our power to mar the beauty of God's design, and indeed so distort it that the result is a grotesque and hideous monster, belonging to no world, neither of God nor of man. If we let a thousand other influences mould and fashion us, God's design must necessarily be spoiled.

The folly of partisanship and sectarianism is finally exhibited in the words "Let no man glory in men. For all things are yours, whether Paul, or Apollos, or Cephas." The man who held to Paul and would learn nothing from Apollos or Peter was defrauding himself of his rights. It has been the weakness of Christians in all ages, and never more than in our own, to see good in only one aspect of truth and listen to no form of teaching but one. The Broad Churchman despises the traditionalist; the Evangelical gathers up his skirts at the approach of a Broad Churchman. Calvinist and

Arminian stand at daggers drawn. Each limits himself to his own fortress, which he thinks he can defend, and starves himself on siege rations while the fields wave white with grain outside. The eye is constructed to sweep round a wide range of vision; but men put on blinkers, and decline even to look at anything which does not lie directly in the line of sight. We know that to confine ourselves to one form of food induces poverty of blood and disease, and yet we fancy a healthy spiritual life can be maintained only by confining ourselves to one form of doctrine and one way of looking at universal truth. To the Evangelical who shrinks with horror from liberal teaching, and to the advanced thinker who turns with contempt from the Evangelical, Paul would say, Ye do yourselves a wrong by listening to one form of the truth only; every teacher who declares what he himself lives on has something to teach you; to despise or neglect any form of Christian teaching is so far to impoverish yourselves. "All things are yours," not this teacher or that, in whom you glory, but all teachers of Christ.

His own expression, "all things are yours," suggests to Paul the whole wealth of the Christian, for whom exist not only all those who have striven to unfold the significance of the Christian revelation, but all things else, whether "the world, or life, or death, or things present, or things to come." As it is true of all teachers, of however commanding genius, that the Church does not exist for them that they may have a field for their genius, and followers to applaud and represent them, but that they exist for the Church, their genius being used for the advancement of the spiritual life of this and that unknown and hidden soul; so is it true of all things,—of life and all its laws, of death and all it leads to,—that these are ordained of God to minister to the growth of His children. This was the regal attitude which Paul himself assumed and maintained towards all events and the whole world of created things. He was incapable of defeat. The outrages and deaths he endured, he bore as proofs of the truth of his gospel. The storms of ill-will and persecution he everywhere encountered, he knew were only bringing him and his gospel more rapidly to all the world. And when he looked at last on the sword of the Roman executioner, he recognised it with joy as the instrument which by one sharp blow was to burst his fetters and set him free to boundless life and the full knowledge of his Lord. The same inheritance belongs to every one who has faith to take it. "All things are yours." The whole course of this world and all its particular incidents, the complete range of human experience from first to last, including all we shrink from and fear,—all are for the good of Christ's people. What thoughts flash from this man's mind.

How his words still entrance and lift and animate the soul. "All things are ours." The catastrophes of life that seem finally to blot out hope, the wild elemental forces in whose presence frail man is as the moth, the unknown future of the physical world, the certain death that awaits every man and listens to no appeal, all things that naturally discourage and compel us to feel our weakness,—yes, says Paul, all these things are yours, serving your highest good, bringing you on towards your eternal joy, more certainly than the things you select and buy, or win, and cherish as your own. You are free men, supreme over all created things, for "ye are Christ's," you belong to Him who rules all, and loves you as His own; and above Christ and His rule there is no adverse will that can rob you of any good, for as ye are Christ's, cherished by Him, so is Christ God's, and the supreme will that governs all, governs all in the interests of Christ.

THE MINISTRY

"Let a man so account of us, as of the ministers of Christ, and stewards of the mysteries of God. Moreover it is required in stewards, that a man be found faithful. But with me it is a very small thing that I should be judged of you, or of man's judgment: yea, I judge not mine own self. For I know nothing by myself; yet am I not hereby justified: but he that judgeth me is the Lord. Therefore judge nothing before the time, until the Lord come, who both will bring to light the hidden things of darkness, and will make manifest the counsels of the hearts: and then shall every man have praise of God. And these things, brethren, I have in a figure transferred to myself and to Apollos for your sakes; that ye might learn in us not to think of men above that which is written, that no one of you be puffed up for one against another. For who maketh thee to differ from another? and what hast thou that thou didst not receive? now if thou didst receive it, why dost thou glory, as if thou hadst not received it? Now ye are full, now ye are rich, ye have reigned as kings without us: and I would to God ye did reign, that we also might reign with you. For I think that God hath set forth us the apostles last, as it were appointed to death: for we are made a spectacle unto the world, and to angels, and to men. We are fools for Christ's sake, but ye are wise in Christ; we are weak, but ye are strong; ye are honourable, but we are despised. Even unto this present hour we both hunger, and thirst, and are naked, and are buffeted, and have no certain dwellingplace: and labour, working with our own hands: being reviled, we bless; being persecuted, we suffer it: being defamed, we intreat: we are made as the filth of the earth, and are the offscouring of all things unto this day. I write not these things to shame you, but as my beloved sons I warn you. For though ye have ten thousand instructers in Christ, yet have ye not many fathers: for in Christ Jesus I have begotten you through the gospel. Wherefore I beseech you, be ye followers of me."—1 Cor. iv. 1-16.

VII
THE MINISTRY

So keenly alive is Paul to the danger and folly of party-spirit in the Church, that he has still one more word of rebuke to utter. He has shown the Corinthians that to give their faith to one teacher, and shut their ears to every other form of truth than that which he delivers, is to impoverish and defraud themselves. All teachers are theirs, and are sent, not to win disciples to themselves, who may spread their fame and reflect credit on their talents, but to serve the people, and be merged in self-obliterating toil. The preachers, Paul tells them, exist for the Church: not the Church for the preachers. The people are the primary consideration, the main end to which the preachers are subordinate. The mistake often made in things civil, that the people exist for the king, not the king for the people, is made also in things ecclesiastical, and has, in some instances, attained such dimensions that the "Church" means the clergy, not the laity, and that when a man enters the ministry he is said to enter the Church,—as if already he were not in it as a layman.

Paul now proceeds to demonstrate the futility of the judgment passed upon their teachers by the Corinthians. Paul and the rest were servants of Christ, stewards sent by Him to dispense to others what he had entrusted to them. The question therefore was, were they faithful, did they dispense what they had received in conformity with Christ's purpose? The question was not, were they eloquent, were they philosophical, were they learned? Criticism no preacher need expect to escape. Sometimes one might suppose sermons were of no other use than to furnish material for a little discussion and pleasant exercise of the critical faculty. Every one considers himself capable of this form of criticism, and once a sermon has been sorted and labelled as of this, that, or the other quality, it is too often put permanently aside. In such criticism, Paul reminds us, it is a great matter to bear in mind that what has no great attraction for us may yet serve some good purpose. The gifts dispensed by Christ are various. The influence of some ministers is most felt in private, while others are shy and stiff, and can only utter themselves freely in the pulpit. In the pulpit again various gifts appear, some having good nerve and a ready and felicitous address which reaches the multitude; while others have more power of thought, and a finer literary gift, or a sympathetic manner of handling peculiarities of spiritual experience. Who shall say which of these styles is most edifying to the Church? And who shall say which teacher is most faithfully serving his Master? Who shall determine whether this preacher or that is the better steward, most truly seeking his Lord's glory, and careless of his own? May it not be expected that when the things at present hidden in darkness, the motives and thoughts of the heart, are brought to light in Christ's judgment, many that are first shall be last, and the last first?

He who is conscious that he is the servant of Christ and must give account to Him, can always say with Paul, "It is a very small thing that I should be judged of man's judgment," whether for acquittal and applause or condemnation and abuse. He who utters what is peculiar to himself must expect to be misjudged by those who do not look at things from his point of view. A teacher who thinks for himself and is not a mere echo of other men, finds himself compelled to utter truths which he knows will be misunderstood by many; but so long as he is conscious that he is faithfully delivering what has been made known to himself, the condemnation of the many can trouble him very little or not at all. It is to his own Master he stands or falls; and if he feels sure that he is doing his Master's will, he may regret the opposition of men, but he can neither be greatly astonished nor greatly perturbed by it. And, on the other hand, the approval and applause of men come to him only as a reminder that there is no finality in man's judgment, and that it is only Christ's approval which avails to give permanent satisfaction. A sympathetic audience every teacher needs, but general approval will be his in the inverse ratio of the individuality of his teaching.

In his whole discussion of this subject Paul has named only himself and Apollos, but he means that what he has said of them should be applied to all. "These things I have in a figure transferred to myself and to Apollos for your sakes; that in us ye might learn not to think of men above that which is written, that no one of you be puffed up for one against another." But great difficulty has always been experienced in tracing the similarities and distinctions which exist between the Apostles and the ordinary ministry of the Church, and had Paul been writing this epistle in our own day he would have felt himself compelled to speak more definitely on these points. For what makes union hopeless in Christendom at present is not that parties are formed round individual leaders, but that Churches are based on diametrically opposed opinions regarding the ministry itself. The Church of Rome unchurches all the rest, and defends her action by the simplest process of reasoning. There can be no true Church, she says, where there is no forgiveness of sins and no sacraments, and there can be no forgiveness and no sacraments where there are no true ministers to administer them, and there are no true ministers save those who can trace their orders to the Apostles. This theory of the ministry proceeds on the idea that the Apostles received from Christ a commission to exercise the apostolic office, and along with it a deposit of grace, with powers to communicate this to those who should succeed them. This deposit of grace derived from Christ Himself has been handed down from generation to generation, through a line of consecrated persons, each member of the series receiving at his ordination, and irrespective of his moral character, both the commission and the powers which belonged to his predecessor in office.

This theory of the efficacy of ministration in the Church, with its entirely external account of its transmission, is but one manifestation of the old superstition that confounds the outward symbol of Christian grace with that grace itself. It is a survival from a time in which religion was treated as a kind of magic, in which it was only needful to observe the right words of incantation and the right outward order. Even supposing that any priest now alive could trace his orders back to the Apostles, which no priest can, is it credible that the mere observance of an outward form should secure the transmission of the highest spiritual functions to those who may or may not have any spirituality of mind? However much grace the ordaining bishop may himself possess, however many of the qualifications of a good minister of Christ he may have, he can transmit none of these by the laying on of his hands. He can confer the external authority in the Church which belongs to the office to which he ordains, but he cannot communicate that which fits a man to use this authority. The laying on of hands is the outward symbol of the bestowal of the Holy Spirit, but it does not confer that Spirit, which is given, not by man, but by Christ alone. The laying on of hands is a fit symbol to use at ordination when those who use it have satisfied themselves that the ordained person is in possession of the Spirit. It is the expression of their reasonable belief that the Spirit is given.

In some Churches reaction against the theory of apostolical succession has led men to distrust and repudiate ordination altogether, and to maintain that any man may preach who can get people to listen to him, and may administer the sacraments to any who apply for them. No outward recognition by the Church is deemed necessary. The middle course is safer, which acknowledges not only the supreme necessity of an inward call, but also the expediency of an outward call by the Church. By an inward call it is meant that it is the inward and spiritual fitness of any person which constitutes his main right of entrance to the ministry. There are certain mental and moral endowments, certain circumstances, and educational advantages, personal inclinations and leanings, which, when they meet in a boy or young man, point him out as suited for the work of the ministry. The evidence that Christ means that any one should take office in His Church,— in other words, calls him to office,—is the fact that He bestows on that person the gifts which fit him for it.

But besides this inward persuasion wrought in the mind of the individual, and which constitutes the inward call, there must be an outward call also by the Church's recognition of fitness and communication of authority. Any man who at his own instance and on his own authority gathers a congregation and dispenses the sacraments is guilty of schism. Even Barnabas and Paul were ordained by the Church. As in the State a prince though legitimate does not succeed to the throne without formal consecration and coronation, so in the Church there is needed a formal recognition of the title which any one claims to office. It is not the consecration which constitutes the prince's right; that he already possesses by birth: so, neither is it the Church's ordination which qualifies and entitles the minister to his office; this he already has by the gift of Christ; but recognition by the Church is needed to give him due authority to exercise the functions of his office. It is a matter of expediency and of order. It is calculated to maintain the unity of the Church. Admission to the ministry being regulated by those already in office, schisms are less likely to occur. Ordination has been a bulwark against fanaticism, against foolish private opinions and doctrines, against divisive courses in worship and in organization. If the Church was to be kept together and to grow as a consistent whole, it was necessary that those already in office should be allowed to scrutinize the claims of aspirants to office, and should not have their order invaded, their work thwarted and obstructed, their doctrine denied and contradicted by every one who might profess to have an inward call to the ministry.

It would therefore seem to be every one's duty to inquire, before he gives himself to another profession or business, whether Christ is not claiming him to serve in His Church. The qualifications which constitute a call to the ministry are such as these: an interest in men, in their ways, and habits, and character; a social disposition, inclining you to mix with other people, to take pleasure in their thoughts and feelings, to be of service to them, to talk frankly with them; a liking for reading, if not for hard study; some capacity for thinking and arranging your thoughts and expressing them, which, however, is to so great an extent the result of study and practice that you may find it impossible to say whether you have it or not. There are negative qualifications equally important, such as an indifference to money-making, a shrinking from the eager competition and hurry of a business life. And, above all, there are the deeper and essential qualifications which are the fruit of the Spirit's sanctifying energy: some genuine sense of your indebtedness to Christ; a strong desire to serve Him; an ambition to preach Him, to proclaim His worth, to invite men to appreciate and love Him. If you have these desires, and if you would fain be of use in things spiritual to your fellow-men, then it would seem that you are called by Christ to the ministry. I do not say that all ministers are so qualified, but only that any one who is so qualified should be careful how he chooses some other calling in preference to the ministry.

Paul concludes this portion of his Epistle with a pathetic comparison of his condition as an Apostle with the condition of those in Corinth who were glorying in this or that teacher. They spoke as if they needed his instructions no more, and as if already they had attained the highest Christian advantages. "Already ye are full; already ye are rich: ye have reigned as kings without us." They behave as if all the trial of the Christian life were over. With the frothy spirit of young converts, they are full of a triumph which they despise Paul for not inculcating. By one leap they had attained, or thought they had attained, a superiority to all disturbance, and to all trial, and to all need of teaching, which, in fact, as Paul's own experience taught him, could only be attained in another life. While they thus triumphed, he who had begotten them in Christ was being treated as the offscouring and filth of the world.

Paul can only compare himself and the other Apostles to those gladiators who were condemned to die, and who came into the arena last, after the spectators had been sated with other exhibitions and bloodless performances. "I think that God hath set forth us the Apostles last, as it were appointed to death. For we are made a spectacle unto the world, and to angels and to men." They came into the arena knowing they should never leave it alive, that they were there for the purpose of enduring the worst their enemies could do to them. It was no fight with buttoned foils Paul and the rest were engaged in. While others sat comfortably looking on, with curtains to shade them from the heat and refreshments to save them from exhaustion or from faintness at the sight of blood, they were in the arena, exposed to wounds, ill-usage, and death. They had as little hope of retiring to live a quiet life as the gladiators who had said farewell to their friends and saluted the Emperor as those about to die. Life became no easier, the world no kinder, to Paul as time went on. "Even unto this present hour of writing," he says, "we both hunger and thirst, and are naked, and are buffeted, and have no certain dwelling-place." Here is the finest mind, the noblest spirit, on earth; and this is how he is treated: driven from place to place, thrust aside as interrupting the proper work of men, passed by with a sneer at his rags, refused the commonest charity, paid for his loving words in blows and insolence. And yet he goes on with his work, and lets nothing interrupt that. "Being reviled, we bless; being persecuted, we suffer it; being defamed, we entreat." Nay, it is a life which he is so far from giving up himself, that he will call to it the easy-going Christians of Corinth. "I beseech you," he says, "be ye followers of me."

And if the contrast between Paul's precarious and self-sacrificing life and the luxurious and self-complacent life of the Corinthians might be expected to shame them into some vigorous Christian service, a similar contrast candidly considered may accomplish some good results in us. Already the Corinthians were accepting that pernicious conception of Christianity which looks upon it as merely a new luxury, that they who are already comfortable in all outward respects may be comforted in spirit as well and purge their minds from all anxieties, questionings, and strivings. They recognised how happy a thing it is to be forgiven, to be at peace with God, to have a sure hope of life everlasting. For them the battle was over, the conquest won, the throne ascended. As yet they had not caught a glimpse of what is involved in becoming holy as Christ is holy, nor had steadily conceived in their minds the profound inward change which must pass upon them. As yet it was enough for them that they were called to be God's children, provided for by a heavenly Father; and Christ's own view of life and of men had not yet possessed or even dawned upon their soul, causing them to feel that until they could live for others they had no true life.

Are there none still who listen to Christianity rather as a voice soothing their fears than as a bugle summoning them to conflict, who are satisfied if through the Gospel they are enabled to comfort their own soul, and who do not yet respond to Christ's call to live under the power of that Spirit of His which prompted Him to all sacrifice? Paul does not summon the whole Church to be homeless, destitute, comfortless, outcast from all joy; and yet there is meaning in his words when he says, "Be ye followers of me." He means that there is not one standard of duty for him and another for us. All is wrong with us until we be made somehow to recognise, and make room in our life for the recognition, that we have no right to be lapping ourselves round with all manner of selfish aggrandizement while Paul is driven through life with scarcely one day's bread provided, that in some way intelligible to our own conscience we must approve ourselves to be his followers, and that no right is secured to any class of Christians to stand selfishly aloof from the common Christian cause. If we be Christ's, as Paul was, it must inevitably come to this with us: that we cordially yield to Him all we are and have; our very selves, with all our tastes and aptitudes and with all we have made by our toil; our life, with all its fruits, we gladly yield to Him. If our hearts be His, this is inevitable and delightful; unless they be so, it is impossible, and seems extravagant. It is vain to say to a man, Serve only yourself in life, seek only to make a reputation for yourself and gather comforts round yourself, and make it the aim of your life to be comfortable and respectable—it is vain to bid a man thus limit and impoverish his life if at the same time you show him a person so attracting human allegiance as Christ does, and so opening to men wider and eternal aims as He does, and if you show him a cause so kindling every right ambition as Christ's cause does.

It was Christ's own self-sacrifice that threw such a spell over the Apostles and gave them so new a feeling towards their fellow-men and so new an estimate of their deepest needs. After seeing how Christ lived, they could never again justify themselves in living for self. After seeing His regardlessness of bodily comfort, His superiority to traditional necessities and customary luxuries, after witnessing how veritably He was but passing through this world, and used it as the stage on which He might serve God and men, and counted His life best spent in giving it for others, they could not settle down into the old life and aim only at passing comfortably, reputably, and religiously through it. That view of life was made for ever impossible to them. The life of Christ had made a new way for itself into a new region, and the horizon rent by the passage never again closed to them. That life became the only spiritual reality to them. And it is because we are so sunk in self-seeking and worldliness, and so blinded by the customs and traditional ideas about spending life, about acquitting ourselves well and making a name, about earning a competence, about everything which turns the regard in upon self instead of outwards upon objects worthy of our exertion—it is therefore that we continue so unapostolic, so unprofitable, so unchanged.

It might encourage us to bring our life more nearly into the line of Paul's were we to see clearly that the cause he served is really inclusive of all that is worth working for. We can scarcely apprehend this with any clearness without feeling some enthusiasm for it. The *kind* of devotedness expected of the Christian is illustrated in the lives of all men of any force of character; the Christian's devotedness is only given to a larger and more reasonable object. There have been statesmen and patriots, and there still are such, who, though possibly not absolutely devoid of some taint of selfish ambition, are yet in the main devoted to their country; its interests are continually on their mind and heart, their time is given wholly to it, and their own personal tastes and pursuits are held in abeyance and abandoned to make room for more important labour. You have seen men become so enamoured of a cause that they will literally sell all they have to forward it, and who obviously have it on their hearts by night and by day, who live for that and for nothing else; you can detect as often as you meet them that the real aim and object of their life is to promote that cause. Some new movement, political or ecclesiastical, some literary scheme, some fresh enterprise of benevolence, some new commercial idea, or no matter what it is, you have seen again and again that men throw themselves so thoroughly into such causes that they cannot be said to be living for themselves. They will part with time, with property, with other important objects, with health, even with life itself, for the sake of their cherished, chosen cause. And when such a cause is worthy, such as the reformation of prison discipline, or the emancipation of slaves, or the liberating of an oppressed nation, the men who adopt it seem to lead the only lives which have some semblance of glory in them; and the sacrifices they make, the obloquy they incur, the toils they endure, make the heart burn and swell as we hear of them. Every one instinctively acknowledges that such self-forgetful and heroic lives are the right and model lives for all. What a man does for himself is jealously examined, criticised, and passed at the most with an exclamation of wonder; but what he does for others is welcomed with acclamation as an honour to our common humanity. So long as a man labours merely for himself, to win himself a name, to get for himself a possession, he makes no valuable contribution to the world's good, and only by accident effects anything for which other men are thankful; but let a man even with small means at his command have the interests of others at his heart, and he sets in motion endless agencies and influences that bless whatever they touch.

It is this then that our Lord does for us by claiming our service; He gives us the opportunity of sinking our selfishness, which is in the last analysis our sin, and of living for a worthier object than our own pleasure or our own careful preservation. When He tells us to live for Him and to seek the things that are His, He but tells us in other words and in a more attractive and practical form to seek the common good. We seek the things that are Christ's when we act as Christ would act were He in our place, when we let Christ live through us, when we, by considering what He would have us do, let His influence still tell on the world and His will still be done in the world. This should be so done by each and every Christian that the result would be the same as if Christ had personally at command all the resources for good that are possessed by His people, as if He were Himself expending all the money, energy, and time that are being expended by His people, so that at every point where there is a Christian Christ's purposes might be being forwarded. This is the devotedness we are called to; this is the devotedness we must cultivate until we do make some considerable attainment in it.

EXCOMMUNICATION; OR, PURGING OUT THE OLD LEAVEN

"For this cause have I sent unto you Timotheus, who is my beloved son, and faithful in the Lord, who shall bring you into remembrance of my ways which be in Christ, as I teach every where in every church. Now some are puffed up, as though I would not come to you. But I will come to you shortly, if the Lord will, and will know, not the speech of them which are puffed up, but the power. For the kingdom of God is not in word, but in power. What will ye? shall I come unto you with a rod, or in love, and in the spirit of meekness?"

"It is reported commonly that there is fornication among you, and such fornication as is not so much as named among the Gentiles, that one should have his father's wife. And ye are puffed up, and have not rather mourned, that he that hath done this deed might be taken away from among you. For I verily, as absent in body, but present in spirit, have judged already as though I were present, concerning him that hath so done this deed. In the name of our Lord Jesus Christ, when ye are gathered together, and my spirit, with the power of our Lord Jesus Christ, to deliver such an one unto Satan for the destruction of the flesh, that the spirit may be saved in the day of the Lord Jesus. Your glorying is not good. Know ye not that a little leaven leaveneth the whole lump? Purge out therefore the old leaven, that ye may be a new lump, as ye are unleavened. For even Christ our passover is sacrificed for us: therefore let us keep the feast, not with old leaven, neither with the leaven of malice and wickedness; but with the unleavened bread of sincerity and truth. I wrote unto you in an epistle not to company with fornicators: yet not altogether with the fornicators of this world, or with the covetous, or extortioners, or with idolaters; for then must ye needs go out of the world. But now I have written unto you not to keep company, if any man that is called a brother be a fornicator, or covetous, or an idolater, or a railer, or a drunkard, or an extortioner; with such an one no not to eat. For what have I to do to judge them also that are without? do not ye judge them that are within? But them that are without God judgeth. Therefore put away from among yourselves that wicked person."—1 Cor. iv. 17-v. 13.

VIII
EXCOMMUNICATION; OR, PURGING OUT THE OLD LEAVEN

From the subject of the factions in the Corinthian Church, which has so long detained Paul, he now passes to the second division of his Epistle, in which he speaks of the relation the Christians should hold to the heathen population around them. The transition is easy and such as befits a letter. Paul had thought it advisable to send Timothy, who perfectly understood his mind, and could represent his views more fully than a letter; but it now occurred to him that this might be construed by some of the vain popular leaders in the Church into a timorous reluctance on his part to appear in Corinth and a sign that they were no longer to be held in check by the strong hand of the Apostle. "Some are puffed up, as though *I* would not come to you." He assures them therefore that he himself will come to Corinth, and also that the leaders of the Church have little reason to be puffed up, seeing that they have allowed in the Church an immorality so gross that even the lower standard of pagan ethics regards it as an unnameable abomination; and if once it is named, it is only to say that not all the waters of ocean can wash away such guilt. Instead of being puffed up, Paul tells them, they should rather be ashamed and at once take steps to put away from them so great a scandal. If not, he must come, not in meekness and love, but with a rod.

The Corinthian Church had fallen into a common snare. Churches have always been tempted to pique themselves on their rich foundations and institutions, on producing champions of the faith, able writers, eloquent preachers, on their cultured ministry, on their rich and æsthetic services, and not on that very thing for which the Church exists: the cleansing of the morals of the people and their elevation to a truly spiritual and godly life. And it is the individuals who give character to any Church. "A little leaven leaveneth the whole lump." Each member of a Church in each day's conduct in business and at home stakes, not only his own reputation, but the credit of the Church to which he belongs. Involuntarily and unconsciously men lower their opinion of the Church and cease to expect to find in her a fountain of spiritual life, because they find her members selfish and greedy in business, ready to avail themselves of doubtful methods; harsh, self-indulgent, and despotic at home, tainted with vices condemned by the least educated conscience. Let us remember that our little leaven leavens what is in contact with us; that our worldliness and unchristian conduct tend to lower the tone of our circle, encourage others to live down to our level, and help to demoralize the community.

In the judgment Paul pronounces on the Corinthian culprit two points are important. First, it is noteworthy that Paul, Apostle though he was, did not take the case out of the hands of the congregation. His own judgment on the case was explicit and decided, and this judgment he does not hesitate to declare; but, at the same time, it is the congregation which must deal with the case and pronounce judgment in it. The excommunication he enjoined was to be their act. "Put away from among yourselves," he says (v. 13), "that wicked person." The government of the Church was in Paul's idea thoroughly democratic; and where the power to excommunicate has been lodged in a priesthood, the results have been deplorable. Either, on the one hand, the people have become craven and have lived in terror, or, on the other hand, the priest has been afraid to measure his strength with powerful offenders. In our own country and in others this power of excommunication has been abused for the most unworthy purposes, political, social, and private; and only when it is lodged in the congregation can you secure a fair judgment and moral right to enforce it. There is little fear that this power will nowadays be abused. Men themselves conscious of strong propensities to evil and of many sins are more likely to be lax in administering discipline than forward to use their power; and so far from ecclesiastical discipline producing in its administrators harsh, tyrannical, and self-righteous feelings, it rather works an opposite effect, and evokes charity, a sense of solemn responsibility, and the longing for the welfare of others which lies latent in Christian minds.

But, second, the precise punishment intended by Paul is couched in language which the present generation cannot readily understand. The culprit is not only to be excluded from Christian communion, but "to be delivered unto Satan for the destruction of the flesh, that the spirit may be saved." Many meanings have been put upon these words; but after all has been said, the natural and obvious meaning of the words asserts itself. Paul believed that certain sins were more likely to be cured by bodily suffering than by any other agency. Naturally sins of the flesh belonged to this class. Bodily suffering of some kinds he believed to be the infliction of Satan. Even his own thorn in the flesh he spoke of as a messenger of Satan sent to buffet him. He expected also that the judgment pronounced by himself and the congregation on this offender would be given effect to in God's providence; and accordingly he bids the congregation hand the man over to this disciplinary suffering, not as a final doom, but as the only likely means of saving his soul.[4] If the offender mentioned in the Second Epistle is the same man, then we have evidence that the discipline was effectual, that the sinner did repent and was overwhelmed with shame and sorrow. Certainly such an experience of punishment, though not invariably or even commonly effectual, is in itself calculated to penetrate to the very depth of a man's spirit and give him new thoughts about his sin. If when suffering he can acknowledge his own wrong-doing as the cause of his misery and accept all the bitter and grievous penalties his sin has incurred, if he can truly humble himself before God in the matter and own that all he suffers is right and good, then he is nearer the kingdom of heaven than ever he was before. Substantially the same idea as Paul's is put in the mouth of the Pope by the most modern of poets:—

> "For the main criminal I have no hope
> Except in such a suddenness of fate.
> I stood at Naples once, a night so dark,
> I could have scarce conjectured there was earth
> Anywhere, sky, or sea, or world at all,
> But the night's black was burst through by a blaze;
> Thunder struck blow on blow; Earth groaned and bore,
> Through her whole length of mountain visible:
> There lay the city thick and plain with spires,
> And, like a ghost disshrouded, white the sea.
> So may the truth be flashed out by one blow,
> And Guido see one instant and be saved."

The necessity for keeping their communion pure, for being a society with no leaven of wickedness among them, Paul proceeds to urge and illustrate in the words, "For even Christ our passover is sacrificed for us; therefore let us purge out the old leaven." The allusion was, of course, much more telling to Jews than it can possibly be to us; still, if we call to mind the outstanding ideas of the Passover, we cannot fail to feel the force of the admonition. That must be the simplest explanation of the Passover which Jewish parents were enjoined to give to their children, in the words, "By strength of hand the Lord brought us out of Egypt, from the house of bondage. And it came to pass when Pharaoh would hardly let us go, that the Lord slew all the firstborn in the land of Egypt, with the firstborn of man and the firstborn of beast. Therefore I sacrifice to the Lord all the firstborn being males, but all the firstborn of my children I redeem." That is to say, all the firstborn of animals they sacrificed to God, slaying them on His altar, but instead of slaying the human firstborns they redeemed them by sacrificing a lamb in their stead. The whole transaction of the night of the first Passover stood thus: God claimed the Israelites as His people; the Egyptians also claimed them as theirs. And as no warning would persuade the Egyptians to let them away to serve God, God at last forcibly delivered them, slaying the flower of the Egyptian people, and so crippling and dismaying them as to give Israel opportunity of escape. Being thus rescued that they might be God's people, they felt bound to continue to own this; and in accordance with the custom of their time they expressed their sense of it by sacrificing their firstborn, by presenting them to God as belonging to Him. By this outward sacrificial act engaged in by every family it was acknowledged that the whole nation belonged to God.

Christ, then, is our Passover or Paschal Lamb, in the first place, because through Him there is made the acknowledgment that we belong to God. He is in very truth the prime and flower, the best representative of our race, the firstborn of every creature. He is the one who can make for all others this acknowledgment that we are God's people. And He does so by perfectly giving Himself up to God. This fact that we belong to God, that we men are His creatures and subjects, has never been perfectly acknowledged save by Christ. No individual or society of people has ever lived entirely for God. No man has ever fully recognised this apparently simple truth, that we are not our own, but God's. The Israelites made the acknowledgment in form, by sacrifice, but Christ alone made it in deed by giving Himself up wholly to do God's will. The Israelites made the acknowledgment from time to time, and with probably more or less truthfulness and sincerity, but Christ's whole spirit and habitual temper of mind was that of perfect obedience and dedication.

Only those of us, then, who see that we ought to live for God can claim Christ as our representative. His dedication to God is unmeaning to us if we do not desire to belong entirely to God. If He is our Passover, the meaning of this is that He gives us liberty to serve God; if we do not mean to be God's people, if we do not resolutely purpose to put ourselves at God's disposal, then it is idle and false of us to talk of Him as our Passover. Christ comes to bring us back to God, to redeem us from all that hinders our serving Him; but if we really prefer being our own masters, then manifestly He is useless to us. It is no matter what we say, nor what rites and forms we go through; the one question is, Do we at heart wish to give ourselves up to God? Does Christ really represent us,—represent, by His devoted unworldly life, our earnest and hearty desire and intention? Do we find in His life and death, in His submission to God and meek acceptance of all God appointed, the truest representation of what we ourselves would fain be and do, but cannot?

It is through this *self-sacrifice* of Christ that we can become God's people, and enjoy all the liberties and advantages of His people. Christ becomes the representative of all whose state of mind His sacrifice represents. If we would fain be of one mind and will with God as Christ was, if we feel the degradation and bitterness of failing God and disappointing the trust He has confided in us His children, if our life is wholly spoiled by the latent feeling that all is wrong because we are not in harmony with the wise and holy and loving Father, if we feel with more and more distinctness, as life goes on, that there is a God, and that the foundation of all happiness and soundness of life must be laid in union with Him, then Christ's perfect surrender of Himself to the will of the Father represents what we would but cannot ourselves achieve. When the Israelite came with his lamb, feeling the attractiveness and majesty of God, and desiring to pour his whole life out in fellowship with God and service of Him, as entirely as the life of the lamb was poured out at the altar, God accepted this symbolic utterance of the worshipper's heart. As the worshipping Israelite saw in the animal yielding its whole life the very utterance of his own desire, and said, Would God I could as freely and entirely devote myself with all my powers and energies to my Father above; so we, looking at the free, and loving, and eager sacrifice of our Lord, say in our hearts, Would God I could thus live in God and for God, and so become one with perfect purity and justice, with infinite love and power.

The Paschal Lamb then was in the first place the acknowledgment by the Israelites that they belonged to God. The lamb was offered to God, not as being itself anything worthy of God's acceptance, but merely as a way of saying to God that the family who offered it gave themselves up as entirely to Him. But by thus becoming a kind of substitute for the family, it saved the firstborn from death. God did not wish to smite Israel, but to save them. He did not wish to confound them with the Egyptians, and make an indiscriminate slaughter. But God did not simply omit the Israelite houses, and pick out the Egyptian ones throughout the land. He left it to the choice of the people whether they would accept His deliverance and belong to Him or not. He told them that every home would be safe, on the door-posts of which there was visible the blood of the lamb. The blood of the lamb thus provided a refuge for the people, a shelter from death which otherwise would have fallen upon them. The angel of judgment was to recognise no distinction between Israelite and Egyptian save this of the sprinkled, stained door-posts. Death was to enter every house where the blood was not visible; mercy was to rest on every family that dwelt under this sign. God's judgment was out that night all over the land, and no difference of race was made anything of. They who had disregarded the use of the blood would have no time to object, We be Abraham's seed. God meant that they should all be rescued, but He knew that it was quite possible that some had become so entangled with Egypt that they would be unwilling to leave it, and He would not force any—we may say He *could* not force any—to yield themselves to Him. This rendering of ourselves to God must be a free act on our part; it must be the deliberate and true act of a soul that feels convinced of the poverty and wretchedness of all life that is not serving God. And God left it in the choice of each family—they might or might not use the blood, as they pleased. But wherever it was used, safety and deliverance were thereby secured. Wherever the lamb was slain in acknowledgment that the family belonged to God, God dealt with them as with His own. Wherever there was no such acknowledgment, they were dealt with as those who preferred to be God's enemies.

And now Christ our Passover is slain, and we are asked to determine the application of Christ's sacrifice, to say whether we will use it or no. We are not asked to add anything to the efficacy of that sacrifice, but only to avail ourselves of it. Passing through the streets of the Egyptian cities on the night of the Passover, you could have told who trusted God and who did not. Wherever there was faith there was a man in the twilight with his bason of blood and bunch of hyssop, sprinkling his lintel and then going in and shutting his door, resolved that no solicitation should tempt him from behind the blood till the angel was by. He took God at His word; he believed God meant to deliver him, and he did what he was told was his part. The result was that he was rescued from Egyptian bondage. God now desires that we be separated from everything which prevents us from gladly serving Him, from every evil bias in us which prevents us from delighting in God, from all that makes us feel guilty and unhappy, from all sin that enchains us and makes our future hopeless and dark. God calls us to Himself, meaning that we shall one day get for ever past all that has made us unfaithful to Him and all that has made it impossible for us to find deep and lasting pleasure in serving Him. To us He throws open a way out from all bondage, and from all that gives us the spirit of slaves; He gives us the opportunity of following Him into real and free life, into glad fellowship with Him and joyful partnership in His ever beneficent and progressive work. What response are we making? In the face of the varied difficulties and deluding appearances of this life, in the face of the complexity and inveterate hold of sin, can you believe that God seeks to deliver you and even now designs for you a life that is worthy of His greatness and love, a life which shall perfectly satisfy you and give play to all your worthy desires and energies?

Sacrifices were in old times accompanied by feasts in which the reconciled God and His worshippers ate together. In the feast of Passover the lamb which had been used as a sacrifice was consumed as food to strengthen the Israelites for their exodus. This idea Paul here adapts to his present purpose. "Christ our passover is sacrificed for us," he says; "let us therefore keep the feast." The whole life of the Christian is a festal celebration; his strength is maintained by that which has given him peace with God. By Christ's death God reconciles us to Himself; out of Christ we continually receive what fits us to serve God as His free people. Every Christian should aim at making his life a celebration of the true deliverance Christ has accomplished for us. We should see that our life is a true exodus, and being so it will bear marks of triumph and of freedom. To feed upon Christ, joyfully to assimilate all that is in Him to our own character, it is this which makes life festal, which turns faintness into abounding strength, and brings zest and appetite into monotonous labour.

But Paul's purpose in introducing the idea of the Passover is rather to enforce his injunction to the Corinthians to purge their communion of all defilement. "Let us keep the feast, not with old leaven, neither with the leaven of malice and wickedness!" Leaven was judged unclean, because fermentation is one form of corruption. This impurity was not to be touched by the holy people during their festival week. This was secured at the first keeping of the Passover by the suddenness of the exodus when the people fled with their kneading boards on their shoulders and had no time to take leaven, and had therefore no choice but to keep God's command and eat unleavened bread. And so scrupulously did the people at all times observe this that before the day of the feast they used to sweep their houses and search the dark corners with candles, lest a morsel of leaven should be found among them. Thus would Paul have all Christians be separate from the rotting, fermenting results of the old life. So suddenly would he have us issue from it and so clean would He have us leave it all behind us. A *little* leaven leaveneth the whole lump; therefore must we be careful, if we would keep this precept and be clean, to search into even unlikely corners in our hearts and lives, and as with the candle of the Lord make diligent search for the tainting remnant.

It is the purpose to keep the feast faithfully, and live as those who are delivered from bondage, which reveals in our consciousness how much we have to put away, and how much of the old life is following on into the new. Habits, feelings, likings and dislikings, all go with us. The unleavened bread of holiness and of a life bound to and ruled by the earnest and godly life of Christ, seems flat and insipid, and we crave something more stimulating to the appetite. The old intolerance of regular, intelligent, continuous prayer, the old willingness to find a rest in this world, must be purged out as leaven which will alter the whole character of our life. Are our holy days holidays, or do we endure holiness of thought and feeling mainly on the consideration that holiness is but for a season? Patiently and believingly resist the stirrings of the old nature. Measure all that rises in you and all that quickens your blood and stirs your appetite by the death and spirit of Christ. Sever yourself determinedly from all that alienates you from Him. The old life and the new should not run parallel with one another so that you can pass from the one to the other. They are not side by side, but end to end; the one all preceding the other, the one ceasing and terminating where the other begins.

The old leaven is to be put away: "the leaven of malice and wickedness," the bad-heartedness that is not seen to be bad till brought into the light of Christ's spirit; the spiteful, vindictive, and selfish feelings that are almost expected in society, these are to be put away; and in their stead "the unleavened bread of sincerity and truth" is to be introduced. Above all things, Paul would say, let us be sincere. The word "sincere" sets before the mind the natural image from which the moral quality takes its name, the honey free from the smallest particle of wax, pure and pellucid. The word which Paul himself, using his own language, here sets down, conveys a similar idea. It is a word derived from the custom of judging the purity of liquids or the texture of cloths by holding them between the eye and the sun. What Paul desiderates in the Christian character is a quality which can stand this extreme test, and does not need to be seen only in an artificial light. He wants a pure transparent sincerity; he wants what is to its finest thread genuine; an acceptance of Christ which is real, and which is rich in eternal results.

Are we living a genuine and true life? Are we living up to what we know to be the truth about life? Christ has given us the true estimate of this world and all that is in it, He has measured for us God's requirements, He has shown us what is the truth about God's love;—are we living in this truth? Do we not find that in our best intentions there is some mixture of foreign elements, and in our most assured choice of Christ some remaining elements which will lead us back from our choice? Even while we own Christ as our Saviour from sin, we are but half-inclined to go out from its bondage. We pray God for deliverance, and when He throws wide open before us the gate that leads away from temptation, we refuse to see it, or hesitate until again it is closed. We know how we may become holy, and yet will not use our knowledge.

Let us, whatever else, be genuine. Let us not trifle with the purpose and requirements of Christ. In our deepest and clearest consciousness we see that Christ does open the way to the true life of man; that it is our part to make room for this self-sacrificing life in our own day and in our own circumstances; that until we do so we can only by courtesy be called

Christians. The convictions and beliefs which Christ inspires are convictions and beliefs about what we should be, and what Christ means all human life to be, and until these convictions and beliefs are embodied in our actual living selves, and in our conduct and life, we feel that we are not genuine. Time will bring us no relief from this humiliating position, unless time brings us at length to yield ourselves freely to Christ's Spirit, and unless, instead of looking at the kingdom He seeks to establish as a quite impossible Utopia, we set ourselves resolutely and wholly to aid in the annexing to His rule our own little world of business and of all the relations of life. To have convictions is well, but if these convictions are not embodied in our life, then we lose our life, and our house is built on sand.

ON GOING TO LAW

"Dare any of you, having a matter against another, go to law before the unjust, and not before the saints? Do ye not know that the saints shall judge the world? and if the world shall be judged by you, are ye unworthy to judge the smallest matters? Know ye not that we shall judge angels? how much more things that pertain to this life? If then ye have judgments of things pertaining to this life, set them to judge who are least esteemed in the Church. I speak to your shame. Is it so, that there is not a wise man among you? no, not one that shall be able to judge between his brethren? But brother goeth to law with brother, and that before the unbelievers. Now therefore there is utterly a fault among you, because ye go to law one with another. Why do ye not rather take wrong? why do ye not rather suffer yourselves to be defrauded? Nay, ye do wrong, and defraud, and that your brethren. Know ye not that the unrighteous shall not inherit the kingdom of God? Be not deceived: neither fornicators, nor idolaters, nor adulterers, nor effeminate, nor abusers of themselves with mankind, nor thieves, nor covetous, nor drunkards, nor revilers, nor extortioners, shall inherit the kingdom of God. And such were some of you: but ye are washed, but ye are sanctified, but ye are justified in the name of the Lord Jesus, and by the Spirit of our God." —1 Cor. vi. 1-11.

IX
ON GOING TO LAW

St. Paul here gives his judgment on the litigiousness of the Corinthians. The Greeks, in general, were fond of going to law. They were not only quarrelsome, but they seemed to derive an excitement pleasant to their frivolous nature in the suspense and uncertainty of cases before the courts. The converts to Christianity seemed not to have discarded this taste, and as a habit of going to law not merely involved great loss of time, but was also dangerous to the feeling of brotherhood which should exist among Christians, St. Paul takes the opportunity to throw in some advice on the subject. He has been telling them they have nothing to do with judging the heathen; he now proceeds to remind them that they ought not to go to law before the heathen. He feared that an unseemly wrangling among Christians might convey to the heathen quite an erroneous impression of the nature of their religion. There was, to his mind, something incongruous, something monstrous, in brother going to law with brother. What was that brotherhood worth that could not bear a little wrong? How could he continue to speak of Christian love, if Christians were to bite and devour one another? How could he preach the superiority of Christianity to heathenism if Christians had so little common sense, so little *esprit de corps*, so little mutual forbearance, that they must call in a heathen to settle their disputes for them? It seemed to Paul to be a losing of caste for Christians to proclaim their insufficiency to carry on their own affairs without the aid of heathen. It seemed to him a public profession that Christianity was not sufficient for the needs of its adherents.

The reasons which St. Paul adduces to give weight to his rebuke are important.

I. The saints are destined to judge the world, to judge angels; that is to say, to judge persons in separation from earthly interests, to judge unclothed detached spirits, to ascertain what is spiritually good and spiritually evil. Shall they not then be considered fit to judge little worldly matters, matters of £. s. d., matters of property and of bargain? This statement that the saints shall judge the world is one of those broad widely-suggestive statements with which St. Paul from time to time surprises us, making them casually, as if he had many more equally astounding facts in his knowledge which he might also reveal if he had leisure. It is difficult to grasp the statements which he makes in this style; it is also difficult to link a truth so revealed to the truths amid which we are now living; it is difficult even to ascertain with precision the bearing and significance of it.

It seems plain, however, that whatever else may be implied in this statement, and in whatever way it is to be fulfilled, St. Paul meant that ultimately, in that final state of things towards which all present things are growing and travelling, the men who are holy shall be at the head of affairs, acknowledged as the fittest to discern between right and wrong; and also that the germ and first principles of this final state of things are already implanted in the world by the Christian religion—two very important truths, certainly, to those who believe them. The precise form of the final judgment and future government of the world we cannot predict; but from this statement a bright ray of light shoots into the darkness, and shows us that the saints, *i.e.*, the servants of Christ, are to have the responsibility of pronouncing judgment on character, and of allotting destiny, reward or punishment. We shrink from such a thought; not, indeed, that we are slow to pronounce judgment upon our fellow-men, but to do so officially, and in connection with definite results, seems a responsibility too heavy for merely human judges to sustain. But why men should not judge men hereafter as they do judge them now, we do not see. If we, in this present world, submit ourselves to those who have knowledge of law and ordinary justice, we may well be content to be judged in the world to come by those whose holiness has been matured by personal strife against evil, by sustained efforts to cleanse their souls from bias, from envy, from haste, from harshness, from all that hinders them from seeing and loving the truth. Holiness, or likeness to God, assimilation to His mind, formed by the constant desire to judge of things in this world as He judges, and to love truly all that He loves, this quality is surely worthy to be at the head. In that future kingdom of God in which all things are to have their proper place, and are to be ranked according to their real worth, holiness must come to the supremacy.

But equally worthy of remark is St. Paul's *inference* from the fact that holiness shall eventually be supreme. His inference is that it ought *now* to be regarded as competent to settle the petty disputes which arise among us. "If we are to judge angels, much more the things that pertain to this life." We can only arrive at any dignity by perseveringly seeking it. If the future kingdom of God is to be a perfect kingdom, it can only be as its subjects carry into it characters which have been strongly tending towards perfection. It is not the future that is to make us, but we who are to make the future. The kingdom of God is within us; if not there, in our own dispositions and likings, it is nowhere. Heaven will be what its inhabitants make it. Earth is not heaven only because men decline to make it so. We do not know the forms which society will assume in the world to come, when men will be grouped, not by families and blood-relationships, and the necessary requirements of physical life, but according to their character and moral value, their spiritual affinities and capacities for usefulness. But though we cannot say exactly how men will be grouped, nor how they will find expression for all that intense emotion and eager activity which in this life creates adventure, war, politics, speculation, inventions of all kinds, we do know that wherever there are men there must be society; there must be men not isolated and solitary, but working together and depending one on the other; and that there will therefore be difficult complications of interest and obscure relations of man to man very similar to those which arise in this world; but that those difficulties will be removed without passion and wrangling and the interference of force. A heaven and an earth there will be; but "a new heaven and a new earth." The outer framework will be very much the same, but the inner spirit and life very different. But it is not the altered place or time that is to produce in us this change of spirit; we are to find it there only if we carry it with us. St. Paul takes for granted that the principles which are to be perfectly and exclusively manifested in the world to come, are now cherished by Christians. And as there will be no differences in heaven which cannot be adjusted without appeal to an authority which can silence and reconcile the disputants, so there ought to be, among the heirs of heaven, no going to law now.

St. Paul, therefore, while he contrasts the subjects in which a lawyer-like mind will find employment in this world and the next, reminds us that those who are here trained to understand character, and to discern where right and justice lie, will be in no want of employment in the world to come. The matters which come before our courts, or which are referred privately to lawyers, may often be in themselves very paltry. A vast proportion of legal business is created by changes from which the future life is exempt, changes consequent on death, on marriage, on pecuniary disasters. But underneath such suits as these the keenest of human feelings are at work, and it is often in the power of a lawyer to give a man advice which will save his conscience from a life-long stain, or which will bring comfort into a family instead of heart-burning, and plenty in place of penury. The physician keeps us in life; the minister of Christ tells us on what principles we ought to live; but the lawyer takes our hand at every great practical step in life, and it is his function (and surely there is none higher) to insist on a conscientious use of money, to point out the just claims which others have upon us, to show us the right and the wrong in all our ordinary affairs, and thus to bring justice and mercy down from heaven and make them familiar to the market-place.

And therefore many of the finest characters and best intellects have devoted themselves, and always will devote themselves, to this profession. It may attract many from less lofty motives; but it always will attract those who are concerned to save men from practical folly, and who wish to see the highest principles brought into direct contact with human affairs. If the legal mind degenerates into a mere memory for technicalities and acuteness in applying forms, nothing can be more contemptible or dangerous to the character; but if it takes to do with real things, and not with forms only, and tries to see what equity requires, and not merely what the letter of the law enjoins, and seeks to forward the well-being of men, then surely there is no profession in which there is such abundant opportunity of earning the beatitude which says, "Blessed are the peacemakers," none in which the senses can better be exercised to discern between good and evil, none in which men may better be prepared for the higher requirements of a heavenly society in which some are made rulers over ten cities.

II. The second confirmation of his rebuke St. Paul brings forward in the fifth verse: "Is there not a wise man among yourselves?" "A wise man" was the technical term for a judge in the Hebrew courts.

To understand Paul's position we must bear in mind that among the Jews there was no distinction between Church and State. The courts appointed for the determination of the minor causes in each locality were composed of the same persons who constituted the eldership of the synagogue. In the synagogue and by the eldership offenders were both tried and punished. The rabbis said, "He who brings lawsuits of Israel before a heathen tribunal profanes the Name, and does homage to idolatry; for when *our enemies* are *judges* (Deut. xxxii. 31) it is a testimony to the superiority of their religion." This idea passed over from Judaism to Christianity; and Paul considers it a scandal that "brother goeth to law with brother, and that before the unbelievers." And even a century after Paul's time the rule of the Christian Church was "Let not those who have disputes go to law before the civil powers, but let them by all means be reconciled by the elders of the Church, and let them readily yield to their decision." And as late as our own day we find an Arab sheikh complaining that Christian Copts come to him, a Mohammedan, to settle their disputes and "won't go and be settled by the priest out of the Gospels."

Did Paul then mean that such legal cases as are now tried in our civil courts should be settled by non-professional men? Did he mean that ecclesiastical courts should take out of the hands of the civil magistrate all pleas regarding property, all disputes about commercial transactions? Did he foresee none of the great evils that have arisen wherever Church or State has not respected the province of the other, and was he prepared to put the power of the sword into the hand of ecclesiastics? We think no one can read either his life or his writings without seeing that this was not his meaning. He taught men to submit themselves to the powers that then were—*i.e.*, to the heathen magistrates of Rome—and he himself appealed to Cæsar. He had no notion of subverting the ordinary legal procedure and civil courts, but he would fain have deprived them of much of their practice. He thought it might be expected that Christians would never be so determinedly rancorous or so blindly covetous but that their disputes might be settled by private and friendly advice. He gives no orders about constituting new courts and appointing new statutes and forms of procedure; he has no idea of transferring into the Church all the paraphernalia of civil courts: but he maintains that if a Christian community be in a healthy state, few quarrels will be referred for settlement to a court of law. Courts of law are necessary evils, which will be less and less patronized in proportion as Christian feeling and principle prevail.

This rebuke is applicable even to a community like our own, in which the courts of law are not heathen, but Christian; and the principle on which the rebuke is based is one that has gradually worked its way into the heart of the community. It is felt, felt now even by nations as well as by individuals, that if a dispute can be settled by arbitration, this is not only cheaper, quicker, and equally satisfactory, but that it is a more generous and Christian way of getting justice done. Those who hold office in the Church may not always happen to be suitable arbitrators; they may not have the technical and special knowledge requisite: but Paul's counsel is acted on if disputes among Christians be somehow adjusted in a friendly way, and without the interference of an external authority. Christian people may need legal advice; they may not know what the right and wrong of a complicated case are; they may be truly at a loss to understand how much is justly theirs and how much their neighbour's; they may often need professional aid to shed light on a transaction: but when two Christians go to law in a spirit of rancour, resolved to make good their own just claims, and to enforce by the authority of law what they cannot compass by right feeling, this only proves that their worldliness is stronger than their Christianity. St. Paul thinks it a scandal and a degradation when Christians need to appeal to law against one another. It is a confession that Christian principle is in their case insufficient by itself to carry them through the practical difficulties of life.

But some one will say to this, as to every unworldly, truly Christian, and therefore novel and difficult counsel, "It savours of theory and of romance; a man cannot act it out unless he is prepared to be duped, and cheated, and imposed upon. It is a theory that if carried out must end in beggary." Just as if the world could be regenerated by anything that is not apparently romantic! If a greater good is to be reached, it must be by some way that men have not tried before. The kingdoms of this world will not become the kingdom of Christ by the admission into our conduct of only that which men have tried and found to be practicable, and void of all risk, and requiring no devotion or sacrifice. If then, any one says, "But if there is to be no going to law, if we are not to force a man to give us our own, we must continually be losers," the reply of a well-known Kincardineshire lawyer might suffice, "Don't go to law if yielding does not cost you more than forty shillings in the pound." And from a different point of view St. Paul replies, "Well, and what though you be losers? The kingdom you belong to is not meat and drink, but righteousness." If a man says, "We must have some redress, some authority to extort the dues that are not freely given; we must strike when we are struck; when a man takes our coat, we must summon him, or he will take our cloak next," St. Paul replies, "Well, if this *be* the alternative, if you must either push your own claims and insist upon your rights, or suffer by assuming the meekness and gentleness of your Master, why do you not rather take wrong? why do you not rather suffer yourselves to be defrauded? It may be quite true that if you turn the other cheek, it also will be smitten. It may be very likely that a greedy competitor will be so little abashed by your meekness, and so little struck by your magnanimity in giving way to some of his demands, that he will even be encouraged to greater extortions. It is quite probable that if you act as your Master did, you will be as ill off in this world as He was. But is that any reason why you should at once call Him your Master and refuse to obey His precepts and follow His example?" One thing is certain: that so long as men honestly accepted Christ's words in their plain meaning, and followed Him in His own way, making light of worldly loss, Christianity was believed in and rapidly extended. It was seen to be a new moral power among men, and was welcomed as such, until a large part of the world received it; but its victory was its defeat. Once it became the fashion, once it became popular, the heart of it was eaten out. As soon as it became a religion without hardship, it became a religion without vitality.

St. Paul then shows no hesitation about pushing his doctrine to its consequences. He sees that the real cure of wrangling, and of fraud, and of war is not litigation, nor any outward restraint that can be laid on the wrong-doer, but meekness, and unselfishness, and unworldliness on the part of those who suffer wrong. The world has laughed at this theory of social regeneration all along; a few men in each generation have believed in it, and have been ridiculed for their belief. At the same time, the world itself is aware, or should be aware, that its own remedies have utterly failed. Has war taught nations moderation in their ambition? Has it saved the world from the calamities which it is said would ensue were any one nation to prefer submitting to injustice rather than going to war? Have the outward restraints of law made men more just or less avaricious? There has been time to test the power of law to repress crime, and to compel men to honesty and justice. Can any one say it has been so successful that it must be looked to as the great means of regenerating society, of bringing society into that healthy and ideal state which statesmen work for, and for which the people inarticulately sigh? Does not St. James come nearer the mark when he says, "Whence come wars and fightings? Come they not hence, even of the lusts that war in your members?"—*i.e.*, from the restless ambitions, and appetites, and longings of men who seek their all in this world? And if that is their source, it is to that we must apply the remedy. Law is necessary for restraining the expressions of a vicious nature, but law is insufficient to remove the possibility of these expressions by healing the nature. This can only be done by the diffusion of unworldliness and unselfishness. And it is Christians who are responsible for diffusing this unworldly spirit, and who must diffuse it, not by talk and advice, but by practice and example, by themselves showing what unselfishness is, rebuking covetousness by yielding to its demands, shaming all wrong-doing by refusing to retaliate while they expose its guilt.

While therefore it is a mistake to suppose that all the laws which are to rule in the perfected kingdom of God can find immediate and unmodified expression in this present world, it is our part to find for them an introduction into the world in every case in which it is possible to apply them. Those laws which are to be our sole rule when we are perfect cannot always be immediately applied now. For example, we all believe that ultimately love will be the only motive, that all service of God and of one another will eventually spring solely from our desire to serve because we love. And because this is so, some persons have thought that love should be the only motive now, and that obedience which is procured by fear is useless; that preachers ought to appeal only to the highest parts of man's nature, and not at all to those which are lower, and that parents should never threaten punishment nor enforce obedience. But the testimony of one of the most genial and successful of preachers is that "of all the persons to whom his ministry had been efficacious *only one* had received the first effectual impressions from the gentle and attractive aspects of religion, all the rest from the awful and alarming ones—the appeals to fear." Take, again, the testimony of one of the wisest and most successful of our schoolmasters. "I can't rule my boys," he says, "by the law of love. If they were angels or professors, I might; but as they are only boys, I find it necessary to make them fear me first, and then take my chance of their love afterwards. By this plan I find that I generally get both; by reversing the process I should in most cases get neither." And God, though slow to anger and not easily provoked, scourgeth every son whom He receiveth, not dealing with us now as He will deal with us when perfect love has cast out its preparative fear. So, in regard to the matter before us, there must be an aiming and striving towards the perfect state in which there shall be no going to law, no settling of matters by appeal to anything outside the heart of the persons interested. But while we aim at this, and seek to give it prevalence, we shall also be occasionally forced back upon the severer and more external means of self-defence. The members of Christ's Church are those on whom the burden falls of giving prevalence to these Christian principles. It is incumbent upon them to show, even at cost to themselves, that there are higher, better, and more enduring principles than law, and the customs of trade, and the ways of the world. And however difficult it may be *theoretically* to hold the balance between justice and mercy, between worldly sharpness and Christian meekness, we all know that there are some who practically exhibit a large measure of this Christian temper, who prefer to take wrong and to suffer quietly rather than to expose the wickedness of others, or to resent their unjust claims, or to complain of their unfair usage. And whatever the most worldly of us may think of such conduct, however we may smile at it as weak, there is no one of us but also pays his tribute of respect to those who suffer wrong, loss, detraction, with a meek and cheerful patience; and whatever be the lot of such sufferers in a world where men are too busy in pushing their worldly prospects to understand those who are not of this world, we have no doubt in what esteem they will be held and what reward they will receive in a world where the Lamb is on the throne, and meek self-sacrifice is honestly worshipped as the highest quality whether in God or in man.

Paul knows that the Christian conscience is with him when he declares that men should rather suffer wrong than bring reproach on the Christian name: "Know ye not that wrong-doers shall not inherit the kingdom of God? Be not deceived; neither covetous, nor drunkards, nor revilers, nor extortioners shall inherit the kingdom of God." And yet how little do men seem to take to heart the great fact that they are travelling forward to a state in which nothing uncongenial to the Spirit of Christ can possibly find place. Do they think of the future at all? Do they believe that a state of things ruled by the Spirit of Christ is to follow this? And what preparation do they make? Is it not the height of folly to suppose that the selfishness and greed, the indolence and frivolity, the dreamy unreality and worldliness, which we suffer to grow upon us here, will give us entrance into the kingdom of God? The seaman who means to winter in the Arctic circle might as reasonably go with a single month's provisions and clothes suited to the tropics. There is a reason and a law in things; and if we are not assimilated to the Spirit of Christ now, we can have no part in His kingdom. If now our interest, and pursuits, and pleasures are all found in what gratifies selfishness and worldliness, it is impossible we can find a place in that kingdom which is all unselfishness and unworldliness. "Be not deceived." The spiritual world is a reality, and the godliness and Christlikeness that compose it must also be realities. Put away from you the fatuous idea that things will somehow come all right, and that your character will adapt itself to changed surroundings. It is not so; nothing that defiles can find entrance into the kingdom of God, but only those who are "sanctified in the name of the Lord Jesus and by the Spirit of our God."

FORNICATION

"All things are lawful unto me, but all things are not expedient: all things are lawful for me, but I will not be brought under the power of any. Meats for the belly, and the belly for meats: but God shall destroy both it and them. Now the body is not for fornication, but for the Lord; and the Lord for the body. And God hath both raised up the Lord, and will also raise up us by His own power. Know ye not that your bodies are the members of Christ? shall I then take the members of Christ, and make them the members of an harlot? God forbid. What? know ye not that he which is joined to an harlot is one body? for two, saith he, shall be one flesh. But he that is joined unto the Lord is one spirit. Flee fornication. Every sin that a man doeth is without the body; but he that committeth fornication sinneth against his own body. What? know ye not that your body is the temple of the Holy Ghost which is in you, which ye have of God, and ye are not your own? For ye are bought with a price: therefore glorify God in your body, and in your spirit, which are God's." —1 Cor. vi. 12-20.

X
FORNICATION

In remonstrating with the Corinthians for their litigiousness, Paul was forcibly reminded how imperfectly his converts understood the moral requirements of the kingdom of God. Apparently, too, he had reason to believe that they were not only content to remain on a low moral plane, but actually quoted some of his own favourite sayings in defence of immoral practices. After warning them therefore that only those who were sanctified could belong to the kingdom of God and specifying certain common kinds of wrong-doing which must for ever be excluded from that kingdom, he goes on to explain how they had misapprehended him if they thought that any principle of his could give colour to immorality. The Corinthians had apparently learned to argue that if, as Paul had so often and emphatically told them, all things were lawful to them, then this commonest of Greek indulgences was lawful; if abstaining from the meat which had been killed in a heathen temple was a matter of moral indifference which Christians might or might not practise, as they pleased, then this other common accompaniment of idolatry was also a matter of indifference and not in itself wrong.

To understand this Corinthian obliquity of moral vision it must be borne in mind that licentious rites were a common accompaniment of pagan worship, and especially in Corinth idolatry might have been briefly described as the performance of Balaam's instructions to the Israelites: the eating of things sacrificed to idols and the committing of fornication. The temples were often scenes of revelry and debauchery such as happily have become incredible to a modern mind. But not at once could men emerging from a religion so slenderly connected with morality apprehend what Christianity required of them. When they abandoned the temple-worship, were they also to abstain from eating the flesh offered for sale in the open market, and which had first been sacrificed to an idol? Might they not by partaking of such flesh become partakers in the sin of idolatry? To this Paul replied, Do not too scrupulously inquire into the previous history of your dinner; the meat has no moral taint; all things are lawful for you. This was reasonable; but then how about the other accompaniment of idolatry? Was it also a thing of indifference? Can we apply the same reasoning to it? It was this insinuation which called forth the emphatic condemnation which Paul utters in this paragraph.

The great principle of Christian liberty, "All things are lawful for me," Paul now sees he must guard against abuse by adding, "But all things are not expedient." The law and its modification are fully explained in a subsequent passage of the Epistle (viii.; x. 23, etc.). Here it may be enough to say that Paul seeks to impress on his readers that the question of duty is not answered by simply ascertaining what is lawful; we must also ask whether the practice or act contemplated is expedient. Though it may be impossible to prove that this or that practice is wrong in every case, we have still to ask, Does it advance what is good in us; is its bearing on society good or evil; will it in present circumstances and in the instance we contemplate give rise to misunderstandings and evil thoughts? The Christian is a law to himself; he has an internal guide that sets him above external rules. Very true; but that guide leads all those who possess it to a higher life than the law leads to, and proves its presence by teaching a man to consider, not how much indulgence he may enjoy without transgressing the letter of the law, but how he can most advantageously use his time and best forward what is highest in himself and in others.

Again, "all things are lawful for me;" all things are in my power. Yes, but for that very reason "I will not be brought under the power of any." "The reasonable use of my liberty cannot go the length of involving my own loss of it."[5] I am free from the law; I will not on that account become the slave of indulgence. As Carlyle puts it, "enjoying things which are pleasant—that is not the evil; it is the reducing of our moral self to slavery by them that is. Let a man assert withal that he is king over his habitudes; that he could and would shake them off on cause shown: this is an excellent law." There are several practices and habits which no one would call immoral or sinful, but which enslave a man quite as much as worse habits. He is no longer a free man; he is uneasy and restless, and cannot settle to his work until he obeys the craving he has created. And it is the very lawfulness of these indulgences which has ensnared him. Had they been sinful, the Christian man would not have indulged in them; but being in his power, they have now assumed power over him. They have power to compel him to waste his time, his money, sometimes even his health. He alone attains the true dignity and freedom of the Christian man who can say, with Paul, "I know both how to be full and to be hungry, both to abound and to suffer need;" "All things are in my power, but I will not be brought under the power of any."

Paul then proceeds more explicitly to apply these principles to the matter in hand. The Corinthians argued that if meats were morally indifferent, a man being morally neither the better nor the worse for eating food which had been offered in an idol's temple, so also a man was neither better nor worse for fornication. To expose the error of this reasoning Paul draws a remarkable distinction between the digestive, nutritive organs of the body and the body as a whole. Paul believed that the body was an essential part of human nature, and that in the future life the natural body would give place to the spiritual body. He believed also that the spiritual body was connected with, and had its birthplace in, the natural body, so that the body we now wear is to be represented by that finer and more spiritual organism we are hereafter to be clothed in. The connection of that future body with the physical world and its dependence on material things we cannot understand; but in some way inconceivable by us it is to carry on the identity of our present body, and thereby it reflects a sacredness and significance on this body. The body of the full-grown man or of the white-bearded patriarch is very different from that of the babe in its mother's arms, but there is a continuity that links them together and gives them identity. So the future body may be very different from and yet the same as the present. At the same time, the organs which merely serve for the maintenance of our present natural body will be unnecessary and out of place in the future body, which is spiritual in its origin and in its maintenance. Paul therefore distinguishes between the organs of nutrition and that body which is part of our permanent individuality, and which by some unimaginable process is to flower into an everlasting body. The digestive organs of the body have their use and their destiny, and the body as a whole has its use and destiny. These two differ from one another; and if you are to argue from the one to the other, you must keep in view this distinction. "Meats for the belly and the belly for meats; and God shall destroy both it and them: but the body is for the Lord, and the Lord for the body, and God shall raise up the one as He has raised up the other." The organs of nutrition have a present use; they are made for meats, and have a natural correspondence with meats. Any meat which the digestive organs approve is allowable. The conscience has to do with meat only through these organs. It must listen to their representations; and if they approve of certain qualities and quantities of food, the conscience confirms this decision: approves when the man uses the food best for these organs; disapproves when he uses consciously and self-indulgently what is bad for them. "Meats for the belly and the belly for meats"—they claim each other as their mutual, God-appointed counterparts. By eating you are not perverting your bodily organs to a use not intended for them; you are putting them to the use God meant them to serve.

Besides, these organs form no part of the future spiritual body. They pass away with the meats for which they were made. God shall destroy both the meats that are requisite for life in this world, and the organs needful for deriving sustenance from them. They serve a temporary purpose, like the houses we live in and the clothes we wear; and as we are not morally better because we live in a stone house, and not in a brick one, or because we wear woollens, and not cotton—so long as we do what is best to keep us in life—so neither is there any moral difference in meats—a remarkable conclusion for a Jew to come to, whose religion had taught him to hold so many forms of food in abhorrence.

But the body as a whole—for what is it made? These organs of nutrition fulfil their function when they lead you to eat such meat as sustains you in life; when does the body fulfil its function? What is its object and end? For what purpose have we a body? Paul is never afraid to suggest the largest questions, neither is he afraid to give his answer. "The body," he says, "is for the Lord, and the Lord for the body." Here also there is a mutual correspondence and fitness.

"The body is for the Lord." Paul was addressing Christians, and this no Christian would be disposed to deny. Every Christian is conscious that the body would not fulfil its end and purpose unless it were consecrated to the Lord and informed by His Spirit. The organism by which we come into contact with the world outside ourselves is not the unwieldy, hindering, irredeemable partner of the spirit, but is designed to be the vehicle of spiritual faculties and the efficient agent of our Lord's purposes. It must not be looked upon with resentment, pity, or contempt, but rather as essential to our human nature and to the fulfilment of the Lord's design as the Saviour of the world and the Head of humanity. It was through the body of the Lord that the great facts of our redemption were accomplished. It was the instrument of the incarnation and of the manifestation of God among men, of the death and the resurrection by which we are saved. And as in His own body Christ was incarnate among men, so now it is by means of the bodily existence and energies of His people on earth that He extends His influence.

The body then is for the Lord. He finds in it His needed instrument; without it He cannot accomplish His will. And the Lord is for the body. Without Him the body cannot develop into all it is intended to be. It has a great future as well as the soul. Our adoption as God's children is, in Paul's view, incomplete until the body also is redeemed and has fought its way through sickness, base uses, death, and dissolution into likeness to the glorified body of Christ. This body which we now identify with ourselves, and apart from which it is difficult to conceive of ourselves, is not the mere temporary lodging of the soul, which in a few years must be abandoned; but it is destined to preserve its identity through all coming changes, so that it will be recognisable still as our body. But this cannot be believed, far less accomplished, save by faith in the fact that God has raised up the Lord Jesus and will with Him raise us also. Otherwise the future of the body seems brief and calamitous. Death seems plainly to say, There is an end of all that is physical. Yes, replies the resurrection of the Lord, in death there is an end of this natural body; but death disengages the spiritual body from the natural, and clothes the spirit in a more fitting garb. Understand this we cannot, any more than we understand why a large mass draws to itself smaller masses; but believe it we can in presence of Christ's resurrection.

The Lord then is for the body, because in the Lord the body has a future opened to it and present connections and uses which prepare it for that future. It is the Spirit of Christ who is, within us, the earnest of that future, and who forms us for it, inclining us while in the body and by means of it to sow to the Spirit and thus to reap life everlasting. Without Christ we cannot have this Spirit, nor the spiritual body He forms. The only future of the body we dare to look at without a shudder is the future it has in the Lord. God has sent Christ to secure for the body redemption from the fate which naturally awaits it, and apart from Christ it has no outlook but the worst. The Lord is for the body, and as well might we try to sustain the body now without food as to have any endurable future for it without the Lord.

But if the body is thus closely united to Christ in its present use and in its destiny, if its proper function and fit development can only be realized by a true fellowship with Christ, then the inference is self-evident that it must be carefully guarded from such uses and impurities as involve rupture with Christ. "Know ye not that your bodies are the members of Christ? Shall I then take the members of Christ and make them the members of an harlot? God forbid." The Christian is one spirit with Christ. There is a real community of spiritual life between them. It is the spirit which possessed Christ which now possesses the Christian. He has the same aims, the same motives, the same view of life, the same hope, as his Lord. It is in Christ he seeks to live, and he has no stronger desire than to be used for His purposes. That Christ would use him as He used the members of His own body while on earth, that there might be the same direct influence and moving power of the Lord's Spirit, the same ready and instinctive response to the Lord's will, the same solidarity between himself and the Lord as between Christ's body and Christ's Spirit—this is the Christian's desire. To have his body a member of Christ—this is his happiness. To be one in will with Him who has brought by His own goodness the light of heaven into the darkness of earth, to learn to know Him and to love Him by serving Him and by measuring His love with all the needs of earth—this is his life. To be so united to Christ in all that is deepest in his nature that he knows he can never be separated from Him, but must go forward to the happy destiny which his Lord already enjoys—this is the Christian's joy; and it is made possible to every man.

Possible to every man is this personal union to Christ, but to be united thus in one Spirit to Christ and at the same time to be united to impurity is for ever impossible. To be one with Christ in spirit and at the same time to be one in body with what is spiritually defiled is impossible, and the very idea is monstrous. Devotedness to Christ is possible, but it is incompatible with any act which means that we become one in body with what is morally polluted. If the Christian is as truly a member of Christ's body as were the hands and eyes of the body He wore on earth, then the mind shrinks, as from blasphemy, from following out the thought of Paul. And if any frivolous Corinthian still objected that such acts went no deeper than the eating of food ceremonially unclean, that they belonged to the body that was to be destroyed, Paul says, It is not so; these acts are full of the deepest moral significance: they were intended by God to be *the expression of inward union*, and they have that significance whether you shut your eyes to it or not.

And this is what Paul means when he goes on to say, "Every sin that a man doeth is without the body; but he that committeth fornication sinneth against his own body." He does not mean that this is the only sin committed by the body, for of many other sins the body is the agent, as in murder, lying, blasphemy, robbery, and thieving. Neither does he mean that this is the only sin to which bodily appetite instigates, for gluttony and drunkenness equally take their rise in bodily appetite. But he means that this is the only sin in which the present connection of the body with Christ and its future destiny in Him are directly sinned against. This is the only sin, he means, which by its very nature alienates the body from Christ, its proper Partner. Other sins indirectly involve separation from Christ; this explicitly and directly transfers allegiance, and sunders our union with Him. By this sin a man detaches himself from Christ; he professes to be united to what is incompatible with Christ.

These weighty reasonings and warm admonitions, into which Paul throws his whole energy, are concluded by the statement of a twofold truth which is of much wider application than to the matter in hand: "Ye are bought with a price to be the temple of the Holy Ghost." We are bought with a price, and are no longer our own. The realities underlying these words are gladly owned in every Christian consciousness. God has caused us to recognise how truly we are His by showing us that He has grudged nothing which can restore us fully to Him. He has bought us, not with any of those prices the wealthy can pay without sacrifice and without profound interest and feeling, but with that price which is coined and issued by love, which carries in it the token and pledge of love, and which therefore wins us wholly. In our relations with God we have never to do with any merely formal transaction performed for the sake of keeping up appearances, saving the proprieties or satisfying the letter of law, but always with what is necessary in the nature of things, with what is real, with the very God of truth, the centre and source of all reality. God has made us His own, has won our hearts and wills to Himself, by manifesting His love in ways that touch and move us, and for purposes absolutely needful. God means that our attachment to Him should be real and permanent, and He has based it on the most reasonable grounds. He means that we should be His, not only because we are His creatures or because He has an indefeasible right to our service as the source of our life; but He means that our hearts should be His, and that we should be drawn to live and labour for His ends, convinced in our reason that this is our happiness and attracted by His love to serve Him. He means this; and accordingly He has bought us, has given us reason to become His, has made such advances as ought to win us has not grudged to show His earnest desire for our love by Himself making sacrifices and declaring that He loves us. It is a thought the humble heart can scarcely endure that it is loved by God, that it has been counted so precious in God's sight that Divine love and sacrifice should have been spent on its restoration. It is a thought that overwhelms the believing heart, but, believed in, it wins the soul eternally to God.

We are not our own; we belong to Him who has loved us most; and His love will be satisfied when we suffer Him to dwell in us, so that we shall be His temples, and shall glorify Him in body and in spirit. God claims our body as well as our spirit; He has a purpose for our body as well as for our spirit. Our body is to glorify Him in the future and now: in the future, by exhibiting how the Divine wisdom has triumphed over all that threatens the body, and has used all the present bodily experiences for preparing a permanent spiritual embodiment of all human faculties and joys; and now, by putting itself at the disposal of God for the accomplishment of His will. We glorify God by allowing Him to fulfil His purpose of love in creating us. What that purpose is we cannot wholly know; but trusting ourselves to His love, we can, by obeying Him, have it more and more accomplished in us. And it is the consciousness that we are God's temples which constantly incites us to live worthily of Him. To say that we are temples of God is not to use a figure of speech. It is the temple of stone that is the figure; the true dwelling-place of God is man. In nothing can God reveal Himself as He can in man. Through nothing else can He express so much of what is truly Divine. It is not a building of stone which forms a fit temple for God; it is not even the heaven of heavens. In material nature only a small part of God can be seen and known. It is in man, able to choose what is morally good, able to resist temptation, to make sacrifices for worthy ends, to determine his own character; it is in man, whose own will is his law, and who is not the mere mechanical agent of another's will, that God finds a worthy temple for Himself. Through you God can express and reveal what is best in Himself. Your love is sustained by His, and reveals His. Your approval of what is pure and hatred of impurity has its source in His holiness, and by transforming you into His own image He discloses Himself as truly dwelling and living within you. Where is God to be found and to be known if not in men? Where can His presence and Divine goodness and reality be more distinctly manifest than in Christ and those who are in any degree like Him? It is in men that the unseen Divine Spirit manifests His nature and His work. But if so, what a profanation is it when we take this body, which is built to be His temple, and put it to uses which it were blasphemous to associate with God! Let us rather find our joy in realizing the ideal set before us by Paul, in keeping ourselves pure as God's temples and in glorifying Him in our body and in our spirit.

MARRIAGE

"Now concerning the things whereof ye wrote unto me: It is good for a man not to touch a woman. Nevertheless, to avoid fornication, let every man have his own wife, and let every woman have her own husband. Let the husband render unto the wife due benevolence: and likewise also the wife unto the husband. The wife hath not power of her own body, but the husband, and likewise also the husband hath not power of his own body, but the wife. Defraud ye not one the other, except it be with consent for a time, that ye may give yourselves to fasting and prayer; and come together again, that Satan tempt you not for your incontinency. But I speak this by permission, and not of commandment. For I would that all men were even as I myself. But every man hath his proper gift of God one after this manner, and another after that. I say therefore to the unmarried and widows, It is good for them if they abide even as I. But if they cannot contain, let them marry: for it is better to marry than to burn. And unto the married I command, yet not I, but the Lord, Let not the wife depart from her husband: but and if she depart, let her remain unmarried, or be reconciled to her husband: and let not the husband put away his wife. But to the rest speak

I, not the Lord: If any brother hath a wife that believeth not, and she be pleased to dwell with him, let him not put her away. And the woman which hath an husband that believeth not, and if he be pleased to dwell with her, let her not leave him. For the unbelieving husband is sanctified by the wife, and the unbelieving wife is sanctified by the husband: else were your children unclean; but now are they holy. But if the unbelieving depart, let him depart. A brother or a sister is not under bondage in such cases: but God hath called us to peace. For what knowest thou, O wife, whether thou shalt save thy husband? or how knowest thou, O man, whether thou shalt save thy wife? But as God hath distributed to every man, as the Lord hath called every one, so let him walk. And so ordain I in all churches. Is any man called being circumcised? let him not become uncircumcised. Is any called in uncircumcision? let him not be circumcised. Circumcision is nothing, and uncircumcision is nothing, but the keeping of the commandments of God. Let every man abide in the same calling wherein he was called. Art thou called being a servant? care not for it: but if thou mayest be made free, use it rather. For he that is called in the Lord, being a servant, is the Lord's freeman: likewise also he that is called, being free, is Christ's servant. Ye are bought with a price; be not ye the servants of men. Brethren, let every man, wherein he is called, therein abide with God. Now concerning virgins I have no commandment of the Lord: yet I give my judgment, as one that hath obtained mercy of the Lord to be faithful. I suppose therefore that this is good for the present distress, I say, that it is good for a man so to be. Art thou bound unto a wife? seek not to be loosed. Art thou loosed from a wife? seek not a wife. But and if thou marry, thou hast not sinned; and if a virgin marry, she hath not sinned. Nevertheless such shall have trouble in the flesh: but I spare you. But this I say, brethren, the time is short: it remaineth, that both they that have wives be as though they had none; and they that weep, as though they wept not; and they that rejoice, as though they rejoiced not; and they that buy, as though they possessed not; and they that use this world, as not abusing it: for the fashion of this world passeth away. But I would have you without carefulness. He that is unmarried careth for the things that belong to the Lord, how he may please the Lord: but he that is married careth for the things that are of the world, how he may please his wife. There is difference also between a wife and a virgin. The unmarried woman careth for the things of the Lord, that she may be holy both in body and in spirit: but she that is married careth for the things of the world, how she may please her husband. And this I speak for your own profit; not that I may cast a snare upon you, but for that which is comely, and that ye may attend upon the Lord without distraction. But if any man think that he behaveth himself uncomely toward his virgin, if she pass the flower of her age, and need so require, let him do what he will, he sinneth not: let them marry. Nevertheless he that standeth stedfast in his heart, having no necessity, but hath power over his own will, and hath so decreed in his heart that he will keep his virgin, doeth well. So then he that giveth her in marriage doeth well; but he that giveth her not in marriage doeth better. The wife is bound by the law as long as her husband liveth; but if her husband be dead, she is at liberty to be married to whom she will; only in the Lord. But she is happier if she so abide, after my judgment: and I think also that I have the Spirit of God."—1 Cor. vii. 1-40.

XI
MARRIAGE

There are two preliminary considerations which throw some light on this much-contested passage. First, Paul had to speak about marriage as he found it, as it existed among those to whom he wished to be of service. Hence he makes no allusion to that which among ourselves is the main argument for, or at least the one only justifying motive to, marriage, viz., love. Marriage is treated here from a lower point of view than it would have been had this letter been originally written for Englishmen. The Church to which it was addressed was composite. Jews, Greeks, and Romans, in what proportions it is not easy to say, brought their peculiar and national usages into it. In the marriages of the Jews and Greeks, love had, as a rule, little to do. The marriage was arranged by the parents of the contracting parties.

"Faces strange and tongues unknown

Make us by a bid their own,"

is the remonstrance of the Greek maiden against the unnatural custom which prevailed of allowing no intimacy, and scarcely any real acquaintance, prior to marriage. The lack of warmth and personal interest which characterizes the Greek plays arises mainly from the circumstance that among the Greeks there was absolutely no such thing as that love prior to marriage on which even our best works of fiction uniformly depend for their interest. Among the Romans there was none of this Eastern seclusion of women, and but for other causes marriage among this section of the Corinthian population might have served as an example to the rest.

Secondly, it is to be considered that not only had Paul to speak of marriage as he found it, but also that he was here only giving answers to some special questions, and not discussing the whole subject in all its bearings. There might be other points which to his mind seemed equally important; but his advice not having been asked about these, he passes them by. He introduces the subject in a manner fitted to remind us that he has no intention of propounding his views on marriage in a complete and systematic form: "Now concerning the things whereof ye wrote unto me." There had arisen in the Corinthian Church certain scruples about marriage; and as the Church was composed of persons who would naturally take very different views on the subject, these scruples might not be easily removed. Among the Jews it was believed that marriage was a duty, "so much so that he who at the age of twenty had not married was considered to have sinned." Among the Gentiles the tendency to celibacy was so strong that it was considered necessary to counteract it by legal enactment. In a community previously disposed to take such opposite views of marriage difficulties were sure to arise. Those who were predisposed to disparage the married state would throw contempt upon it as a mere concession to the flesh; they apparently even urged that, Christians being new creatures, their whole previous relationships were dissolved. To Paul therefore appeal is made.

The questions referred to Paul resolve themselves into two: whether the unmarried are to marry, and whether the married are to continue to live together.

In reply to the former question, whether the unmarried are to marry, he first states the duty of unmarried persons themselves (in vers. 2, 7-9); and afterwards (in vers. 25-39) he explains the duty of parents to their unmarried daughters.

I. First then we have Paul's counsel to the unmarried. This is summed up in the words, "I say therefore to the unmarried and widows, It is good for them if they abide even as I;" that is to say, if they remain unmarried, Paul being probably the only unmarried Apostle. But if any man's temperament be such that he cannot settle undistractedly to his work without marrying; if he is restless and ill at ease, and full of natural cravings which make him think much of marriage, and make him feel sure he would be less distracted in married life—then, says Paul, let such an one by all means marry. But do not misunderstand me, he says; this is permission I am giving you, not commandment. I do not say you *must* or ought to marry; I say you *may*, and in certain circumstances *ought*. Those among you who say a man sins if he do not marry, talk nonsense. Those among you who feel a quiet superiority because you are married, and think of unmarried people as undergraduates who have not attained a degree equal to yours, are much mistaken if you suppose that I am of your mind. When I say, "Let every man have his own wife, and let every woman have her own husband," I do not mean that every man who wishes to come as near perfection as possible must go and marry, but what I speak I speak by way of permission; I permit every man to marry who deliberately believes he will be the better of marrying. So far from thinking that every man ought to marry, or that married men have somehow the advantage over single men, I think the very opposite, and would that *all* men were even as I myself, only I know that to many men it is not so easy as it is to me to live unmarried; and therefore I do not advise them to a single life.

But this advice of Paul's proceeds, not from any ascetic tendency, but from the practical bias of his mind. He had no idea that marriage was a morally inferior condition; on the contrary, he saw in it the most perfect symbol of the union of Christ and the Church. But he thought that unmarried men were likely to be most available for the work of Christ; and therefore he could not but wish it possible, though he knew it was not possible, that all unmarried men should remain unmarried.

His reason for thinking that unmarried men would be more efficient in the service of Christ is given in the thirty-second and thirty-third verses: "He that is unmarried careth for the things that belong to the Lord, how he may please the Lord; but he that is married careth for the things that are of the world, how he may please his wife," an opinion quite similar to that which Lord Bacon pronounced when he said, "Certainly the best works, and of greatest merit for the public, have proceeded from the unmarried or childless men, who both in affection and means have married and endowed the public." Given two men with equal desire to serve Christ, but the one married and the other unmarried, it is obvious that the unmarried man has more means and opportunities of service than he who has a large family to support. No doubt a good wife may stimulate a man to liberality, and may greatly increase his tenderness towards deserving objects of charity; but the fact remains that he who has seven or ten mouths to fill cannot have so much to give away as if he had but himself to support. Then, again, however alike in sentiment husband and wife may be, there are sacrifices which a married man may not make. With the unmarried man there need be no other consideration than this: How can I best serve Christ? With the married man there must always be other considerations. He cannot ignore or forswear the ties with which he has bound himself; he cannot act as if he had only himself to consider. The unmarried man has life and the world before him, and may choose the most ideal and perfect style of life he pleases. He may seek to realize, as many in recent times have realized, the exact apostolic idea of how it is best to spend a human life. He may choose to devote himself to the elevation of some one class of the community, or he is free to go to the ends of the earth to preach the Gospel. He has no one thing to consider but how he may please the Lord. But the married man has limited his range of choice, and has cut himself off from some at least of the most influential ways of doing good in the world. It is therefore to the unmarried that the State looks for the manning of the army and navy; it is to the unmarried that society looks for the nursing of the sick and for the filling of posts of danger; and it is on the unmarried that the Church depends for a large part of her work, from teaching in Sunday-schools to occupying unhealthy and precarious outposts in the mission field.

But while Paul makes no scruple of saying that for many purposes the unmarried man is the more available, he says also, Beware how *you* individually think yourself a hero, and able to forego marriage. Beware lest, by choosing a part which you are not fit for, you give Satan an advantage over you, and expose yourself to constant temptation, and pass through life distracted by needless deprivation. "Far be it from me," says Paul, "to cast a snare upon you," to invite or encourage you into a position against which your nature would unceasingly rebel, to prompt you to attempt that for which you are constitutionally unfit, and thereby to make your life a chronic temptation. "Every man hath his proper gift of God, one after this manner, another after that." And if any man fancies that, because there are advantages in being unmarried, therefore that is the best state for him, or if, on the other hand, any man fancies that, because most men seem to find great happiness in marriage, he also needs marriage to complete his happiness, both of these men leave out of account that which is chiefly to be taken into account, viz., the special temperament, calling, and opportunities of each.

The common-sense and wise counsel of this chapter are sometimes half jestingly put aside by the idle remark that Paul, being himself unmarried, takes a biassed view of the subject. But the chief merit of the whole passage is that Paul positively and expressly declines to judge others by himself, or himself by others. What is good for one man in this respect is not good, he says, for another; every man must ascertain for himself what is best for him. And this is precisely what is lacking in popular feeling and talk about marriage. People start in life, and are encouraged to start in life, on the understanding that their happiness cannot be complete till they are married; that they are in some sense incomplete and unsatisfactory members of society until they marry. Now, on the contrary, people should be taught not to follow one another like sheep, nor to suppose that they will infallibly find happiness where others have found it. They should be taught to consider their own make and bent, and not to take for granted that the cravings they feel for an indefinite addition to their happiness will be satisfied by marriage. They should be taught that marriage is but one out of many paths to happiness, that it is possible celibacy may be the straightest path to happiness for them, and that many persons are so constituted that they are likely to be much more useful unmarried than married. They should, above all, be taught that human life is very wide and multifarious, and that, to effect His ends, God needs persons of all kinds and conditions, so that to prejudge the direction in which our usefulness and happiness are to run is to shut God out of our life. There can be no doubt that the opposite way of speaking of marriage as the great settlement in life has introduced much misery and uselessness into the lives of thousands.

It is this then which not only signally illustrates the judicial balance of the Apostle's mind, but at the same time gives us the key to the whole chapter. The capacity for celibacy is a gift of God to him who possesses it, a gift which may be of eminent service, but to which no moral value can be attached. There are many such diversities of gifts among men, gifts of immense value, but which may belong to bad as well as to good men. For example, two men travel together; the one can go without food for twelve hours, the other cannot, but if you repair his strength every five hours, he can go through as much fatigue as the other. This power of abstinence is a valuable gift, and has frequently enabled men in certain circumstances to save life or perform other important service. But no one would dream of arguing that because a man possessed this gift, he was therefore a *better* man than his less enduring friend. Unfortunately, so simple a distinction has not been kept in view. In the most powerful Church in the world celibacy is regarded as a virtue in itself, so that men with no natural gift for it have been encouraged to aim at it, with what results we need not say.

But while there is no virtue in remaining unmarried, there is virtue in remaining unmarried for the sake of serving Christ better. Some persons are kept single by mere selfishness; having been accustomed to orderly and quiet ways, they shrink from having their personal peace broken in upon by the claims of children. Some shrink from being tied down to any definite settlement in life; they like to feel unencumbered, and free to shift their tent at short notice. Some dread responsibility and the little and great anxieties of family life. A few have the feeling of the miser, and prefer the possibility of many conceivable marriages to the actuality of one. For such persons to make a virtue of their celibacy is absurd. But all honour to those who recognise that they are called to some duty they could not discharge if married! All honour to that eldest son of an orphaned family who sees that it is not for him to please himself, but to work for those who have none to look to but him! There are here and there persons who from the highest motives decline marriage: persons conscious of some hereditary weakness, physical or mental; persons who, on a deliberate survey of human life, have seemed to themselves to recognise that they are called to a kind of service with which marriage is incompatible. We may be thankful that in our own country and time there are men and women of sufficiently heroic mould to exemplify the wisdom of the Apostle's counsel. Such devotion is not for every one. There are persons of a soft and domestic temperament who need the supports and comforts of home-life, and nothing can be more cruel and ill-advised than to encourage such persons to turn their life into a channel in which it was never intended to run. But it is equally to be lamented that, where there are women quite capable of a life of self-devotion to some noble work, they should be discouraged from such a life by the false, and foolish, and petty notions of society, and should be taught to believe that the only way in which they can serve their Lord is by caring for the affairs of a single household. No calling is nobler or more worthy of a Christian woman than marriage; but it is not the only calling. There are other callings as noble, and there are callings in which many women will find a much wider field for doing good.

II. St. Paul's counsel to the married. Some of the Corinthians seem to have thought that, because they were new creatures in Christ, their old relations should be abandoned; and they put to Paul the question whether a believing man who had an unbelieving wife ought not to forsake her. Paul had shrewdness enough to see that if a Christian might separate from an unbelieving wife on the sole ground that he was a Christian, this easy mode of divorce might lead to a large and most unwelcome influx of pretended Christians into the Church. He therefore lays down the law that the power of separation is to rest with the unbelieving, and not with the believing, partner. If the unbelieving wife wishes to separate from her Christian husband, let her do so; but the change from heathenism to Christianity was no reason for sundering the marriage union. It frequently happened in the early ages of the Church that when a man was converted to the Christian faith in middle life, and judged he could serve God better without the encumbrance of a family, he forsook his wife and children and betook himself to a monastery. This directly contravened the law here laid down to abide in the vocation wherein God's call had found him.

The principle, "Let every man abide in the same calling wherein he was called," is of wide application. The slave who heard God's call to him to become His child was not to think he must resent being a slave and assert his Christian liberty by requiring emancipation from earthly servitude. On the contrary, he must be content with the inward possession of the freedom Christ had given him, and must show his liberty by the willingness and spontaneity of his submission to all his outward conditions. It is not externals that make a Christian; and if God's grace has found a man in unlikely circumstances, that is the best evidence he can have that he will find opportunity of serving God in those circumstances, if there be no sin in them. It throws great light on the relation which we as Christians hold to the institutions of our country, and generally to outward things, when we understand that Christianity does not begin by making external changes, but begins within and gradually finds its way outwards, modifying and rectifying all it meets.

But the principle to which Paul chiefly trusts, he enounces in the twenty-ninth verse: "This I say, brethren, the time is short: it remaineth that both they that have wives be as though they had none, and they that weep as though they wept not; ... for the fashion of this world passeth away." The forms in which human life is now moulded, the kind of business we are now engaged in, the pleasures we enjoy, even the relationships we hold to one another, pass away. There are no doubt relationships which time cannot dissolve, marriages so fit and uniting spirits so essentially kindred that no change can dissolve them, affections so pure and clinging that if the future does not renew them, it loses a large part of its charm for us. But whatever is temporary in our relation to the present world it is foolish so to set our heart on, that death may seem to end all our joy and all our usefulness. We may resent being asked to be moderate and self-restrained in our devotedness to this or that pursuit, but the fact is that the time is short and that the fashion of this world passeth away; and it is surely the part of wisdom to accommodate one's self to fact. In this life we now lead, and underneath all its activities, and forms, and relationships, we have opportunity of laying hold on what is permanent; and if, instead of penetrating through the outward things to the eternal significance and relations they bear, we give ourselves wholly to them, we abuse the world, and pervert it to an end for which it was not intended. The man who is sent abroad for five years would consider it folly to accumulate a large collection of the luxuries of life, furniture, and paintings, and encumbrances; how many times five years do we expect to live, that we should be much concerned to amass goods which we cannot remove to another world? This world is a means, and not an end; and those use it best who use it in relation to what is to be. They use it not less vigorously, but more wisely, not despising the mould which fashions them to their eternal form, but ever bearing in mind that the mould is to be broken and that what is fashioned by it alone remains. It is the thought of our great future which alone gives us sufficient courage and wisdom to deal with present things intensely and in earnest. For, as a heathen long ago saw and said, "if God make so much of creatures in whom there is nothing permanent, He is like women who sow the seeds of plants within the soil enclosed in an oyster-shell." The very intensity of our interests and affections reminds us that we cannot root ourselves in this present life, but need a larger room.

"Now as touching things offered unto idols, we know that we all have knowledge. Knowledge puffeth up, but charity edifieth. And if any man think that he knoweth anything, he knoweth nothing yet as he ought to know. But if any man love God, the same is known of him. As concerning therefore the eating of those things that are offered in sacrifice unto idols, we know that an idol is nothing in the world, and that there is none other God but one. For though there be that are called gods, whether in heaven or in earth, (as there be gods many, and lords many,) but to us there is but one God, the Father, of whom are all things, and we in Him; and one Lord Jesus Christ, by whom are all things, and we by Him. Howbeit there is not in every man that knowledge: for some with conscience of the idol unto this hour eat it as a thing offered unto an idol; and their conscience being weak is defiled. But meat commendeth us not to God: for neither, if we eat, are we the better; neither, if we eat not, are we the worse. But take heed lest by any means this liberty of yours become a stumbling-block to them that are weak. For if any man see thee which hast knowledge sit at meat in the idol's temple, shall not the conscience of him which is weak be emboldened to eat those things which are offered to idols; and through thy knowledge shall the weak brother perish, for whom Christ died? But when ye sin so against the brethren, and wound their weak conscience, ye sin against Christ. Wherefore, if meat make my brother to offend, I will eat no flesh while the world standeth, lest I make my brother to offend." —1 Cor. viii. 1-13.

"All things are lawful for me, but all things are not expedient: all things are lawful for me, but all things edify not. Let no man seek his own, but every man another's wealth. Whatsoever is sold in the shambles, that eat, asking no question for conscience' sake: for the earth is the Lord's, and the fulness thereof. If any of them that believe not bid you to a feast, and ye be disposed to go; whatsoever is set before you, eat, asking no question for conscience' sake. But if any man say unto you, This is offered in sacrifice unto idols, eat not for his sake that showed it, and for conscience' sake: for the earth is the Lord's, and the fulness thereof: conscience, I say, not thine own, but of the other: for why is my liberty judged of another man's conscience? For if I by grace be a partaker, why am I evil spoken of for that for which I give thanks? Whether therefore ye eat, or drink, or whatsoever ye do, do all to the glory of God. Give none offence, neither to the Jews, nor to the Gentiles, nor to the Church of God: even as I please all men in all things, not seeking mine own profit, but the profit of many, that they may be saved. Be ye followers of me, even as I also am of Christ." —1 Cor. x. 23-xi. 1.

XII
LIBERTY AND LOVE

The next question which had been put to Paul by the Corinthian Church, and to which he now replies, is "touching things offered unto idols," whether a Christian had liberty to eat such things or not. This question necessarily arose in a society partly heathen and partly Christian. Every meal was in a manner dedicated to the household gods by laying some portion of it on the family altar. Where one member of a heathen family had become a Christian, he would at once be confronted with the question, rising in his own conscience, whether by partaking of such food he might not be countenancing idolatry. On the occasion of a birthday, or a marriage, or a safe return from sea, or any circumstance that seemed to call for celebration, it was customary to sacrifice in some public temple. And after the legs of the victim, enclosed in fat, and the entrails had been burnt on the altar, the worshipper received the remainder, and invited his friends and guests to partake of it either in the temple itself, or in the surrounding grove, or at his own home. Here again a young convert might very naturally ask himself whether he was justified in attending such a feast and actually sitting down to meat in the idol's presence. Nor was it only personal friendships and the harmony of family life that were threatened; but on public occasions and national celebrations the Christian was in a strait betwixt two; fearful, on the one hand, of branding himself as no good citizen by abstaining from participation in the feast, fearful, on the other hand, lest by compliance he should be found unfaithful to his new religion. And even though his own family was entirely Christian, the difficulty was not removed, for much of the meat offered in worship found its way into the common market, so that at every meal the Christian ran the risk of eating things sacrificed to idols.

Among the Jews it had always been considered pollution to eat such food. Instances are on record of men dying cheerfully rather than suffer such contamination. Few Jewish Christians could rise to the height of our Lord's maxim, "Not that which goeth into a man defileth him." The Gentile converts also felt the difficulty of at once throwing off all the old associations. When they entered the temple where but a few months ago they had worshipped, the atmosphere of the place intoxicated them; and the long-accustomed sights quickened their pulse and exposed them to serious temptation. Others, less sensitive, could use the temple as they would an ordinary eating-house, without the slightest stirring of idolatrous feeling. Some went to the houses of heathen friends as often as they were invited, and partook of what was set before them, making no minute inquiries as to how the meat had been provided, asking no questions for conscience' sake, but believing that the earth and its fulness were the Lord's, and that what they ate they received from God, and not from an idol. Others, again, could not shake off the feeling that they were countenancing idolatry when they partook of such feasts. Thus there arose a diversity of judgment and a variance in practice which must have given rise to much annoyance, and which did not appear to be approaching any nearer to a final and satisfactory settlement.

In answer to the appeal made to him on this subject, it might seem that Paul had nothing to do but quote the deliverance of the Council of Jerusalem, which determined that Gentile converts should be commanded to abstain from meats offered to idols. Paul himself had obtained that deliverance, and was satisfied with it; but now he makes no reference to it, and treats the question afresh. In the epistles of the Lord to the Churches, embodied in the Book of Revelation, the eating of things sacrificed to idols is spoken of in strongly condemnatory language; and in one of the very earliest non-canonical documents of the primitive Church we find the precept, "Abstain carefully from things offered to idols, for that is worship of dead gods." Paul's disregard of the decision of the Council is probably due to his belief that that decision was merely provisional and temporary. He had founded Churches which could scarcely be expected to go past himself for guidance; and as the situation in the Corinthian Church was different from what it had been in Antioch, he felt justified in treating the matter afresh. And while in the early Church the partaking of sacrificial food which Paul allowed was sometimes vehemently condemned, this was due to the circumstance that it was sometimes used as a test of a man's abandonment of idolatry. Of course where this was the case no Christian could possibly be in doubt regarding the proper course to follow. What a man may freely do in ordinary circumstances, he may not do if he is warned that certain inferences will be drawn from his action.

The case laid before Paul then belongs to the class known as matters morally indifferent. These are matters upon which conscience does not uniformly give the same verdict even among persons brought up under the same moral law. On mingling with society, every one finds that there are many points of conduct regarding which there is not an unanimous consent of judgment among the most delicately conscientious people, and upon which it is difficult to decide even when we are anxious to do right. Such points are the lawfulness of attending certain places of public amusement, the propriety of allowing one's self to be implicated in certain kinds of private amusements or entertainments, the way of spending Sunday, and the amount of pleasure, refinement, and luxury one may admit into his life.

The state of feeling produced in Corinth by the discussion of such topics is apparent from Paul's mode of treating the question put to him. His answer is addressed to the party who claimed superior knowledge, who wished to be known as the party which stood for liberty of conscience, and probably for the Pauline axiom, "All things are lawful for me." Paul does not directly address those who had scruples about eating, but those who had none. He does not speak to, but only of, the "weak" brethren who had still conscience of the idol. And apparently a good deal of ill-feeling had been engendered in the Corinthian Church by the different views taken. This is always the trouble in connection with morally indifferent matters. They do little harm if each holds his own opinion genially and endeavours to influence others by a friendly statement of his own practice and the grounds of it. But in most instances it happens as in Corinth: those who saw that they could eat without contamination scorned those who had scruples; while, on their side, the scrupulous judged the eaters to be worldly time-servers, in a perilous state, less godly and consistent than themselves.

As a first step towards the settlement of this matter, Paul makes the largest concession to the party of liberty. Their clear perception that an idol was nothing in the world, a mere bit of timber, and of no more significance to a Christian than a pillar or a doorpost—this knowledge is sound and commendable. At the same time, they need not make quite so much of it as they were doing. In their letter of inquiry they must have emphasized the fact that they were the party of enlightenment, who saw things as they really were, and had freed themselves from fantastic superstitions and antiquated ideas. Quite true, says Paul, "we all have knowledge;" but you need not remind me at every turn of your superior discernment of the Christian's true position nor of your wonderfully sagacious discovery that an idol is nothing in the world. Any Jewish schoolboy could have told you this. I know that you understand the principles which should regulate your intercourse with the heathen much better than the scrupulous do, and that your views of liberty are my own. Let us then hear no more of this. Do not always be returning upon this, as if this settled the whole matter. You are in the right so far as regards knowledge, and your brethren are weak; let that be conceded: but do not suppose you settle the question or impress me more strongly with the righteousness of your conduct by reiterating that you, whom your brethren call lax and misguided, are better instructed in the principle of Christian conduct than they. Once for all, I know this.

Does this then not settle the question? If—the party of liberty might say—if we are right, if the idol is nothing, and an idol's temple no more than an ordinary dining-room, does this not settle the whole matter? By no means, says Paul. "Knowledge puffeth up, but charity edifieth." You have as yet grasped only one end, and that the weaker end, of the Christian rule. You must add love, consideration of your neighbour to your knowledge. Without this, knowledge is unwholesome and as likely to do harm as to do good. In very similar terms the founder of the Positive philosophy speaks of the evil results of loveless knowledge. "I am free to confess," he says, "that hitherto the Positive spirit has been tainted with the two moral evils which peculiarly wait on knowledge. It puffs up, and it dries the heart, by giving free scope to pride and by turning it from love." It is indeed matter of everyday observation that men of ready insight into moral and spiritual truth are prone to despise the less enlightened spirits that stumble among the scruples which, like the bats of the moral twilight, fly in their faces. The knowledge which is not tempered by humility and love does harm both to its possessor and to other Christians; it puffs up its possessor with scorn, and it alienates and embitters the less enlightened. Knowledge without love, knowledge which does not take into consideration the difficulties and scruples of brethren, cannot be admired or commended, for though in itself a good thing and capable of being used for the advancement of the Church, knowledge dissociated from charity can do good neither to him who possesses it nor to the Christian community. However the possessors of such knowledge vaunt themselves as the men of progress and the hope of the Church, it is not by knowledge alone the Church can ever solidly grow. Knowledge does produce an appearance of growth, a puffing up, an unhealthy, morbid growth, a mushroom, fungous growth; but that which builds up the Church stone by stone, a strong, enduring edifice, is love. It is a good thing to have clear views of Christian liberty, to have definite, firmly held ideas of Christian conduct, to discard fretting scruples and idle superstitions; add love to this knowledge, exercise it in a tender, patient, self-denying, considerate, loving way, and you edify both yourself and the Church: but exercise it without love, and you become a poor inflated creature, puffed up with a noxious gas destructive of all higher life in yourself and in others.

Paul's law then is that liberty must be tempered by love; that the individual must consider the society of which he forms a part; and that, after his own conscience is satisfied regarding the legitimacy of certain actions, he must further consider how the conscience of his neighbour will be affected if he uses his liberty and does these actions. He must endeavour to keep step with the Christian community of which he forms a part, and must beware of giving offence to less enlightened persons by his freer conduct. He must consider not only whether he himself can do this or that with a good conscience, but also how the conscience of those who know what he does will be affected by it.

Applying this law to the matter in hand, Paul declares that, for his own part, he has no scruples at all about meat. "Meat commendeth us not to God: for neither, if we eat, are we the better; neither, if we eat not, are we the worse." If therefore I had to consult only my own conscience, the matter would admit of prompt and easy solution. I would as soon eat in an idol's temple as anywhere else. But all have not the conviction we have that an idol is nothing in the world. Some are unable to rid themselves of the feeling that in eating sacrificial meat they are paying an act of homage to the idol. "Some with conscience of the idol," with the feeling that the idol is present and accepting the worship, "eat the sacrificial meat as a thing offered unto an idol, and their conscience being weak is defiled." Their conscience is weak, not fully enlightened, not purged of old superstition; but their conscience is their conscience: and if they feel they are doing a wrong thing and yet do it, they do a wrong thing, and defile their conscience. Therefore we must consider them as well as ourselves, for as often as we use our liberty and eat sacrificial meat we tempt them to do the same, and so to defile their conscience. They know that you are men of sound and clear spiritual discernment; they look up to you as guides: and if they see you who have knowledge sitting at meat in the idol's temple, must not they be emboldened to do the same, and so to stain and harden their own conscience?

It is easy to imagine how this would be exemplified at a Corinthian table. Three Christians are invited, with other guests, to a party in the house of a heathen friend. One of these invited Christians is weakly scrupulous, unable to disentangle himself from the old idolatrous associations connected with sacrificial meat. The other two Christians are men of ampler view and more enlightened conscience, and have the deepest conviction that scruples about eating at a heathen table are baseless. All three recline at the table; but, as the meal goes on, the anxious, scrutinizing eye of the weak brother discerns some mark which identifies the meat as sacrificial, or, fearing it may be so, he inquires of the servant, and finds it has been offered in the temple: and at once he draws the attention of his Christian friends to this, saying, "This has been offered in sacrifice to idols." One of his friends, knowing that heathen eyes are watching, and wishing to show how superior to all such scruples the enlightened Christian is and how genial and free a religion is the religion of Christ, smiles at his friend's scruples, and accepts the meat. The other, quite as clear-sighted and free from superstition, but more generous and more truly courageous, accommodates himself to the scruple of the weak brother, and declines the dish, lest by eating and leaving the scrupulous man without support he should tempt him to follow their example, contrary to his own conviction, and so lead him into sin. It need not be said which of these men acts the friendly part and comes nearest to the Christian principle of Paul.

In our own society similar cases necessarily arise. I, as a Christian man, and knowing that the earth and its fulness are the Lord's, may feel at perfect liberty to drink wine. Had I only myself to consider, and knowing that my temptation does not lie that way, I might use wine regularly or as often as I felt disposed to enjoy a needed stimulant. I may feel quite convinced in my own mind that morally I am not one whit the worse of doing so. But I cannot determine whether I am to indulge myself or not without considering the effect my conduct will have on others. There may be among my friends some who know that their temptation does lie that way, and whose conscience bids them altogether refrain. If by my example such persons are encouraged to silence the voice of their own conscience, then I incur the incalculable guilt of helping to destroy a brother for whom Christ died.

Or again, a lad has had the great good fortune to be brought up in a Puritanic household, and has imbibed stringent moral principles, with perhaps somewhat narrow ideas. He has been taught, together with much else of the same character, that the influence of the theatre is in our country demoralizing, that one day in the week is little enough to give to the claims of spiritual education, and so forth. But on entering the life of a great city he is soon brought in contact with men whose uprightness, and sagacity, and Christian spirit he cannot but respect, but who yet read their weekly paper, or any book they are interested in, as freely on Sunday as on Saturday, and who visit the theatre without the slightest twinge of conscience. Now either of two things will probably happen in such a case. The young man's ideas of Christian liberty may become clearer. He may attain the standpoint of Paul, and may see that fellowship with Christ can be maintained in conditions of life he once absolutely condemned. Or the young man may not grow in Christian perception, but being daunted by overpowering example, and chafing under the raillery of his companions, may do as others do, though still uneasy in his own conscience.

What is to be observed about this process, which is ceaselessly going on in society, is that the emboldening of conscience is one thing, its enlightenment quite another. And were it possible to get statistics of the proportion of cases in which the one process goes on without the other, these statistics might be salutary. But we need no statistics to assure us that Christian people by selfishly using their own liberty do continually lead less enlightened persons to trample on their scruples and disregard their own conscience. Constantly it happens in every department of human life that men who once shrank from certain practices as wrong now freely engage in them, although they are not in their own mind any more clearly convinced of their legitimacy than they were before, but are merely emboldened by the example of others. Such persons, if possessed of any self-observation and candour, will tell you that at first they felt as if they were stealing the indulgence or the gain the practice brings, and that they had to drown the voice of conscience by the louder voice of example.

The results of this are disastrous. Conscience is dethroned. The ship no longer obeys her helm, and lies in the trough of the sea swept by every wave and driven by every wind. It may indeed be said, What harm can come of persons less enlightened being emboldened to do as we do if what we do is right? Is not that, most strictly speaking, edification? It is not as if we emboldened any one to transgress the moral law; we are merely bringing our weak brother's conduct up to the level of our own. Do we not act wisely and well in so doing? Again it must be answered, No, because, while yielding themselves to the influence of your example, these persons abandon the guidance of their own conscience, which may be a less enlightened, but is certainly a more authoritative, guide than you. If the weak brother does a right thing while his conscience tells him it is a wrong thing, to him it is a wrong thing. "Whatsoever is not of faith is sin;" that is to say, whatsoever is not dictated by a thorough conviction that it is right is sin. It is sin which in some respects is more dangerous than a sin of passion or impulse. By a sin of passion the conscience is not directly injured, and may remain comparatively tender and healthy; but when you refuse to acknowledge conscience as your guide and accept some other person's conduct as that which may dictate to you what you may or may not do, you dethrone conscience, and sap your moral nature. You shut your own eyes, and prefer to be led by the hand of another person, which may indeed serve you on this occasion; but the end will be a dog and a string.

Two permanent lessons are preserved in this exposition which Paul gives of the matter laid before him. The first is the sacredness or supremacy of conscience. "Let every man be fully persuaded in his own mind;" that is the one legitimate source of conduct. A man may possibly do a wrong thing when he obeys conscience; he is certainly wrong when he acts contrary to conscience. He may be helped to a decision by the advice of others, but it is his own decision by which he must abide. He must act, not on the conviction of others, but on his own. It is what he himself sees that must guide him. He is bound to use every means to enlighten his conscience and to learn with accuracy what is right and allowable, but he is also bound always to act upon his own present perception of what is right. His conscience may not be as enlightened as it ought to be. Still his duty is to enlighten, not to violate, it. It is the guide God has given us, and we must not choose another.

The second lesson is that we must ever use our Christian liberty with Christian consideration of others. Love must mingle with all we do. There are many things which are lawful for a Christian, but which are not compulsory or obligatory, and which he may refrain from doing on cause shown. Duties he must of course discharge, regardless of the effect his conduct may have on others. He may be quite sure he will be misunderstood; he may be sure evil motives will be imputed to him; he may be sure disastrous consequences will be the first result of his action; but if conscience says this or that *must* be done, then all thought of consequences must be thrown to the winds. But where conscience says, not "You must," but only "You may," then we must consider the effect our using our liberty will have on others. We lie as Christians under an obligation to consider others, to lay aside all pride of advanced ideas, and this not merely that we may submit ourselves to those who know better than we, but that we may not offend those who are bound by prejudices of which we are rid. We must limit our liberty by the scrupulosity of prejudiced, narrow-minded, weak people. We must forego our liberty to do this or that if by doing it we should shock or disturb a weak brother or encourage him to overstep his conscience. As the Arctic voyager who has been frozen up all winter does not seize the first opportunity to escape, but waits till his weaker companions gain strength enough to accompany him, so must the Christian accommodate himself to the weaknesses of others, lest by using his liberty he should injure him for whom Christ died. Never was there a man who more fully understood the freedom of the Christian position than Paul; no man was ever more entirely lifted out of the mist of superstition and formalism into the clear light of free, eternal life: but with this freedom he carried a sympathy with weak and entangled beginners which prompted him to exclaim, "If meat make my brother to offend, I will eat no flesh while the world standeth, lest I make my brother to offend."

Our conduct must be limited and to a certain extent regulated by the narrow-mindedness, the scruples, the prejudices, the weakness in short, of others. We cannot say, I see my way to do so-and-so, let my friend think what he pleases; I am not to be trammelled by his superstition or ignorance; let my conduct have what effect it will on him; I am not responsible for that; if he does not see it to be right, I do, and I will act accordingly. We cannot speak thus if the matter be indifferent; if it be a matter we can lawfully abstain from, then abstain we must if we would follow the Apostle who followed Christ. This is the practical law which stands in the forefront of Christ's teaching and was sealed by every day of His life. It is enounced not only by

St. Paul: "Destroy not him with thy meat for whom Christ died;" "Through thy knowledge shall the weak brother perish, for whom Christ died," but also in our Lord's still more emphatic words, "Whoso shall offend one of these little ones which believe in Me, it were better for him that a millstone were hanged about his neck, and that he were drowned in the depth of the sea." Paul could not look on his weak brethren as narrow-minded bigots, could not call them hard names and ride rough-shod over their scruples; and to this delicate consideration he was aided by the remembrance that these were the persons for whom Christ died. For them Christ sacrificed, not merely a little feeling or a little of His own way, but His own will and self entirely. And the spirit of Christ is still manifested in all in whom He dwells, specially in a humility and yieldingness of disposition which is not led by self-interest or self-complacency, but seeks the weal of other men. Nothing shows us more distinctly the thorough manner in which St. Paul partook of the spirit of Christ than his ability to say, "I please all men in all things, not seeking mine own profit, but the profit of many, that they may be saved. Be ye followers of me, even as I also am of Christ."

MAINTENANCE OF THE MINISTRY

"Am I not an apostle? am I not free? have I not seen Jesus Christ our Lord? are not ye my work in the Lord? If I be not an apostle unto others, yet doubtless I am to you: for the seal of mine apostleship are ye in the Lord. Mine answer to them that do examine me is this, Have we not power to eat and to drink? Have we not power to lead about a sister, a wife, as well as other Apostles, and as the brethren of the Lord, and Cephas? Or I only and Barnabas, have not we power to forbear working? Who goeth a warfare any time at his own charges? who planteth a vineyard, and eateth not of the fruit thereof? or who feedeth a flock, and eateth not of the milk of the flock? Say I these things as a man? or saith not the Law the same also? For it is written in the law of Moses, Thou shalt not muzzle the mouth of the ox that treadeth out the corn. Doth God take care for oxen? Or saith He it altogether for our sakes? For our sakes, no doubt, this is written: that he that ploweth should plow in hope; and that he that thresheth in hope should be partaker of his hope. If we have sown unto you spiritual things, is it a great thing if we shall reap your carnal things? If others be partakers of this power over you, are not we rather? Nevertheless we have not used this power; but suffer all things, lest we should hinder the

Gospel of Christ. Do ye not know that they which minister about holy things live of the things of the temple? and they which wait at the altar are partakers with the altar? Even so hath the Lord ordained that they which preach the Gospel should live of the Gospel. But I have used none of these things: neither have I written these things, that it should be so done unto me: for it were better for me to die, than that any man should make my glorying void. For though I preach the Gospel, I have nothing to glory of: for necessity is laid upon me; yea, woe is unto me, if I preach not the Gospel! For if I do this thing willingly, I have a reward: but if against my will, a dispensation of the Gospel is committed unto me. What is my reward then? Verily that, when I preach the Gospel, I may make the Gospel of Christ without charge, that I abuse not my power in the Gospel. For though I be free from all men, yet have I made myself servant unto all, that I might gain the more. And unto the Jews I became as a Jew, that I might gain the Jews; to them that are under the Law, as under the Law, that I might gain them that are under the Law; to them that are without law, as without law, (being not without law to God, but under the Law to Christ,) that I might gain them that are without law. To the weak became I as weak, that I might gain the weak: I am made all things to all men, that I might by all means save some." — 1 Cor. ix. 1-22.

XIII
MAINTENANCE OF THE MINISTRY

In the preceding chapter Paul has disposed of the question put to him regarding meats offered in sacrifice to idols. He has taken occasion to point out that in matters morally indifferent Christian men will consider the scruples of weak, and prejudiced, and superstitious people. He has inculcated the duty of accommodating ourselves to the consciences of less enlightened persons, if we can do so without violating our own. For his own part, he is prepared, while the world standeth, to abridge his Christian liberty, if by his using that liberty he may imperil the conscience of any weak brother. But keeping pace, as Paul always does, with the thought of those he writes to, he no sooner makes this emphatic statement than it occurs to him that those in Corinth who are ill-affected towards him will make a handle even of his self-denial, and will whisper or boldly declare that it is all very fine for Paul to use this language, but that, in point of fact, the precarious position he holds in the Church makes it incumbent on him to deny himself and become all things to all men. His apostleship stands on so insecure a basis that he has no option in the matter, but must curry favour with all parties. He is not on the same platform as the original Apostles, who may reasonably stand upon their apostleship, and claim exemption from manual labour, and demand maintenance both for themselves and their wives. Paul remains unmarried, and works with his hands to support himself, and makes himself weak among the weak, because he has no claim to maintenance and is aware that his apostleship is doubtful. He proceeds therefore, with some pardonable warmth and righteous indignation, to assert his freedom and apostleship (vers. 1, 2), and to prove his right to the same privileges and maintenance as the other Apostles (3-14); and then from the fifteenth to the eighteenth verse he gives the true reason for his foregoing his rightful claim; and in vers. 19-22 he reaffirms the principle on which he uniformly acted, becoming "all things to all men," suiting himself to the innocent prejudices and weaknesses of all, "that he might by all means save some."

Paul then had certain rights which he was resolved should be acknowledged, although he waived them. He maintains that if he saw fit, he might require the Church to maintain him, and to maintain him not merely in the bare way in which he was content to live, but to furnish him with the ordinary comforts of life. He might, for example, he says, require the Church to enable him to keep a wife and to pay not only his own, but her, travelling expenses. The other Apostles apparently took their wives with them on their apostolic journeys, and may have found them useful in gaining access for the Gospel to the secluded women of Eastern and Greek cities. He might also, he says, "forbear working;" might cease, that is to say, from his tent-making and look to his converts for support. He is indignant at the sordid, or malicious, or mistaken spirit which could deny him such support.

This claim to support and privilege Paul rests on several grounds. 1. He is an apostle, and the other Apostles enjoyed these privileges. "Have we not power to take with us a Christian woman as a wife, as well as other Apostles?... Or I only and Barnabas, have not we power to forbear working?" His proof of his apostleship is summary: "Have I not seen Jesus Christ our Lord? are not ye my work in the Lord?" No one could be an apostle who had not seen Jesus Christ after His resurrection. The Apostles were to be witnesses to the Resurrection, and were qualified to be so by seeing the Lord alive after death. But it seems to have been commonly urged against Paul that he had not been among those to whom Christ showed Himself after He rose from the dead. Paul therefore both in his reported speeches and in his letters insists upon the fact that on the way to Damascus he had seen the risen Lord.

But not every one who had seen the Lord after His resurrection was an apostle, but those only who by Him were commissioned to witness to it; and that Paul had been thus commissioned he thinks the Corinthians may conclude from the results among themselves of his preaching. The Church at Corinth was the seal of his apostleship. What was the use of quibbling about the time and manner of his ordination, when the reality and success of his apostolic work were so apparent? The Lord had acknowledged his work. In presence of the finished structure that draws the world to gaze, it is too late to ask if he who built it is an architect. Would that every minister could so prove the validity of his orders!

2. Paul maintains his right to support on the principle of remuneration everywhere observed in human affairs. The soldier does not go to war at his own expense, but expects to be equipped and maintained in efficiency by those for whom he fights. The vinedresser, the shepherd, every labourer, expects, and is certainly warranted in expecting, that the toil he expends will at least have the result of keeping him comfortably in life. However difficult it is to lay down an absolute law of wages, this may at least be affirmed as a natural principle: that labour of all kinds must be so paid as to maintain the labourer in life and efficiency; and it may be added that there are certain

inalienable human rights, such as the right to bring up a family the members of which shall be useful and not burdensome to society, the right to some reserve of leisure and of strength which the labourer may use for his own enjoyment and advantage, which rights will be admitted and provided for when out of the confused war of theories, and strikes, and competition a just law of wages has been won. Happily no one now needs to be told that one of the most striking results of our modern civilisation is that the nineteenth century labourer has less of the joy of life than the ancient slave, and that we have forgotten the fundamental law that the husbandman that laboureth must be first partaker of the fruits.

And lest any one should sanctimoniously or ignorantly say, "These secular principles have no application to sacred things," Paul anticipates the objection, and dismisses it: "Say I these things as a man? or saith not the Law the same also?" I am not introducing into a sacred region principles which rule only in secular matters. Does not the Law say, "Thou shalt not muzzle the ox that treadeth out the corn"? It must be allowed to live by its labour. As it threshes out the wheat, it must be allowed to feed itself, mouthful by mouthful, as it goes on with its work. And this was not said in the Law because God had any special care for oxen, but in order to give expression to the law which must regulate the connection between all labourers and their work that he that plougheth may plough in hope, may have a personal interest in his work, and may give himself ungrudgingly to it, assured that he himself will be the first to benefit by it.

This law that a man shall live by his labour is a two-edged law. If a man produce what the community needs, he should himself profit by the production; but, on the other hand, if a man will not work, neither should he eat. Only the man who produces what other men need, only the man who by his industry or capability contributes to the good of the community, has any right to profits. Quick and easy manipulations of money, shrewd and risky dexterities which yield no real benefit to the community, deserve no remuneration. It is a blind, sordid, and contemptible spirit that hastes to be rich by one or two successful transactions that profit no one. A man should be content to live on what he is worth to the community. Here also our minds are often confused by the complexities of business; but on that account it is all the more necessary that we firmly adhere to the few essential canons, such as that "trading ceases to be just when it ceases to benefit both parties," or that a man's wealth should truly represent his value to society. Conscience enlightened by allegiance to the Spirit of Christ is a much more satisfactory guide for the individual in trade, speculation, and investment than any trade customs or economic theories.

3. A third ground on which Paul rests his claim to be supported by the Church is ordinary gratitude: "If we have sown unto you spiritual things, is it a great thing if we shall reap your carnal things?" Some of the Churches founded by Paul spontaneously acknowledged this claim, and wished to free him from the necessity of labouring for his own support. They felt that the benefit they had derived from him could not be stated in terms of money; but prompted by irrepressible gratitude, they could not but seek to relieve him from manual labour and set him free for higher work. This method of gauging the amount of spiritual benefit absorbed, by its overflow in material aid given to the propagation of the Gospel would, I daresay, scarcely be relished by that monstrous development the niggardly Christian.

4. Lastly, Paul argues from the Levitical usage to the Christian. Both in heathen countries and among the Jews it was customary that they who ministered in holy things should live by the offerings of the people to the temple. Levites and priests alike had been thus maintained among the Jews. "Even so hath the Lord ordained that they which preach the Gospel should live of the Gospel." Were there no recorded command of the Lord to this effect, we might suppose Paul merely argued that this was the Lord's will; but among the original instructions given to the seventy who were first sent to preach the kingdom of heaven, we find this: "Into whatsoever house ye enter, there remain, eating and drinking such things as they give, for the labourer is worthy of his hire."

That evils may result from the existence of a paid ministry no one will be disposed to deny. Some of the most disastrous abuses in the Church of Christ, as well as some of the gravest political troubles, could never have arisen had there been no desirable benefices. Lucrative ecclesiastical posts and offices have necessarily excited the avarice of unworthy aspirants, and have weakened instead of strengthening the Church's influence. Many wealthy ecclesiastics have done nothing for the benefit of the people, whereas many laymen by their unpaid devotedness have done much. In view of these and other evils, it cannot surprise us to find that again and again it has occurred to good men to suppose that on the whole Christianity might be more effectively propagated were there no separate class of men set apart to this work as their sole occupation. But this idea is reactionary and extreme, and is condemned both by common-sense and by the express declarations of our Lord and His Apostles. If the work of the ministry is to be thoroughly done, men must give their whole time to it. Like every other professional work, it will often be done inadequately; and I daresay there is much in our methods which is unwise and susceptible of improvement: but the ministry keeps pace with the general intelligence of the country, and may be trusted to adapt its methods, even though too tardily for some ardent spirits, to the actual necessities. And if men give their whole time to the work, they must be paid for it, a circumstance which is not likely to lead to much evil in our own country so long as the great mass of ministers are paid as they presently are. It is hardly the profession which is likely to be chosen by any one who is anxious to coin his life into money. If the laity consider that covetousness is more unseemly in a Christian minister than in a Christian man, they have taken an effectual means of barring out that vice.

Paul felt himself the more free to urge these claims because his custom was to forego them all in his own case. "I have used none of these things: neither have I written these things, that it should be so done unto me; for it were better for me to die, than that any man should make my glorying void." Here again we come upon the sound judgment and honest heart that are never biassed by his own personal circumstances or insist that what is fit for him is fit for every one. How apt are self-denying men to spoil their self-denial by dropping a sneer at the weaker souls that cannot follow their heroic example. How ready are men who can live on little and accomplish much to leave the less robust Christians to justify on their own account their need of human comforts. Not so Paul. He first fights the battle of the weak for them, and then disclaims all participation in the spoils. What a nobility and sagacity in the man who himself would accept no remuneration for his work, and who yet, so far from thinking slightingly of those who did or even being indifferent to them, argues their case for them with an authoritative force they did not themselves possess!

Nor does he consider that his self-denial is at all meritorious. He has no desire to signalize himself as more disinterested than other men. On the contrary, he strives to make it appear as if this course were compulsory and as if no choice were left to him. His fear was that if he took remuneration, he "should hinder the Gospel of Christ." Some of the best incomes in Greece in Paul's day were made by clever lecturers and talkers, who attracted disciples, and initiated them into their doctrines and methods. Paul was resolved he should never be mistaken for one of these. And no doubt his success was partly due to the fact that men recognised that his teaching was a labour of love, and that he was impelled by the truth and importance of his message. Every man finds an audience who is inwardly impelled to speak; who speaks, not because he is paid for doing so, but because there is that in him which must find utterance.

This, says Paul, was his case. "Though I preach the Gospel, I have nothing to glory of: for necessity is laid upon me; yea, woe is unto me, if I preach not the Gospel!" His call to the ministry had been so exceptional, and had so distinctly and emphatically declared the grace and purpose of Christ, that he felt bound by all that can constrain a man to the devotedness of a lifetime. Paul felt what we now so clearly see: that on him lay the gravest responsibilities. Had he declined to preach, had he complained of bad usage, and stipulated for higher terms, and withdrawn from the active propagation of Christianity, who would or could have taken up the task he laid down? But while Paul could not but be conscious of his importance to the cause of Christ, he would arrogate to himself no credit on account of his arduous toil, for from this, he says, he could not escape; necessity was laid upon him. Whether he does his work willingly or unwillingly, still he must do it. He dare not flinch. If he does it willingly, he has a reward; if he does it unwillingly, still he is entrusted with a stewardship he dare not neglect. What then is the reward he has, giving himself, as he certainly does, *willingly* to the work? His reward is that "when he preaches the Gospel he makes the Gospel of Christ without charge." The deep satisfaction he felt in dissociating the Gospel of self-sacrifice from every thought of money or remuneration and in offering it freely to the poorest as his Master's fit representative was sufficient reward for him and incalculably greater than any other he ever got or could conceive.

In other words, Paul saw that however it might be with other men, with him there was no alternative but to preach the Gospel; the only alternative was—was he to do it as a slave entrusted with a stewardship, and who was compelled, however reluctant he might be, to be faithful, or was he to do it as a free man, with his whole will and heart? The reluctant slave could expect no reward; he was but fulfilling an obligatory, inevitable duty. The free man might, however, expect a reward; and the reward Paul chose was that he should have none—none in the ordinary sense, but really the deepest and most abiding of all: the satisfaction of knowing that, having freely received, he had freely given, and had lifted the Gospel into a region quite undimmed by the suspicion of self-seeking or any mists of worldliness.

In declining pecuniary remuneration, Paul was acting on his general principle of making himself the servant of all and of living entirely and exclusively for the good of others. "Though I be free from all men, yet have I made myself servant unto all, that I might gain the more." It was from Paul that Luther derived his two propositions which he uttered as the keynote of the resonant blast "on Christian Liberty" with which he stirred all Europe into new life: "A Christian man is the most free lord of all, and subject to none; a Christian man is the most dutiful servant of all, and subject to every one." So Paul's independence of all men was assumed and maintained for the very purpose of making himself the more effectually the servant of all. To the Jew and to those under the Law he became as a Jew, observing the seventh day, circumcising Timothy, abstaining from blood, accommodating himself to all their scruples. To those who were without the Law, and who had been brought up in Greece, he also conformed himself, freely entering into their innocent customs, calling no meats unclean, appealing, not to the law of Moses, but to conscience, to common-sense, to their own poets. "I am made all things to all men, that I might by all means save some"—a course which none but a man of wide sympathy and charity, clear intellect, and thorough integrity can adopt.

For Paul was no mere latitudinarian. While accommodating himself to the practice of those around him in all matters of mere outward observance, and which did not touch the essentials of morality and faith, he at the same time held very definite opinions on the chief articles of the Christian creed. No amount of liberality of sentiment can ever induce a thoughtful man to discourage the formation of opinion on all matters of importance. On the contrary, the only escape from mere traditionalism or the tyranny of authority in matters of religion is in individual inquiry and ascertainment of the truth. Free inquiry is the one instrument we possess for the discovery of truth; and by pursuing such inquiry men may be expected to come to some agreement in religious belief, as in other things. No doubt righteousness of life is better than soundness of creed. But is it not possible to have both? It is better to live in the Spirit, to be meek, chaste, temperate, just, loving, than to understand the relation of the Spirit to God and to ourselves; but the human mind can never cease to seek satisfaction: and truth, the more clearly it is seen, will the more effectually nourish righteousness.

Again, Paul had an end in view which preserved his liberality from degenerating. He sought to recommend himself to men, not for his sake, but for theirs. He saw that conscientious scruples were not to be confounded with malignant hatred of truth, and that if we are to be helpful to others, we must begin by appreciating the good they already possess. Hostile criticism or argument for the sake of victory produces no results worth having. Vain exultation in the victors, obstinacy and bitterness in the vanquished—these are worse than useless, the retrograde results of unsympathetic argument. In order to remove a man's difficulties, you must look at them from his point of view and feel the pressure he feels. "The greatest orator save one of antiquity has left it on record that he always studied his adversary's case with as great, if not still greater, intensity than even his own;"[6] and certainly those who have not entered into the point of view of those who differ from them are not likely to have anything of importance to say to them. In order to "gain" men, you must credit them with some desire to see the truth, and you must have sympathy enough to see with their eyes. Parents sometimes weaken their influence with their children by inability to look at things with the eyes of youth, and by an insistence upon the outward expressions of religion which are distasteful to children and suitable only for adults. Children have a high esteem for justice and courage, and can respond to exhibitions of self-sacrifice, and truth, and purity; that is to say, they have a capacity for admiring and adopting the essentials of the Christian character, but if we insist upon them exhibiting feelings which are alien to their nature and practices necessarily distasteful and futile, we are more likely to drive them from religion than to attract them to it. Let us beware of insisting on alterations in conduct where these are not absolutely necessary. Let us beware of identifying religion in the minds of the young with a rigid conformity in outward things, and not with an inward spirit of love and goodness. Are you striving to gain some? Then let these words of the Apostle warn you not to seek for the wrong thing, not to begin at the wrong end, not to measure the hold which truth has over those you seek to win, by the exactness with which all your ideas are carried out and all your customs observed. Human nature is an infinitely various thing, and often there is the truest regard for what is holy and Divine disguised under a violent departure from all ordinary ways of manifesting reverence and piety. Put yourself in the place of the inquiring, perplexed, embittered soul, find out the good that is in it, patiently accommodate yourself to its ways so far as you legitimately may, and you will be rewarded by "gaining some."

NOT ALL WHO RUN WIN

"And this I do for the Gospel's sake, that I might be partaker thereof with you. Know ye not that they which run in a race run all, but one receiveth the prize? So run, that ye may obtain. And every man that striveth for the mastery is temperate in all things. Now they do it to obtain a corruptible crown; but we an incorruptible. I therefore so run, not as uncertainly; so fight I, not as one that beateth the air: but I keep under my body, and bring it into subjection: lest that by any means, when I have preached to others, I myself should be a castaway." —1 Cor. ix. 23-27.

XIV
NOT ALL WHO RUN WIN

In the preceding part of this chapter Paul has proved his right to claim remuneration from those to whom he preached the Gospel, and he has also given his reasons for declining to urge this claim. He was resolved that no one should have any ground for misapprehending his motive in preaching the Gospel. He was quite content to live a bare, poor life, not merely that he might keep himself above suspicion, but that those who heard the Gospel might see it simply as the Gospel and not be hindered from accepting it by any thought of the preacher's motives. This was his main reason for supporting himself by his own labour. But he had another reason, namely, "that he might be himself a partaker of the benefits he preached" (ver. 23). Apostle though he was, he had his own salvation to work out. He was not himself saved by proclaiming salvation to others, no more than the baker is fed by making bread for others or the physician kept in health by prescribing for others. Paul had a life of his own to lead, a duty of his own to discharge, a soul of his own to save; and he recognised that what was laid before him as the path to salvation was to make himself entirely the servant of others. This he was resolved persistently to do, "lest that by any means, when he had preached to others, he himself should be a castaway."

Paul had evidently felt this danger to be a serious one. He had found himself tempted from time to time to rest in the name and calling of an apostle, to take for granted that his salvation was a thing past doubt and on which no more thought or effort need be expended. And he saw that in a slightly altered form this temptation was common to all Christians. All have the name, not all the reality. And the very possession of the name is a temptation to forget the reality. It might almost seem to be in the proportion of runners to winners in a race: "All run, but one receiveth the prize."

In endeavouring to warn Christians against resting in a mere profession of faith in Christ, he cites two great classes of instances which prove that there is often ultimate failure even where there has been considerable promise of success. First, he cites their own world-renowned Isthmian games, in which contests, as they all well knew, not every one who entered for the prizes was successful: "All run, but one receiveth the prize." Paul does not mean that salvation goes by competition; but he means that as in a race not all who run run so as to obtain the prize for which they run, so in the Christian life not all who enter it put out sufficient energy to bring them to a happy issue. The mere fact of recognising that the prize is worth winning and even of entering for it is not enough. And then he cites another class of instances with which the Jews in the Corinthian Church were familiar. "*All* our fathers," he says, "were under the cloud, and *all* passed through the sea, and *all* were baptized unto Moses in the cloud and in the sea." All of them without exception enjoyed the outward privileges of God's people, and seemed to be in a fair way of entering the promised land; and yet the majority of them fell under God's displeasure, and were overthrown in the wilderness. Therefore "let him that thinketh he standeth take heed lest he fall."

The Isthmian games, then, one of the most ancient glories of Corinth, furnished Paul with the readiest illustration of his theme. These games, celebrated every second year, had in ancient times been one of the chief means of fostering the feeling of brotherhood in the Hellenic race. None but Greeks of pure blood who had done nothing to forfeit their citizenship were allowed to contend in them. They were the greatest of national gatherings; and even when one State was at war with another, hostilities were suspended during the celebration of the games. And scarcely any greater distinction could be earned by a Greek citizen than victory in these games. When Paul says that the contending athletes endured their severe training and underwent all the privations necessary "to obtain a corruptible crown," we must remember that while it is quite true that the wreath of pine given to the victor might fade before the year was out, he was welcomed home with all the honours of a victorious general, the wall of his town being thrown down that he might pass in as a conqueror, and his statue being set up by his fellow-citizens. In point of fact, the names and deeds of many of the victors may yet be read in the verses of one of the greatest of Greek poets, who devoted himself, as laureate of the games, to the celebration of the annual victories.

But however highly we raise the value of the Greek crown, the force of Paul's comparison remains. The wreath of the victor in the games was at the best corruptible, liable to decay. No permanent, eternal satisfaction could result from being victorious in a contest of physical strength, activity, or skill. But for every man it is possible to win an incorruptible crown, that which shall always and for ever be to him a joy as thrilling and a distinction as honourable as at the moment he received it. There is that which is worthy of the determined and sustained effort of a lifetime. Put into the one scale all perishable distinctions, and honours, and prizes, all that has stimulated men to the most strenuous endeavours, all that a grateful nation bestows on its heroes and benefactors, all for which men "scorn delights and live laborious days;" and all these kick the beam when you put in the other scale the incorruptible crown. The two are not necessarily opposed or incompatible; but to choose the less in preference to the greater is to repudiate our birthright. As victory in the games was the actual incentive which stimulated the youth of Greece to attain the perfection of physical strength, beauty, and development, so there is laid before us an incentive which, when clearly apprehended, is sufficient to carry us forward to perfect moral attainment. The brightest jewel in the incorruptible crown is the joy of having become all God made us to become, of perfectly fulfilling the end of our creation, of being able to find happiness in goodness, in closest fellowship with God, in promoting what Christ lived and died to promote. Must we say that there are men who have no ambition to experience perfect rectitude and purity? Are we to conclude that there are men of so grovelling, besotted, and blind a spirit that when opportunity is given them to win true glory, perfect expansion and growth of spirit, and perfect joy they turn away to salaries and profits, to meat and drink, to frivolity and the world's routine? The incorruptible crown is held over their head; but so intent are they on the muck-rake, they do not even see it.

To those who would win it Paul gives these directions:—

1. Be temperate. "Every man that striveth for the mastery is temperate in all things." Contentedly and without a murmur he submits himself to the rules and restrictions of his ten months' training, without which he may as well not compete. The little indulgences which other men allow themselves he must forego. Not once will he break the trainer's rules, for he knows that some competitors will refrain even from that once and gain strength while he is losing it. He is proud of his little hardships, and fatigues, and privations, and counts it a point of honour scrupulously to abstain from anything which might in the slightest degree diminish his chance of success. He sees other men giving way to appetite, resting while he is panting with exertion, luxuriating in the bath, enjoying life at pleasure; but he has scarce a passing thought of envy, because his heart is set on the prize, and severe training is indispensable. He knows that his chances are gone if in any point or on any occasion he relaxes the rigour of the discipline.

The contest in which Christians are engaged is not less, but more, severe. The temperance maintained by the athlete must be outdone by the Christian if he is to be successful. There are many things in which men who have no thought of the incorruptible prize may engage, but from which the Christian must refrain. All that lowers the tone and slackens the energies must be abandoned. If the Christian indulges in the pleasures of life as freely as other men, if he is unconscious of any severity of self-restraint, if he denies himself nothing which others enjoy, he proves that he has no higher aim than they and can of course win no higher prize. The temperance here enjoined, and which the Christian practises, not because it is enjoined, but because a higher aim truly cherished compels him to practise it, is a habitual sober-mindedness and detachment from what is worldly in the world. It is that temper of spirit and that sustained attitude towards life which enable a man to rule his own desires, to endure hardness and find pleasure in so doing. No spasmodic, occasional efforts and partial abstinences will ever bring a man victorious to the goal. Many a man denies himself in one direction and indulges himself in another. He macerates the flesh, but pampers the spirit by vanity, ambition, or self-righteousness. Or he denies himself some of the pleasures of life, but is more besotted by its gains than other men. Temperance to be effectual must be complete. The athlete who drinks more than is good for him may save himself the trouble of observing the trainer's rules as to what he eats. It is lost labour to develop some of his muscles if he do not develop all of them. If he offends in one point, he breaks the whole law.

Temperance must be continuous as well as complete. One day's debauch was enough to undo the result of weeks during which the athlete had carefully attended to the rules prescribed. And we find that one lapse into worldliness undoes what years of self-restraint have won. Always the work of growth is very slow, the work of destruction very quick. One indiscretion on the part of the convalescent will undo what the care of months has slowly achieved. One fraud spoils the character for honesty which years of upright living have earned. And this also is one of the great dangers of the spiritual life: that a little carelessness, a brief infidelity to our high calling, or a passing indulgence suddenly demolishes what long and patient toil has been building up. It is like the taking out of a pin or a ratchet that lets all we have gained run down to its old condition.

Beware then of giving place to the world or the flesh at any point. Be reasonable and true. Recognise that if you are to succeed in winning eternal life, all the spiritual energy you can command will be required. So set your heart on the attainment of things eternal that you will not grudge missing much that other men enjoy and possess. Measure the invitations of life by their fitness or unfitness to develop within you true spiritual energy.

2. Be decided. "I run," says Paul, "not as uncertainly," not as a man who does not know where he is going or has not made up his mind to go there. To be among those who win as well as among those who run, we must know where we are going, and be quite sure we mean to be there. We have all some kind of idea about what God offers and calls us to. But this idea must be clear if we are to make for it straight. No man can run

straight to a mere will-o'-the-wisp, and no man can run straight who first means to go to one house or station and then changes his mind and thinks he should go to another. We must count the cost and see clearly what we are to gain and what we must lose by making for the incorruptible prize. We must be resolved to win and have no thought of defeat, of failure, of doing something better. It is the absence of deliberate choice and reasonable decision which causes such "uncertain" running on the part of many who profess to be in the race. Their faces are as often turned from the goal as towards it. They are evidently not clear in their own minds that all strength spent in any other direction than towards the goal is wasted. They do not distinctly know what they mean to be at, what they wish to make of life. Paul did know. He had made up his mind not to pursue comfort, learning, money, respect, position, but to seek first the kingdom of God. He judged that to spread the knowledge of Christ was the best use to which he could put his life. He knew where he was going and to what all his efforts tended. Every life is unsatisfactory until its owner has made up his mind what he means to do with it, until it is governed by a clearly conceived and firmly held aim. Then it flies like the arrow to its mark.

What then do the traces of our past life show? Do we see the straight track of a well-steered ship, which has deviated not a yard from its course nor wasted an ounce of power? Has every footfall been in direct advance of the last, and has all expenditure of energy brought us nearer the ultimate goal? Or are the traces we look back on like ground trodden by dancers, a confused medley all in one spot, or like the footsteps of saunterers in a garden backwards and forwards, according as this or that has attracted them? Has not the course of many of us been like that of persons lost, uncertain which direction to pursue, eagerly starting off, but after a little slackening their pace, stopping, looking round, and then going off in another direction? For some weeks a great deal of ardour has been apparent, the whole man girt up, every nerve strained, the whole attention directed towards spiritual victory, arrangements made to facilitate communion with God, new methods devised for subordinating all our work to the one great aim, everything gone about as if now at last we had found the secret of living; and then in a surprisingly short time all this eagerness cools down, doubt takes the place of decision, discouragement and failure breed distrust of our methods, and we lapse into contentment with easier attainments and more worldly aims. And at length, after many false starts, we are ashamed to begin any arduous spiritual task for fear of ceasing it next week. We think that the surest way to make fools of ourselves is to adopt a thorough-going Christian practice, so much do we count upon ourselves flagging, wearying, altering our course. How many times have we been rekindled to some true zeal, how often have we gathered up our scattered energies and concentrated our efforts on the Christian life, and yet as often have we gone back to a dreamy, listless sauntering, as if we had nothing to secure, no end to reach, no work to accomplish.

Are we likely ever to reach the goal thus? Will the goal come to us, or how are we ever to reach it? Are we nearer to it to-day than ever before? Are not our minds yet made up that it is worth reaching, and that whatever does not help us towards it must be abandoned? Let us be clear in our own minds as to the matters which tempt us aside from the straight path to the goal and are incompatible with progress; and let us determine whether these things are to prevail with us or not.

3. Be in earnest. "So fight I, not as one that beateth the air," not as one amusing himself with idle flourishes, but as one who has a real enemy to encounter. What a blush does this raise on the cheek of every Christian who knows himself! How much of this mere parade and sham-fighting is there in the Christian army! We learn the art of war and the use of our weapons as if we were forthwith to use them in the field; we act over and learn many varieties of offensive and defensive movements, and know the rules by which spiritual foes may be subdued; we read books which direct us about personal religion, and delight in those which most skilfully lay open our weaknesses and show us how we may overcome them. But all this is mere fencing-school work; it kills no enemy. It is but a species of accomplishment like that of those who learn the use of the sword, not because they mean to use it in battle, but that they may have a more elegant carriage. A great part of our spiritual strength is spent in mere parade. It is not meant to have any serious effect. It is not directed against anything in particular. We seem to be doing everything that a good soldier of Jesus Christ need do save the one thing: we slay no enemy. We leave no foe stone-dead on the field. We are well trained: no one can deny it; we could instruct others how to conquer sin; we spend much time, and thought, and feeling on exercises which are calculated to make an impression on sin; and yet is it not almost entirely a beating the air? Where are our slain foes? This apparent eagerness to be holy, this professed devotedness to the cause of Christ—are they not mere flourish? We do not mean to strike our enemies; we for the most part only wish to make ourselves believe we are striking them and are zealous and faithful soldiers of Christ.

Even where there is some reality in the contest we may still be beating the air. We may be able to say that we have apprehended the reality of the moral warfare to which every man is called in this life. We may be able honestly to say that if our sins are not slain, it is neither because we have not recognised them, nor because we have aimed no blows at them. We have made serious and honest efforts to destroy sin, and yet our blows seem to fall short; and sin stands before us vigorous and lively, and as ready as ever to give us a fall. Many persons who level blows at their sins do not after all strike them. Spiritual energy is put forth; but it is not brought fully, fairly, and firmly into contact with the sin to be destroyed. In most Christian people there is a great expenditure of thought and of feeling about sin; their spirit is probably more exercised about their sins than about anything else: and a great deal of spiritual life is expended in the shape of shame, compunction, penitence, resolve, self-restraint, watchfulness, prayer. All this, were it brought directly to bear on some definite object, would produce great effect; but in many cases no good whatever seems to result.

Paul's language suggests that possibly the reason may be that there remains in the heart some reluctance quite to kill and put an end to sin, to beat all the life out of it. It is like a father fighting with his son: he wishes to defend himself and disarm his son, but not to kill him. We may be willing or even intensely anxious to escape the blows sin aims at us; we may be desirous to wound, hamper, and limit our sin, and keep it under control; we may wish to tame the wild animal and domesticate it, so as to make it yield some pleasure and profit, and yet be reluctant to slay it outright. The soul and life of every sin is some lust of our own; and while quite anxious to put an end to some of the evils this lust produces in our life, we may not be prepared to extinguish the lust itself. We pray God, for example, to preserve us from the evils of praise or of success; and yet we continue to court praise and success. We are unable to sacrifice the pleasure for the sake of the safety. Therefore our warfare against sin becomes unreal. Our blows are not delivered home, but beat the air. Unconsciously we cherish the evil desire within us which is the soul of the sin, and seek to destroy only some of its manifestations.

The result of such unreal contest is detrimental. Sin is like something floating in the air or the water: the very effort we make to grasp and crush it displaces it, and it floats mockingly before us untouched. Or it is like an agile antagonist who springs back from our blow, so that the force we have expended merely racks and strains our own sinews and does him no injury. So when we spend much effort in conquering sin and find it as lively as ever, the spirit is strained and hurt by putting out force on nothing. It is less able than before to resist sin, less believing, less hopeful, inwardly ill at ease and distracted. It becomes confused and disheartened, disbelieves in itself, and scoffs at fresh resolves and endeavours.

Finally, Paul tells us what that enemy was against which he directed his well-aimed, firmly planted blows. It was his own body. Every man's body is his enemy when, instead of being his servant, it becomes his master.

The proper function of the body is to serve the will, to bring the inner man into contact with the outer world and enable him to influence it. When the body mutinies and refuses to obey the will, when it usurps authority and compels the man to do its bidding, it becomes his most dangerous enemy. When Paul's body presumed to dictate to his spirit, and demanded comforts and indulgences, and shrank from hardship, he beat it down. The word he uses is an exceptionally strong one: "I keep under;" it is a technical term of the games, and means to strike full in the face. It was the word used of the most damaging blow one boxer could give another. This unmerciful, overpowering blow Paul dealt to his body, resisting its assaults and making it helpless to tempt him. He thus brought it into subjection, made it his slave, as the winner in some of the games had a right to carry the vanquished into slavery.

It was probably by sheer strength of will and by the grace of Christ that Paul subdued his body. Many in all ages have striven to subdue it by fasting, by scourging, by wakefulness; and of these practices we have no right to speak scornfully until we can say that by other means we have reduced the body to its proper position as the servant of the spirit. Can we say that our body is brought into subjection; that it dare not curtail our devotions on the plea of weariness; that it dare not demand a dispensation from duty on the score of some slight bodily disturbance; that it never persuades us to neglect any duty on the score of its unpleasantness to the flesh; that it never prompts us to undue anxiety either about what we shall eat or drink or wherewithal we shall be clothed; that it never quite treads the spirit under foot and defiles it with wicked imaginings? There is a fair and reasonable degree in which a man may and ought to cherish his own flesh, but there is also needful a disregard to many of its claims and a hardhearted obduracy to its complaints. In an age when Spartan simplicity of life is almost unknown, it is very easy to sow to the flesh almost without knowing it until we find ourselves reaping corruption.

Probably nothing more effectually slackens our efforts in the spiritual life than the sense of unreality which haunts us as we deal with God and the unseen. With the boxer in the games it was grim earnest. He did not need any one to tell him that his life depended on his ability to defend himself against his trained antagonist. Every faculty must be on the alert. No dreamer has here a chance. What we need is something of the same sense of reality, that it is a life-and-death contest we are engaged in, and that he that treats sin as a weak or pretended antagonist will shortly be dragged a mangled disgrace out of the arena.

FALLACIOUS PRESUMPTIONS

"Moreover, brethren, I would not that ye should be ignorant, how that all our fathers were under the cloud, and all passed through the sea; and were all baptized unto Moses in the cloud and in the sea; and did all eat the same spiritual meat; and did all drink the same spiritual drink: for they drank of that spiritual Rock that followed them: and that Rock was Christ. But with many of them God was not well pleased: for they were overthrown in the wilderness. Now these things were our examples, to the intent we should not lust after evil things, as they also lusted. Neither be ye idolaters, as were some of them; as it is written. The people sat down to eat and drink, and rose up to play. Neither let us commit fornication, as some of them committed, and fell in one day three-and-twenty thousand. Neither let us tempt Christ, as some of them also tempted, and were destroyed of serpents. Neither murmur ye, as some of them also murmured, and were destroyed of the destroyer. Now all these things happened unto them for ensamples: and they are written for our admonition, upon whom the ends of the world are come. Wherefore let him that thinketh he standeth take heed lest he fall. There hath no temptation taken you but such as is common to man: but God is faithful, who will not suffer you to be tempted above that ye are able; but will with the temptation also make a way to escape, that ye may be able to bear it. Wherefore, my dearly beloved, flee from idolatry. I speak as to wise men; judge ye what I say. The cup of blessing which we bless, is it not the communion of the blood of Christ? The bread which we break, is it not the communion of the body of Christ? For we being many are one bread, and one body: for we are all partakers of that one bread. Behold Israel after the flesh: are not they which eat of the sacrifices partakers of the altar? What say I then? that the idol is anything, or that which is offered in sacrifice to idols is anything? But I say, that the things which the Gentiles sacrifice, they sacrifice to devils, and not to God: and I would not that ye should have fellowship with devils. Ye cannot drink the cup of the Lord, and the cup of devils: ye cannot be partakers of the Lord's table, and of the table of devils. Do we provoke the Lord to jealousy? are we stronger than He?" — 1 Cor. x. 1-22.

XV
FALLACIOUS PRESUMPTIONS

In discussing the question regarding "things offered unto idols," Paul is led to treat at large of Christian liberty, a subject to which he was always drawn. And partly to encourage the Christians of Corinth to consider their weak and prejudiced brethren, partly for other reasons, he reminds them how he himself abridged his liberty and departed from his just claims in order that the Gospel he preached might find readier acceptance. Besides, not only for the sake of the Gospel and of other men, but for his own sake also, he must practise self-denial. It would profit him nothing to have been an apostle unless he practised what he preached. He had felt that in considering the spiritual condition of other men and trying to advance it he was apt to forget his own; and he saw that all men were more or less liable to the same temptation, and were apt to rest in the fact that they were Christians and to shrink from the arduous life which gives that name its meaning. By means of two illustrations Paul fixes this idea in their minds, first pointing them to their own games, in which they saw that not all who entered for the race obtained the prize, and then pointing them to the history of Israel, in which they might plainly read that not all who began the journey to the promised land found entrance into it.

The Israelites of the Exodus are here introduced as exemplifying a common experience. They accepted the position of God's people, but failed in its duties. They perceived the advantages of being God's subjects, but shrank from much which this implied. They were willing to be delivered from bondage, but found themselves overweighted by the responsibilities and risks of a free life. They were in contact with the highest advantages men need possess, and yet failed to use them.

The amount of conviction which prompts us to form a connection with Christ may be insufficient to stimulate us to do and endure all that results from that connection. The children of Israel were all baptized unto Moses, but they did not implement their baptism by a persistent and faithful adherence to him. They were baptized unto Moses by their acceptance of his leadership in the Exodus. By passing through the Red Sea at his command they definitely renounced Pharaoh and abandoned their old life, and as definitely pledged and committed themselves to throw in their lot with Moses. By passing the Egyptian frontier and following the guidance of the pillar of cloud they professed their willingness to exchange a life of bondage, with its security and occasional luxuries, for a life of freedom, with its hazards and hardships; and by that passage of the Red Sea they were as certainly sworn to support and obey Moses as ever was Roman soldier who took the oath to serve his emperor. When, at Brederode's invitation, the patriots of Holland put on the beggar's wallet and tasted wine from the beggar's bowl, they were baptized unto William of Orange and their country's cause. When the sailors on board the *Swan* weighed anchor and beat out of Plymouth they were baptized unto Drake and pledged to follow him and fight for him to the death. Baptism means much; but if it means anything, it means that we commit and pledge ourselves to the life we are called to by Him in whose name we are baptized. It draws a line across the life, and proclaims that to whomsoever in time past we have been bound, and for whatsoever we have lived, we now are pledged to this new Lord, and are to live in His service. Such a pledge was given by every Israelite who turned his back on Egypt and passed through that sea which was the defence of Israel and destruction to the enemy. The crossing was at once actual deliverance from the old life and irrevocable committal to the new. They died to Pharaoh, and were born again to Moses. They were baptized unto Moses.

And as the Israelites had thus a baptism analogous to the one Christian sacrament, so had they a spiritual food and drink in the wilderness which formed a sacrament analogous to the Christian communion. They were not shut out of Egypt, and imprisoned in the desert, and left to do the best they could on their own resources. If they failed to march steadily forward and fulfil their destiny as the emancipated people of God, this failure was not due to any neglect on God's part. The fare might be somewhat Spartan, but a sufficiency was always provided. He who had encouraged them to enter on this new life was prepared to uphold them in it and carry them through.

One of the expressions used by Paul in describing the sustenance of the Israelites has given rise to some discussion. "They did all drink," he says, "the same spiritual drink, for they drank of that spiritual Rock that followed them; and that Rock was Christ." Now there happened to be a Jewish tradition which gave out that the rock smitten by Moses was a detached block or boulder, "globular, like a beehive," which rolled after the camp in its line of march, and was always at hand, with its unfailing water-supply. This is altogether too grotesque an idea. The fact is that the Israelites did not die of thirst in the wilderness. It was quite likely they should; and but for the providential supply of water, so large a company could not have been sustained. And no doubt not only in the rock at Rephidim at the beginning of their journey and the rock of Kadesh at its close, but in many most unlikely places during the intervening years, water was found. So that in looking back on the entire journey it might very naturally be said that the rock had followed them, not meaning that wherever they went they had the same source to draw from, but that throughout their journeyings they were supplied with water in places and ways as unexpected and unlikely.

Paul's point is that in the wilderness the food and drink of the Israelites were "spiritual," or, as we should more naturally say, sacramental; that is to say, their sustenance continually spoke to them of God's nearness and reminded them that they were His people. And as Christ Himself, when He lifted the bread at the Last Supper, said, "This is My body," so does Paul use analogous language and say, "That Rock was Christ," an expression which gives us considerable insight into the significance of the Israelitish types of Christ, and helps to rid our minds of some erroneous impressions we are apt to cherish regarding them.

The manna and the water from the rock were given to sustain the Israelites and carry them towards their promised land, but they were so given as to quicken faith in God. To every Israelite his daily nourishment might reasonably be called spiritual, because it reminded him that God was with him in the wilderness, and prompted him to think of that purpose and destiny for the sake of which God was sustaining the people. To the devout among them their daily food became a means of grace, deepening their faith in the unseen God and rooting their life in a true dependence upon Him. The manna and the water from the rock were sacramental, because they were continuous signs and seals of God's favour and redeeming efficiency and promise. They were types of Christ, serving for Israel in the wilderness the purpose which Christ serves for us, enabling them to believe in a heavenly Father who cared for them and accomplishing the same spiritual union with the unseen God which Christ accomplishes for us.

It was in this sense that Paul could say that the rock was Christ. The Israelites in the wilderness did not know that the rock was a type of Christ. They did not, as they drank of the water, think of One who was to come and satisfy the whole thirst of men. The types of Christ in the old times did not enable men to forecast the future; it was not through the future they exercised an influence for good on the mind. They worked by exciting there and then in the Jewish mind the same faith in God which Christ excites in our mind. It was not knowledge that saved the Jew, but faith, attachment to the living God. It was not the fragmentary and disjointed picture of a Redeemer thrown on the screen of his hopes by the types, nor was it any thought of a future Deliverer, which saved him, but his belief in God as his Redeemer there and then. This belief was quickened by the various institutions, providences, and objects by which God convinced the Jews that He was their Friend and Lord. Sacrifice they accepted as an institution of God's appointment intended to encourage them to believe in the forgiveness of sin and in God's favour; and without any thought of the realized ideal of sacrifice in Christ, the believing and devout Israelite entered through sacrifice into fellowship with God. Every sacrifice was a type of Christ; it did foreshadow that which was to be: but it was a type, not because it revealed Christ to those who saw or offered it, but because for the time being it served the same purpose as Christ now serves, enabling men to believe in the forgiveness of sins.

But while in the mind of the Israelite there was no connection of the type with the Christ that was to come, there was in reality a connection between them. The redemption of men is one whether accomplished in the days of the Exodus or in our own time. The idea or plan of salvation is one, resting always on the same reasons and principles. The Israelites were pardoned in view of the incarnation and atonement of Christ just as we are. If it was needful for our salvation that Christ should come and live and suffer in human nature, it was also needful for their salvation. The Lamb was slain "from the foundation of the world," and the virtue of the sacrifice of Calvary was efficacious for those who lived before as well as for those who lived after it. To the mind of God it was present, and in His purpose it was determined, from the beginning; and it is in view of Christ's incarnation and work that sinners early or late have been restored to God. So that everything by which God instructed men and taught them to believe in His mercy and holiness was connected with Christ. It was to Christ it owed its existence, and really it was a shadow of the coming substance. And as the shadow is named from the substance, it may truly be said, "That Rock was Christ."

These outward blessings then of which St. Paul here speaks had very much the same nature as the Christian sacraments to which he tacitly compares them. They were intended to convey greater gifts and be the channels of a grace more valuable than themselves. But to most of the Israelites they remained mere manna and water, and brought no firmer assurance of God's presence, no more fruitful acceptance of God's purpose. The majority took the husk and threw away the kernel; were so delayed by the wrappings that they forgot to examine the gift they enclosed; accepted the physical nourishment, but rejected the spiritual strength it contained. Instead of learning from their wilderness experience the sufficiency of Jehovah and gathering courage to fulfil His purpose with them, they began to murmur and lust after evil things, and were destroyed by the destroyer. They had been baptized unto Moses, pledging themselves to his leadership and committing themselves to the new life he opened to them; they had been sustained by manna and water from the rock, which plainly told them that all nature would work for them if they pressed forward to their God-appointed destiny: but the most of them shrank from the hardships and hazards of the way, and could not lift their heart to the glory of being led by God and used to fulfil His greatest purposes.

And so, says Paul, it may be with you. It is possible that you may have been baptized and may have professedly committed yourself to the Christian career, it is possible you may have partaken of that bread and wine which convey undying life and energy to believing recipients, and may yet have failed to use these as spiritual food, enabling you to fulfil all the duties of the life you are pledged to. Had it been enough merely to show a readiness to enter on the more arduous life, then all Israel would have been saved, for "all" without exception passed through the Red Sea and committed themselves to life under God's leadership. Had it been enough outwardly to participate in that which actually links men to God, then all Israel would have been inspired by God's Spirit and strength, for "all" without exception partook of the spiritual food and the spiritual drink. But the disastrous and undeniable result was that the great mass of the people were overthrown in the wilderness and did never set foot in the land of promise. And men have not yet outlived this same danger of committing themselves to a life they find too hard and full of risk. They see the advantages of a Christian career, and connect themselves with the Christian Church; they instinctively perceive that it is there God is most fully known, and that the purposes of God are there concentrated and running on to direct and perfect results; they are drawn by their better self to throw in their lot with the Church, to forget competing advantages, and spend themselves wholly on what is best: and yet the difficulty of standing alone and acting on individual conviction rather than on current understandings, the wearing depression of personal failure and insufficiency for high and spiritual attainment, the distraction of the haunting doubt that after all they are making sacrifices and suffering privations which are fruitless, unwise, unnecessary, gradually betray the spirit into virtual renunciation of all Christian hopes and into a practical willingness to return to the old life. And thus as the wilderness came to be spotted all over with the burial-places of those who had left the Red Sea behind them with shouts of triumph and with hopes that broke out in song and dancing, as the route of that once jubilant host might at last have been traced, as the great slave-routes of Africa are traceable, by the bones of men and the skeletons of children, so, alas! might the Church's march through the centuries be recognised by the far more horrifying remains of those who once, with liveliest hope and unbroken sense of security, joined themselves to the people of Christ, but silently lost hold of the hope that once drew them on and either stole away on private enterprises of their own and were destroyed of the destroyer, or withered in helpless imbecility, murmuring at their lot and stone-blind to its glory. As the retreat of Napoleon's "grand army" from Moscow was marked by corpses wearing the French uniform, but bringing neither strength nor lustre to their cause, so must shame be reflected on the Church by the countless numbers of those who can be identified with Christ's cause only by the uniform they wear, and not by any victories they have won. There were in the wilderness districts through which no Israelite would willingly pass, districts in which many thousands had fallen, and which were branded as vast "graves of lust," places whose very name stirred a deeper horror and raised a quicker blush on the Israelite's cheek than is raised on the Englishman's by the mention of Majuba Hill or Braddon's defeat. And the Church's territory also is spotted with those vast charnel-houses and places of defeat where even her mighty have fallen, where the earth refuses to cover the disgrace and blot out the stain. These are not things of the past. While women and children are starved though they toil all day and half the night, with eagerest energy and the skill necessity gives; while life is to so many thousands in our land a joyless and hopeless misery; while trade not only panders to covetousness and selfishness, but directly contributes to what is immoral and destructive, we can scarcely speak of the "glorious marching" of the Church of Christ. We have our places of horror, which no right-hearted Christian can think of without a shudder.

But while the distinction between the life we naturally seek and that to which God calls us is felt by all from age to age, the forms in which this distinction makes itself felt vary as the world grows older. To all men living in a world of sense it is difficult to live by faith in the unseen. To every man it is the ultimate, severest test of character to determine for what ends he will live and to carry out this determination; but the temptations which avail to draw men aside from their reasonable decision are various as the men themselves. Paul names the temptations to which the Corinthians, in common with the Israelites, were exposed: idolatry, fornication, murmuring, tempting Christ. He saw clearly how difficult it was for the Corinthians to discard all heathen customs, how much of what had been brightest in their life they must sacrifice if they were to renounce absolutely the religion of their parents and friends and all the joyous, if licentious, customs associated with that religion. Apparently some of them thought they might pass from the Christian communion to the heathen temple, and after partaking of Christ's sacrament eat and drink in the idolatrous festival, entering into the entire service. They seemed to think that they might be both Christians and pagans.

Against this vain attempt to combine the incompatible Paul warns them. Do not tempt Christ, he says, by experimenting how far He will bear with your conformity to idolatry. Some of the Israelites did so, and were destroyed by serpents. Do not murmur that you are hereby severed from all the enjoyments of life, dissociated from your heathen friends, blackballed in society and in business, excluded from all national festivals and from many private entertainments; do not count up your losses, but your gains. Your temptations are severe, but "there hath no temptation taken you but such as is common to man." Every man must make up his mind to a certain kind of life and go through with it. No man can unite in his own life all advantages. He must deliberate and choose; and having made his choice, he must not lament what he loses or be tempted from striving to gain what he judges best by weakly and greedily craving for the second-best also. He may win the first prize; he may win the second: he cannot win both, and if he tries, he will win neither.

The practical outcome of all that Paul has thus rapidly passed in review he utters in the haunting words, "Let him that thinketh he standeth take heed lest he fall." In this life we are never beyond the reach of temptation. And these temptations to which all of us are exposed are real; they do sufficiently test character and show what it actually is. Our suppositions regarding ourselves are often untrue. There is no reality corresponding. Our state is actually not such as we conceive it to be. We are at ease and complacent when we ought not to be at ease. We think we stand secure when we are on the point of falling. We live as if we had reached the goal when the whole journey is yet before us. Our future may be very different from what we wish or expect. Mere satisfaction with our present condition is a very insecure foundation on which to build our hope for the future. Mere reliance on a profession we have made, or on the fact that we are within reach of means of grace, tends only to slacken our energies. Heedlessness, taking things for granted, failure to sift matters thoroughly out, an indolent unwillingness to probe our spiritual condition to the quick—this is what has betrayed multitudes of Christians. "Wherefore let him that thinketh he standeth take heed lest he fall."

If determined wickedness has slain its thousands, heedlessness has slain its tens of thousands. Through lack of watchfulness men fall into sin which entangles them for life and thwarts their best purposes. Through want of watchfulness men go on in sin which exceedingly provokes God, till at last His hand falls heavily upon them. Every man is apt to lay too much stress on the circumstance that he has joined himself to the number of those who own the leadership of Christ. The question remains, How far has he gone with his Leader? Many an Israelite compassionated the poor heathen whom he left behind in the land of Egypt, and yet found that, with all his own apparent nearness to God, his heart was heathen still. Whoever takes it for granted that things are well with him, whoever "thinketh he standeth"—he is the man who has especial and urgent need to "take heed lest he fall."

THE VEIL

"Be ye followers of me, even as I also am of Christ. Now I praise you, brethren, that ye remember me in all things, and keep the ordinances, as I delivered them to you. But I would have you know, that the head of every man is Christ; and the head of the woman is the man; and the head of Christ is God. Every man praying or prophesying, having his head covered, dishonoureth his head. But every woman that prayeth or prophesieth with her head uncovered dishonoureth her head: for that is even all one as if she were shaven. For if the woman be not covered, let her also be shorn: but if it be a shame for a woman to be shorn or shaven, let her be covered. For a man indeed ought not to cover his head, forasmuch as he is the image and glory of God: but the woman is the glory of the man. For the man is not of the woman; but the woman of the man. Neither was the man created for the woman; but the woman for the man. For this cause ought the woman to have power on her head because of the angels. Nevertheless neither is the man without the woman, neither the woman without the man, in the Lord. For as the woman is of the man, even so is the man also by the woman; but all things of God. Judge in yourselves: is it comely that a woman pray unto God uncovered? Doth not even nature itself teach you, that, if a man have long hair, it is a shame unto him? But if a woman have long hair, it is a glory to her: for her hair is given her for a covering. But if any man seem to be contentious, we have no such custom, neither the Churches of God."—1 Cor. xi. 1-16.

XVI
THE VEIL

At this point of the Epistle Paul passes from the topics regarding which the Corinthians had requested him to inform them, to make some remarks on the manner in which, as he had heard, they were conducting their meetings for public worship. The next four chapters are occupied with instructions as to what constitutes seemliness and propriety in such meetings. He desires to express in general his satisfaction that on the whole they had adhered to the instructions he had already given them and the arrangements he had himself made while in Corinth. "I praise you, brethren, that ye remember me in all things, and keep the ordinances, as I delivered them to you." Yet there are one or two matters which cannot be spoken of in terms of commendation. He heard, in the first place, with surprise and vexation, that not only were women presuming to pray in public and address the assembled Christians, but even laid aside while they did so the characteristic dress of their sex, and spoke, to the scandal of all sober-minded Orientals and Greeks, unveiled. To reform this abuse he at once addresses himself. It is a singular specimen of the strange matters that must have come before Paul for decision when the care of all the Churches lay upon him. And his settlement of it is an admirable illustration of his manner of resolving all practical difficulties by means of principles which are as true and as useful for us to-day as they were for those primitive Christians who had heard his own voice admonishing them. In treating ethical or practical subjects, Paul is never superficial, never content with a mere rule.

In order to see the import and importance of this matter of dress, we must first of all know how it came to pass that the Christian women should have thought of making a demonstration so unfeminine as to shock the very heathen around them. What was their intention or meaning in doing so? What idea was possessing their minds? Throughout this long and interesting letter, Paul is doing little else than endeavouring to correct the hasty impressions which these new believers were receiving regarding their position as Christians. A great flood of new and vast ideas was suddenly poured in upon their minds; they were taught to look differently on themselves, differently on their neighbours, differently on God, differently on all things. Old things had in their case passed away with a will, and all things had become new. They were made alive from the dead, they were born again, and did not know how far this affected the relationships with this world into which their natural birth had brought them. The facts of the second birth and the new life took such hold upon them, that they could not for a time understand how they were yet connected with the old life. So that for some of them Paul had to solve the simplest problems, as, for example, we find that the believing husband was in doubt whether he should live with his wife who remained an unbeliever, for was it not abhorrent to nature that he, the living, should be bound to the dead, that a child of God should remain in the most intimate connection with one who was yet a child of wrath? Was this not a monstrous anomaly, for which prompt divorce was the fit remedy? That such questions as these should be put shows us how difficult these early Christians found it to adjust themselves as children of God to their position in a corrupt condemned world.

Now one of the ideas in Christianity which was newest to them was the equality of all before God, an idea well calculated to take powerful and absorbing hold of a world half slaves, half masters. The emperor and the slave must equally give account to God. Cæsar is not above responsibility; the barbarian who swells his triumph and is afterwards slaughtered in his dungeon or his theatre is not beneath it. Each man and each woman must stand alone before God, and for himself and herself give account of the life received from God. Alongside of this idea came that of the one Saviour for all alike, the common salvation accessible to all on equal terms, and partaking of which all became brethren and on a level, one with Christ and one therefore with each other. There was neither Greek nor barbarian, male nor female, bond nor free, now. These three mighty distinctions that had tyrannized over the ancient world were abolished, for all were one in Christ Jesus. It dawned on the barbarian that though there was no Roman citizenship for him nor any entrance into the mighty commonwealth of Greek literature, he had a citizenship in heaven, was the heir of God, and could command even with his barbaric speech the ear of the Most High. It dawned on the slave as his fetter galled him, or as his soul sank under the sad hopelessness of his life, that he was God's redeemed, rescued from the bondage of his own evil heart, and superior to all curse, being God's friend. And it dawned on the woman that she was neither man's toy nor man's slave, a mere luxury or appendage to his establishment, but that she also had herself a soul, a responsibility equally momentous with the man's, and therefore a life to frame for herself. The astonishment with which such ideas must have been received, so subversive of the principles on which heathen society was proceeding, it is impossible now to realize; but we cannot wonder that they should by their fresh power and absorbing novelty have carried the Christians to quite the opposite extremes from those at which they had been living.

In the case before us the women who had been awakened to a sense of their own personal, individual responsibility and their equal right to the highest privileges of men began to think that in all things they should be recognised as the equals of the other sex. They were one with Christ; men could have no higher honour: was it not obvious that they were on an equality with those who had held them so cheap? They had the Holy Ghost dwelling in them; might not they, as well as the men, edify Christian assemblies by uttering the inspirations of the Spirit? They were not dependent on men for their Christian privileges; ought not they to show this by laying aside the veil, which was the acknowledged badge of dependence? This laying aside of the veil was not a mere change of fashion in dress, of which, of course, Paul would have had nothing to say; it was not a feminine device for showing themselves to better advantage among their fellow-worshippers; it was not even, though this also, also! falls within the range of possible supposition, the immodest boldness and forwardness which are sometimes seen to accompany in both sexes the profession of Christianity; but it was the outward expression and easily read symbol of a great movement on the part of women in assertion of their rights and independence.

The exact meaning of the laying aside of the veil thus becomes plain. It was the part of female attire which could most readily be made the symbol of a change in the views of women regarding their own position. It was the most significant part of the woman's dress. Among the Greeks it was the universal custom for the women to appear in public with the head covered, commonly with the corner of their shawl drawn over their head like a hood. Accordingly Paul does not insist on the face being covered, as in Eastern countries, but only the head. This covering of the head could be dispensed with only in places where they were secluded from public view. It was therefore the recognised badge of seclusion; it was the badge which proclaimed that she who wore it was a private, not a public, person, finding her duties at home, not abroad, in one household, not in the city. And a woman's whole life and duties ought to lie so much apart from the public eye, that both sexes looked upon the veil as the truest and most treasured emblem of woman's position. In this seclusion there was of course implied a limitation of woman's sphere of action and a subordination to one man's interests instead of to the public. It was the man's place to serve the State or the public, the woman's place to serve the man. And so thoroughly was it recognised that the veil was a badge setting forth this private and subordinate position of the woman, that it was the one significant rite in marriage that she assumed the veil in token that now her husband was her head, to whom she was prepared to hold herself subordinate. The laying aside the veil was therefore an expression on the part of the Christian women that their being assumed as members of Christ's body raised them out of this position of dependence and subordination.

This movement of the Corinthian women towards independence, on the ground that all are one in Christ Jesus, Paul meets by reminding them that personal equality is perfectly consistent with social subordination. It was quite true, as Paul himself had taught them, that, so far as their connection with Christ went, there was no distinction of sex. To the woman, as to the man, the offer of salvation was made directly. It was not through her father or her husband that the woman had to deal with Christ. She came into contact with the living God and united herself to Christ independently of any male representative and on the same footing as her male relatives. There is but one Christ for all, rich and poor, high and low, male and female; and all are received by Him on the same footing, no distinction being made. While then in things civil and social the husband represents the wife, he cannot do so in matters of religion. Here each person must act for himself or herself. And the woman must not confound these two spheres in which she moves, or argue that because she is independent of her husband in the greater, she must also be independent of him in the less. Equality in the one sphere is not inconsistent with subordination in the other. "I would have you know, that the head of every man is Christ; and the head of the woman is the man; and the head of Christ is God."

The principle enounced in these words is of incalculable importance and very wide and constant application. Whatever is meant by the natural equality of men, it cannot mean that all are to be in every respect on the same level, and that none are to have authority over others. The application of Paul's principle to the matter in hand alone here concerns us. The woman must recognise that as Christ, though equal with the Father, is subordinate to Him, so is she herself subordinate to her husband or her father. In her private worship she deals with Christ independently; but when she appears in public and social worship, she appears as a woman with certain social relations. Her relation to Christ does not dissolve her relations to society. Rather does it intensify them. The inward change that has passed upon her and the new relation which she has formed independently of her husband only strengthen the bond by which she is tied to him. When a boy becomes a Christian, that confirms, and in no degree relaxes, his subordination to his parents. He holds a relation to Christ which they could not form for him, and which they cannot dissolve; but this independence in one matter does not make him independent in everything. A commissioned officer in the army holds his commission from the Crown; but this does not interfere with, but only confirms, his subordination to officers who, like himself, are servants of the Crown, but above him in rank. In order to the harmony of society, there is a gradation of ranks; and social grievances result, not from the existence of social distinctions, but from their abuse.

This gradation then involves Paul's inference that "every man praying or prophesying, having his head covered, dishonoureth his head. But every woman that prayeth or prophesieth with her head uncovered dishonoureth her head." The veil being the recognised badge of subordination, when a man appears veiled he would seem to acknowledge some one present and visible as his head, and would thus dishonour Christ, his true Head. A woman, on the other hand, appearing unveiled would seem to say that she acknowledges no visible human head, and thereby dishonours her head — that is, her husband — and so doing, dishonours herself. For a woman to appear unveiled on the streets of Corinth was to proclaim her shame. And so, says Paul, a woman who in public worship discards her veil might as well be shaven. She puts herself on the level of the woman with a shaven head, which both among Jews and Greeks was a brand of disgrace. In the eye of the angels, who, according to the Jewish belief, were present in meetings for worship, the woman is disgraced who does not appear with "power on her head;" that is to say, with the veil by which she silently acknowledges the authority of her husband.

This subordination of the woman to the man belongs not merely to the order of the Christian Church, but has its roots in nature. "Man is the image and glory of God: but the woman is the glory of the man." Paul's idea is that man was created to represent God and so to glorify Him, to be a visible embodiment of the goodness, and wisdom, and power of the unseen God. Nowhere so clearly or fully as in man can God be seen. Man is the glory of God because he is His image and is fitted to exhibit in actual life the excellencies which make God worthy of our love and worship. Looking at man as he actually and broadly is, we may think it a bold saying of Paul when he says, "Man is the glory of God;" and yet on consideration we see that this is no more than the truth. We should not scruple to say of the Man Christ Jesus that He is the glory of God, that in the whole universe of God nothing can more fully reveal the infinite Divine goodness. In Him we see how truly man is God's image, and how fit a medium human nature is for expressing the Divine. We know of nothing higher than what Christ said, did, and was during the few months He went about among men. He is the glory of God; and every man in his degree, and according to his fidelity to Christ, is also the glory of God.

This is of course true of woman as well as of man. It is true that woman can exhibit the nature of God and be His glory as well as man. But Paul is placing himself at the point of view of the writer of Genesis and speaking broadly of God's purpose in creation. And he means that God's purpose was to express Himself fully and crown all His works by bringing into being a creature made in His image, able to subdue, and rule, and develop all that is in the world. This creature was man, a masculine, resolved, capable creature. And just as it appeals to our sense of fitness that when God became incarnate He should appear as man, and not as woman, so does it appeal to our sense of fitness that it is man, and not woman, who should be thought of as created to be God's representative on earth. But while man directly, woman indirectly, fulfils this purpose of God. She is God's glory by being man's glory. She serves God by serving man. She exhibits God's excellencies by creating and cherishing excellence in man. Without woman man cannot accomplish aught. The woman is created for the man, because without her he is helpless. "For as the woman is of the man, even so is the man also by the woman."

But as man becomes actually the glory of God when he perfectly subordinates himself to God with the absolute devotedness of love, so does woman become the glory of man when she upholds and serves man with that perfect devotedness of which woman so constantly shows herself to be capable. It is in winning the self-sacrificing love of man and his entire devotion that God's glory appears, and man's glory appears in his power to kindle and maintain the devotion of woman. Not in independence of God does man find either his own glory or God's, and not in independence of man does woman find either her own glory or man's. The desire of woman shall be to her husband; in the honourable devotedness to man which love prompts, woman fulfils the law of her creation; and it is only the imperfect and ignoble woman who has any sense of humiliation, degradation, or limitation of her sphere in following the lead of love for the individual. It is through this honourable service of man she serves God and fulfils the purpose of her existence. The woman who is most womanly will most readily recognise that her function is to be the glory of man, to mould, and elevate, and sustain the individual, to find her joy and her life in the private life, in which the affections are developed, principles formed, and all personal wants provided for. And man, on his part, must say,

> "If aught of goodness or of grace
> Be mine, hers be the glory."

For, as a French writer says, "her influence embraces the whole of life. A wife, a mother—two magical words, comprising the sweetest sources of man's felicity! Theirs is the reign of beauty, of love, of reason, always a reign. A man takes counsel with his wife; he obeys his mother: he obeys her long after she has ceased to live, and the ideas he has received from her become principles even stronger than his passions."[7]

The position assigned to woman as the glory of man is therefore far removed from the view which cynically proclaims her man's mere convenience, whose function it is "to fatten household sinners," "to suckle fools and chronicle small beer." Paul's view, though adopted and exhibited in individual instances, is far as yet from commanding universal consent. But certainly nothing so distinguishes, elevates, purifies, and balances a man in life as a high esteem for woman. A man shows his manliness chiefly by a true reverence for all women, by a clear recognition of the high service appointed to them by God, and by a tender sympathy with them in all the various endurance their nature and their position demand.

That this is woman's normal sphere is indicated even by her unalterable physical characteristics. "Doth not even nature itself teach you, that, if a man have long hair, it is a shame unto him? But if a woman have long hair, it is a glory to her; for her hair is given her for a covering." By nature woman is endowed with a symbol of modesty and retirement. The veil, which signifies her devotement to home duties, is merely the artificial continuation of her natural gift of hair. The long hair of the Greek fop or of the English cavalier was accepted by the people as an indication of effeminate and luxurious living. Suitable for women, it is unsuitable for men; such is the instinctive judgment. And nature, speaking through this visible sign of the woman's hair, tells her that her place is in private, not in public, in the home, not in the city or the camp, in the attitude of free and loving subordination, not in the seat of authority and rule. In other respects also the physical constitution of woman points to a similar conclusion. Her shorter stature and slighter frame, her higher pitch of voice, her more graceful form and movement, indicate that she is intended for the gentler ministries of home life rather than for the rough work of the world. And similar indications are found in her mental peculiarities. She has the gifts which fit her for influencing individuals; man has those qualities which enable him to deal with things, with abstract thought, or with persons in the mass. Quicker in perception and trusting more to her intuitions, woman sees at a glance what man is sure of only after a process of reasoning.

These arguments and conclusions introduced by Paul of course apply only to the broad and normal distinction between man and woman. He does not argue that women are inferior to men, nor that they may not have equal spiritual endowments; but he maintains that, whatever be their endowments, there is a womanly mode of exercising them and a sphere for woman which she ought not to transgress. Not all women are of the distinctively womanly type. A Britomarte may arm herself and overthrow the strongest knights. A

Joan of Arc may infuse into a nation her own warlike and patriotic ardour. In art, in literature, in science, feminine names may occupy some of the highest places. In our own day many careers have been opened to women from which they had hitherto been debarred. They are now found in Government offices, in School Boards, in the medical profession. Again and again in the history of the Church attempts have been made to institute a female order in the ministry, but as yet both the clerical and the legal professions are closed to women.[8] And we may reasonably conclude that as the army and navy will always be manned by the physically stronger sex, so there are other employments in which women would be entirely out of place.

But it will be asked, Why was Paul so exact in describing how a woman should comport herself while praying or prophesying in public, when he meant very shortly in this same Epistle to write, "Let your women keep silence in the Churches: for it is not permitted unto them to speak; but they are commanded to be under obedience, as also saith the Law. And if they will learn anything, let them ask their husbands at home; for it is a shame for women to speak in the Church"? It has been suggested that although it was the standing order that women should not speak, there might be occasions when the Spirit urged them to address an assemblage of Christians; and the regulation here given is intended for these exceptional cases. This may be so, but the connection in which the absolute prohibition is given rather militates against this view, and I think it more likely that in his own mind Paul held the two matters quite distinct and felt that a mere prohibition preventing women from addressing public meetings would not touch the more serious transgression of female modesty involved in the discarding of the veil. He could not pass over this violent assertion of independence without separate treatment; and while he is treating it, it is not the speaking in public which is before his mind, but the unfeminine assertion of independence and the principle underlying this manifestation.

Besides the direct teaching of this passage on the position of woman, there are inferences to be drawn from it of some importance. First, Paul recognises that the God of nature is the God of grace, and that we may safely argue from the one sphere to the other. "All things are of God." It is profitable to be recalled to the teaching of nature. It saves us from becoming fantastic in our beliefs, from cherishing fallacious expectations, from false, pharisaic, extravagant conduct.

Again, we are here reminded that every man and woman has to do directly with God, who has no respect of persons. Each soul is independent of all others in its relation to God. Each soul has the capacity of direct connection with God and of thus being raised above all oppression, not only of his fellows, but of all outward things. It is here man finds his true glory.

His soul is his own to give it to God. He is dependent on nothing but on God only. Admitting God into his spirit, and believing in the love and rectitude of God, he is armed against all the ills of life, however little he may relish them. To all of us God offers Himself as Friend, Father, Saviour, Life. No man need remain in his sin; none need be content with a poor eternity; no man need go through life trembling or defeated: for God declares Himself on our side, and offers His love to all without respect of persons. We are all on the same footing before Him. God does not admit some freely, while He shrinks from the touch of others. It is as full and rich an inheritance that He puts within the reach of the poorest and most wretched of earth's inhabitants as He offers to him on whom the eyes of men rest in admiration or in envy. To disbelieve or repudiate this privilege of uniting ourselves to God is in the truest sense to commit spiritual suicide. It is in God we live now; He is with us and in us: and to shut Him out from that inmost consciousness to which none else is admitted is to cut ourselves off, not only from the deepest joy and truest support, but from all in which we can find spiritual life.

Lastly, although there is in Christ an absolute levelling of distinctions, no one being more acceptable to God or nearer to Him because he belongs to a certain race, or rank, or class, yet these distinctions remain and are valid in society. A woman is a woman still though she become a Christian; a subject must honour his king although by becoming a Christian he is himself in one aspect above all authority; a servant will show his Christianity, not by assuming an insolent familiarity with his Christian master, but by treating him with respectful fidelity. The Christian, above all men, needs sober-mindedness to hold the balance level and not allow his Christian rank entirely to outweigh his social position. It forms a great part of our duty to accept our own place without envying others and to do honour to those to whom honour is due.

ABUSE OF THE LORD'S SUPPER

"Now in this that I declare unto you I praise you not, that ye come together not for the better, but for the worse. For first of all, when ye come together in the Church, I hear that there be divisions among you; and I partly believe it. For there must be also heresies among you, that they which are approved may be made manifest among you. When ye come together therefore into one place, this is not to eat the Lord's Supper. For in eating every one taketh before other his own supper: and one is hungry, and another is drunken. What? have ye not houses to eat and to drink in? or despise ye the

Church of God, and shame them that have not? What shall I say to you? shall I praise you in this? I praise you not. For I have received of the Lord that which also I delivered unto you, that the Lord Jesus the same night in which He was betrayed took bread: and when He had given thanks, He brake it, and said, Take, eat: this is My body which is broken for you: this do in remembrance of Me. After the same manner also He took the cup, when He had supped, saying, This cup is the new testament in My blood: this do ye, as oft as ye drink it, in remembrance of Me. For as often as ye eat this bread, and drink this cup, ye do show the Lord's death till He come. Wherefore whosoever shall eat this bread, and drink this cup of the Lord, unworthily, shall be guilty of the body and blood of the Lord. But let a man examine himself, and so let him eat of that bread, and drink of that cup. For he that eateth and drinketh unworthily, eateth and drinketh damnation to himself, not discerning the Lord's body. For this cause many are weak and sickly among you, and many sleep. For if we would judge ourselves, we should not be judged. But when we are judged, we are chastened of the Lord, that we should not be condemned with the world. Wherefore, my brethren, when ye come together to eat, tarry one for another. And if any man hunger, let him eat at home; that ye come not together unto condemnation. And the rest will I set in order when I come." — 1 Cor. xi. 17-34.

XVII
ABUSE OF THE LORD'S SUPPER

In this paragraph of his letter Paul speaks of an abuse which can scarcely be credited, still less tolerated, in our times. The most sacred of all Christian ordinances had been allowed to degenerate into a bacchanalian revel, not easily to be distinguished from a Greek drinking party. A respectable citizen would hardly have permitted at his own table the licence and excess visible at the Table of the Lord. How such disorders in worship should have arisen calls for explanation.

It was common in Corinth and the other cities of Greece for various sections of the community to form themselves into associations, clubs, or guilds; and it was customary for such societies to share a common meal once a week, or once a month, or even when convenient daily. Some of these associations were formed of persons very variously provided with this world's goods, and one of the objects of some of the clubs was to make provision for the poorer members in such a manner as to subject them to none of the shame which is apt to attend the acceptance of promiscuous charity. All members had an equal right to present themselves at the table; and the property held by the society was equally distributed to all.

This custom, not unknown in Palestine itself, had been spontaneously adopted by the primitive Church of Jerusalem. The Christians of those early days felt themselves to be more closely related than the members of any trade guild or political club. If it was convenient and suitable that persons of similar political opinions or belonging to the same trade should to some extent have common property and should exhibit their community by sharing a common meal, it was certainly suitable among Christians. Speedily it became a prevalent custom for Christians to eat together. These meals were called *agapæ*—love-feasts—and became a marked feature of the early Church. On a fixed day, generally the first day of the week, the Christians assembled, each bringing what he could as a contribution to the feast: fish, poultry, joints of meat, cheese, milk, honey, fruit, wine, and bread. In some places the proceedings began by partaking of the consecrated bread and wine; but in other places physical appetite was first appeased by partaking of the meal provided, and after that the bread and wine were handed round.

This mode of celebrating the Lord's Supper was recommended by its close resemblance to its original celebration by the Lord and His disciples. It was at the close of the Paschal Supper, which was meant to satisfy hunger as well as to commemorate the Exodus, that our Lord took bread and brake it. He sat with His disciples as one family, and the meal they partook of was social as well as religious. But when the first solemnity passed away, and Christ's presence was no longer felt at the common table, the Christian love-feast was liable to many corruptions. The wealthy took the best seats, kept hold of their own delicacies, and, without waiting for any common distribution, each looked after himself, and went on with his own supper, regardless of the fact that others at the table had none. "Every one taketh before other his own supper," so that, while one is hungry and has received nothing, another at this so-called common love-feast has already taken too much and is intoxicated. Those who had no need to use the common stock, but had houses of their own to eat and to drink in, yet, for the sake of appearances, brought their contribution to the meal, but consumed it themselves. The consequence was that from being truly love-feasts, exhibiting Christian charity and Christian temperance, these meetings became scandalous as scenes of greedy selfishness, and profane conduct, and besotted excess. "What shall I say to you? shall I praise you in this? I praise you not." In this Paul anticipates the condemnation of these occasions of revelry and discord which the Church was obliged to pronounce after no great lapse of time.[9]

Thus then arose these disorders in the celebration of the Lord's Supper. By the conjunction of this rite with the social meal of the Christians it degenerated into an occasion of much that was unseemly and scandalous. To the reform of this abuse Paul now addresses himself; and it is worth our while to observe what remedies he does not propose as well as those he recommends.

First, he does not propose to disjoin absolutely and in all cases the religious rite from the ordinary meal. In the case of the richer members of the Church this disjunction is enjoined. They are directed to take their meals at home. "Have ye not houses to eat and to drink in? or despise ye the Church of God, and shame them that have not?... If any man hunger, let him eat at home." But with the destitute or those who had no well-provided homes another rule must be adopted. It would shame the Christian community, and quite undo its quickly won reputation for brotherly love and charity, were its members observed begging their daily bread on the streets. It was equally unseemly for the rich to accept and for the poor to be denied the meal furnished at the expense of the Church. And therefore Paul's recommendation is that those who can conveniently eat at home should do so. But as no quality of the Christian Church is more strictly her own than charity and no duty more incumbent or more lovely than to feed the hungry, it could not dishonour the Church to spread in it a meal for whosoever should be in need of it.

Again, although the wine of Holy Communion had been so sadly abused, Paul does not prohibit its use in the ordinance. His moderation and wisdom have not in this respect been universally followed. On infinitely less occasion alterations have been introduced into the administration of the ordinance with a view to preventing its abuse by reclaimed drunkards, and on still slighter pretext a more sweeping alteration was introduced many centuries ago by the Church of Rome. In that Church the custom still prevails of receiving communion only under one kind; that is to say, the communicant partakes of the bread, but not of the wine. The reason for this is given by one of their most authoritative writers as follows: "It is well known that this custom was not first established by any ecclesiastical law; but, on the contrary, it was in consequence of the general prevalence of the usage that this law was passed in approval of it. It is a matter of no less notoriety that the monasteries in whose centre this observance had its rise, and thence spread in ever wider circles, were led by a very nice sense of delicacy to impose on themselves this privation. A pious dread of desecrating, by spilling and the like, even in the most conscientious ministration, the form of the sublimest and the holiest whereof the participation can be vouchsafed to man, was the feeling which swayed their minds.... However, we should rejoice if it were left free to each one to drink or not out of the consecrated chalice; and this permission would be granted if with the same love and concord a universal desire were expressed for the use of the cup as from the twelfth century the contrary wish has been enounced."[10] One cannot but regret that this reverence for the ordinance did not take the form of a humble acceptance of it, in accordance with its original institution; and one cannot but think that the "pious dread of desecrating" the ordinance would have sufficiently prevented any spilling of the wine or other abuse, or have sufficiently atoned for any little accident which might occur. And certainly, in contrast to all such contrivances, the sanity of Paul's judgment comes out in strong relief; and we more clearly recognise the sagacity which directed that the ordinance should not be tampered with to suit the avoidable weaknesses of men, but that men should learn to live up to the requirements of the ordinance.

Again, Paul does not insist that because frequent communion had been abused this must give place to monthly or yearly communion. In after-times, partly from the abuses attending frequent communion and partly from the condition of the cities into which Christianity found its way, a change to rarer celebration was found advisable; and, for reasons that need not here be detailed, the Church catholic, both in the East and in the West, settled down to the custom of celebrating the Lord's Supper weekly: and for some centuries it was expected that all members of the Church should partake weekly. Paul's reluctance to lay down any law on the subject suggests that the abuse of this or any other ordinance does not arise simply from the frequency of its administration. It is quite natural to suppose that the inevitable result of frequent communion is an undue familiarity with holy things and a profane carelessness in handling what should only be approached with the deepest reverence. That familiarity breeds contempt, or at any rate heedlessness, is certainly a rule that ordinarily holds good. As Nelson said of his sailors, hardened by familiarity with danger, they cared no more for round-shot than for peas. The medical student who faints or sickens at his first visit to the operating theatre soon looks with unblenching face on wounds and blood. And by the same law it is feared, and not without reason, that if we observed frequent communion, we should cease to cherish that proper awe, and cease to feel that flutter of hesitation, and cease to be subdued by that sacredness of the ordinance which yet are the very feelings through which in great measure the rite influences us for good. We think it would be impossible to pass every week through those trying moments in which the soul trembles before God's majesty and love as exhibited in the Lord's Supper; and we fear that the heart would instinctively shrink from the reality, and protect itself against the emotion, and find a way of observing the ordinance with ease to itself, and that thus the life would die out from the celebration, and the mere husk or form be left.

It is, however, obvious that these fears need not be verified, and that an effort on our part would prevent the consequences dreaded. Our method of procedure in all such cases is first to find out what it is right to do, and then, though it cost us an effort, to do it. If our reverence for the ordinance in question depends on its rare celebration, every one must see that such reverence is very precarious. May it not be a merely superstitious or sentimental reverence? Is it not produced by some false idea of the rite and its signification, or does it not spring from the solemnity of the paraphernalia and human surroundings of it? Paul seeks to restore reverence in the Corinthians not by prohibiting frequent communion, but by setting more clearly before them the solemn facts which underlie the rite. In presence of these facts every worthy communicant is at all times living; and if it be merely the outward equipment and presentation of these facts which solemnize us and quicken our reverence, then this itself is rather an argument for a more frequent celebration of the rite, that so this false reverence at least might be dissipated.

The instincts of men are, however, in many cases a safer guide than their judgments; and there is a feeling prevalent that very frequent communion is not advisable, and that if it be advisable it should be reached not at a bound, but step by step. The main point on which the individual should insist on coming to some clear understanding with himself is whether his own reluctance to frequent communion does not arise from his fear of the ordinance being too profitable rather than from any fear of its ceasing to profit. Does not our shrinking from it often mean that we shrink from being more distinctly confronted with the love and holiness of Christ and with His purpose in dying for us? Does it not mean that we are not quite reconciled to be always living on the holiest motives, always under the most subduing and purifying influences, always living as the children of God, whose citizenship is in heaven? Do we shrink from the additional restraint and the fresh and effectual summons to a life, not higher and purer than we ought to be living—for there is no such life—but higher and purer than we are quite prepared to live? Putting to ourselves these questions, we use this rite as the thermometer, which shows us whether we are cold, lukewarm, or hot, or as the lead heaved from time to time, which shows us the depth of water we have and the kind of bottom over which we are holding our course.

The two most instructive writers on the sacraments are Calvin and Waterland. The latter, in his very elaborate treatment of the Eucharist, offers some remarks upon the point before us. "There can," he says, "be no just bar to frequency of communion but the want of preparation, which is only such a bar as men may themselves remove if they please; and therefore it concerns them highly to take off the impediment as soon as possible, and not to trust to vain hopes of alleviating one fault by another.... The danger of misperforming any religious duty is an argument for fear and caution, but no excuse for neglect; God insists upon the doing it, and the doing it well also.... It was no sufficient plea for the slothful servant under the Gospel that he thought his master hard to please, and thereupon neglected his bounden duty, for the use he ought to have made of that thought was to have been so much the more wakeful and diligent in his master's service. Therefore in the case of the Holy Communion it is to very little purpose to plead the strictness of the self-examination or preparation by way of excuse either for a total, or for a frequent, or for a long neglect of it. A man may say that he comes not to the Table because he is not prepared, and so far he assigns a good reason; but if he should be further asked why he is not prepared when he may, then he can only make some trifling, insufficient excuse or remain speechless."[11]

The positive counsel Paul gives regarding suitable preparation for participation in this Sacrament is very simple. He offers no elaborate scheme of self-examination which might fill the mind with scruples and induce introspective habits and spiritual hypochondria. He would have every man answer the plain question, Do you discern the Lord's body in the Sacrament? This is the one cardinal point on which all revolves, admitting or excluding each applicant. He who clearly understands that this is no common meal, but the outward symbol by means of which God offers to us Jesus Christ, is not likely to desecrate the Sacrament. "This is My body," says the Lord, meaning that this bread will ever remind the communicant that his Lord freely gave His own body for the life of the world. And whoever accepts the bread and the wine because they remind him of this and bring him into a renewed attitude of faith is a worthy communicant. The Corinthians were chastened by sickness and apparently by death that they might see and repent of the enormity of using these symbols as common food; and in order that they might escape this chastening, they had but to recall the institution of the Sacrament by our Lord Himself.

The brief narrative of this first institution which Paul here inserts gives prominence to the truth that the Sacrament was intended primarily as a memorial or remembrance of the Saviour. Nothing could be simpler or more human than our Lord's appointment of this Sacrament. Lifting the material of the Supper before Him, He bids His disciples make the simple act of eating and drinking the occasion of remembering Him. As the friend who is setting out on a long absence or is passing for ever from earth puts into our hands his portrait or something he has used, or worn, or prized, and is pleased to think that we shall treasure it for his sake, so did Christ on the eve of His death secure this one thing: that His disciples should have a memento by which to remember Him. And as the dying gift of a friend becomes sacred to us as his own person, and we cannot bear to see it handed about by unsympathetic hands and remarked upon by those who have not the same loving reverence as ourselves, and as when we gaze at his portrait, or when we use the very pen or pencil worn smooth by his fingers, we recall the many happy times we spent together and the bright and inspiring words that fell from his lips, so does this Sacrament seem sacred to us as Christ's own person, and by means of it grateful memories of all He was and did throng into the mind.

Again, the form of this memorial is fitted to recall the actual life and death of the Lord. It is His body and blood we are invited by the symbols to remember. By them we are brought into the presence of an actual living Person. Our religion is not a theory; it is not a speculation, a system of philosophy putting us in possession of a true scheme of the universe and guiding us to a sound code of morals; it is, above all, a personal matter. We are saved by being brought into right personal relations. And in this

Sacrament we are reminded of this and are helped to recognise Christ as an actual living Person, who by His body and blood, by His actual humanity, saved us. The body and blood of Christ remind us that His humanity was as substantial as our own, and His life as real. He redeemed us by the actual human life He led and by the death He died, by His use of the body and soul we make other uses of. And we are saved by remembering Him and by assimilating the spirit of His life and death.

But especially, when Christ said, "Do this in remembrance of Me," did He mean that His people to all time should remember that He had given Himself wholly to them and for them. The symbols of His body and blood were intended to keep us in mind that all that gave Him a place among men He devoted to us. By giving His flesh and blood He means that He gives us His all, Himself wholly; and by inviting us to partake of His flesh and blood He means that we must receive Him into the most real connection possible, must admit His self-sacrificing love into our heart as our most cherished possession. He bade His disciples remember Him, knowing that the death He was about to die would "draw all men unto Him," would fill the despairing with hopes of purity and happiness, would cause countless sinners to say to themselves with soul-subduing rapture, "He loved me, and gave Himself for me." He knew that the love shown in His death and the hopes it creates would be prized as the world's redemption, and that to all time men would be found turning to Him and saying, "If I forget Thee, let my right hand forget her cunning; if I do not remember Thee, let my tongue cleave to the roof of my mouth, if I do not prefer Thee above my chief joy." And therefore He presents Himself to us as He died: as One whose love for us actually brought Him to the deepest abasement and sorest suffering, and whose death opens for us a way to the Father.

But these symbols were appointed to be for a remembrance of Christ in order that, remembering Him, we might renew our fellowship with Him. In the Sacrament there is not a mere representation of Christ or a bare commemoration of events in which we are interested; but there is also an actual, present communion between Christ and the soul. Encouraged and stimulated by the outward signs, we, in our own soul and for ourselves, accept Christ and the blessings He brings. There is in the bread and wine themselves nothing that can profit us, but we are by their means to "discern the Lord's body." When Christ is said to be present in the bread and the wine, nothing mysterious or magical is meant. It is meant that He is spiritually present to those who believe. He is present in the Sacrament as He is present to faith at any time and in any place; only, these signs which God puts into our hands to assure us of His gift of Christ to us help us to believe that Christ is given, and make it easier for us to rest in Him.

CONCERNING SPIRITUAL GIFTS

"Now concerning spiritual gifts, brethren, I would not have you ignorant. Ye know that ye were Gentiles, carried away unto these dumb idols, even as ye were led. Wherefore I give you to understand, that no man speaking by the Spirit of God calleth Jesus accursed: and that no man can say that Jesus is the Lord, but by the Holy Ghost. Now there are diversities of gifts, but the same Spirit. And there are differences of administrations, but the same Lord. And there are diversities of operations, but it is the same God which worketh all in all. But the manifestation of the Spirit is given to every man to profit withal. For to one is given by the Spirit the word of wisdom; to another the word of knowledge by the same Spirit; to another faith by the same Spirit; to another the gifts of healing by the same Spirit; to another the working of miracles; to another prophecy; to another discerning of spirits; to another divers kinds of tongues; to another the interpretation of tongues: but all these worketh that one and the selfsame Spirit, dividing to every man severally as He will. For as the body is one, and hath many members, and all the members of that one body, being many, are one body: so also is Christ. For by one Spirit are we all baptized into one body, whether we be Jews or Gentiles, whether we be bond or free; and have been all made to drink into one Spirit. For the body is not one member, but many. If the foot shall say, Because I am not the hand, I am not of the body; is it therefore not of the body? And if the ear shall say, Because I am not the eye, I am not of the body; is it therefore not of the body? If the whole body were an eye, where were the hearing? If the whole were hearing, where were the smelling? But now hath God set the members every one of them in the body, as it hath pleased Him. And if they were all one member, where were the body? But now are they many members, yet but one body. And the eye cannot say unto the hand, I have no need of thee: nor again the head to the feet, I have no need of you. Nay, much more those members of the body, which seem to be more feeble, are necessary: and those members of the body, which we think to be less honourable, upon these we bestow more abundant honour; and our uncomely parts have more abundant comeliness. For our comely parts have no need: but God hath tempered the body together, having given more abundant honour to that part which lacked: that there should be no schism in the body; but that the members should have the same care one for another. And whether one member suffer, all the members suffer with it; or one member be honoured, all the members rejoice with it. Now ye are the body of Christ, and members in particular. And God hath set some in the Church, first apostles, secondarily prophets, thirdly teachers, after that miracles, then gifts of healings, helps, governments, diversities of tongues. Are all apostles? are all prophets? are all teachers? are all workers of miracles? Have all the gifts of healing? do all speak with tongues? do all interpret?"—1 Cor. xii. 1-30.

XVIII
CONCERNING SPIRITUAL GIFTS

This Epistle is well fitted to disabuse our minds of the idea that the primitive Church was in all respects superior to the Church of our own day. We turn page after page, and find little but contention, jealousies, errors, immorality, fantastic ideas, immodesty, irreverence, profanity. At this point in the Epistle we do come upon a state of things which differentiates the primitive Church from our own; but here too the superior advantages of those early Christians were sadly abused by ignorance and envy. The members of the Corinthian Church were possessed of "spiritual gifts." They were endowed at their conversion or at baptism with certain powers which they had not previously possessed, and which were due to the influence of the Holy Spirit. It would have been surprising had so entire a revolution in human feelings and prospects as Christianity introduced not been accompanied by some extraordinary and abnormal manifestation. The new Divine life which was suddenly poured into human nature stirred it to unusual power. Men and women who yesterday could only sit and condole with their sick friends found themselves to-day in so elevated a state of mind that they could impart to the sick vital energy. Young men who had been brought up in idolatry and ignorance suddenly found their minds filled with new and stimulating ideas which they felt impelled to impart to those who would listen. These and the like extraordinary gifts, which were very helpful in calling attention to the young Christian community, speedily passed away when the Christian Church took its place as an established institution.

If we are disposed to question the genuineness of those manifestations because in our own day the Spirit of Christ does not produce them, there are two considerations which should weigh with us. First, that which Browning urges: that miracles which were once needed are now no longer required, because they served the purpose for which they were given. As when you sow a plot in a garden you stick twigs round it, that no careless person may tread down and destroy the young and yet unseen plant, but when the plants have themselves become as tall and visible as the twigs, then these are useless, so if the miracles actually served to help the young

Church's growth, she by their means has now become sufficiently visible and sufficiently understood to need them no more.[12]

And, secondly, it was to be expected that the first impact of these new Christian forces on the spirit of man should produce disturbance and violent emotions, such as could not be expected to continue as the normal condition of things. New political or social ideas suddenly possessing a people, as at the French Revolution, carry them to many actions and inspire them with an energy which cannot be normal. And gentle and without observation as were the Spirit and the kingdom of Christ, yet it was impossible but that, under the pressure of the most influential and inspiring ideas which ever possessed our race, there should be some extraordinary manifestations.

Nothing could be more natural than that these gifts should be overrated and should almost be considered as the most substantial and advantageous blessings Christianity had to offer. First being accepted as evidence of the real indwelling of the Holy Spirit, they came to be prized for their own sake. Originally designed as signs of the reality of the communication between the risen Lord and His Church, and therefore as assurances that the holiness and blessedness promised by Christ were not unattainable, they came to be regarded as themselves more precious than the holiness they promised. Given to this individual and to that in order that each might have some gift by which he could profit the community, they came to be looked upon as distinctions of which the individual was proud, and therefore introduced vanity, envy, and separation, instead of mutual esteem and helpfulness. One gift was measured with another and rated above or below it; and, as usual, what was useful could not compete with what was surprising. The gift of speaking for the spiritual profit of the hearers was little thought of in comparison with the gift of speaking in unknown tongues. Throughout this and the two following chapters Paul explains the object of these gifts and the principle of their distribution and employment; he enounces the supremacy of love, and lays down certain rules for the guidance of meetings in which these gifts were displayed.

Paul introduces his remarks by reminding them that their previous history sufficiently explained their need of instruction. "In your former heathen state you had no experience whatever similar to that which you now have in the Church. The dumb idols to the worship of which you let yourselves be carried did not communicate powers similar to those which the Spirit now communicates to you. Consequently, novices as you are in this domain, you need a guiding thread to prevent you from going astray. This is why I instruct you."[13] And the first thing you need to guide you is a criterion by which you can judge whether so-called manifestations of the Spirit are genuine or spurious. The test is a simple one. Every one whose words or actions disparage Jesus proclaims himself to be under some other influence than that of the Spirit; every one who owns Jesus as Lord, serving Him and promoting His cause, is animated by the Spirit.

"No man speaking by the Spirit of God calleth Jesus accursed." But was there any possibility of such an utterance being heard in a Christian Church? It seems there was. It seems that very early in the history of Christianity men were found in the Church who could not reconcile themselves to the accursed death of Christ. They believed in the Gospel He proclaimed, the miracles He wrought, the kingdom He founded; but the Crucifixion was still a stumbling-block to them. And so they framed a theory to suit their own prejudices, and held that the Divine Logos descended upon Jesus at His baptism and spoke and acted through Him, but abandoned Him before the Crucifixion. It was Jesus, a mere man, who died on the Cross the accursed death. This degradation of Jesus was not to be tolerated in the Christian Church, and was decisive as to a man's possession of true spiritual gifts. To own the lordship of Jesus was the test of a man's Christianity. Did he acknowledge as supreme that Person who had lived and died under the name of Jesus? Did he employ his spiritual gifts for the furtherance of His kingdom and as one who was really endeavouring to serve this unseen Master? Then no hesitation need be shown in admitting his claim to be animated by the Spirit of God.

In other words, Paul wishes them to understand that, after all, the only sure test of a man's Christianity is his actual submission to Christ. No wonderful works he may accomplish in the Church or in the world prove his possession of Christ's Spirit. "Many will say to Me in that day, Lord, Lord, have we not prophesied in Thy name, and in Thy name have cast out devils, and in Thy name done many wonderful works? And then will I profess unto them, I never knew you; depart from Me, ye that work iniquity." A man may gather and edify a large congregation, he may write ably in defence of Christianity, he may be recognised as a benefactor of his age, or he may be considered the most successful of missionaries, but the only test of a man's claim to be listened to by the Church is his actual submission to Christ. He will seek not his own glory, but the good of men. And as to the gifts themselves, they should be no cause of discord, for they have everything in common: they have their source in God; they are for Christ's service; they are forms of the same Spirit. "There are diversities of gifts, but the same Spirit. And there are differences of administrations, but the same Lord. And there are diversities of operations, but it is the same God which worketh all in all."

The new life then introduced by Christ into the individual and society was found to assume various forms and to suffice for all the needs of human nature in this world. Paul delighted to survey the variety of endowment and faculty which appeared in the Church. Wisdom, knowledge, faith, power to work miracles, extraordinary gifts of exhortation or prophecy and also of speaking in unknown tongues, capacity for managing affairs and general helpfulness—these and other gifts were the efflorescence of the new life. As the sun in spring develops each seed according to its own special kind and character, so this new spiritual force develops in each man his most intimate and special character. Christian influence is not an external appliance that clips all men after one pattern as trees in an avenue are clipped into one shape; but it is an inward and vital power which causes each to grow according to his own individuality, one with the rugged irregularity of the oak, another with the orderly richness of the plane. Variety in harmony is said to be the principle of all beauty, and it is this which the Divine Spirit in man produces. Individual distinctions are not obliterated, but developed and directed for the service of the community. At one in their allegiance to Christ, bound into one body by common affections, beliefs, and hopes, and aiming at the advancement of one cause, Christians are yet as different as other men in faculty, in temperament, in attainment.

There is no truth coming more determinedly to the front in our own day than this: that society is an organism similar to the human body. This indeed is no new idea, nor is it an exclusively Christian idea. That man was made for society and that it was each man's business to labour for the good of the whole was common Stoic doctrine. It was taught that every man should believe himself to be born, not for himself, but for the whole world. Take one out of many expressions of this truth: "You have seen a hand cut off, or a foot, or a head, lying apart from the rest of the body; that is what a man makes himself when he separates himself from others or does anything unsocial. You were made by nature a part; and it is due to the benevolence of God that, if you have become detached from the whole, you can be reunited to it." And in the very earliest days, when the populace of Rome became disaffected and seditious and retired outside the city walls to a camp of their own, Menenius Agrippa went out to them and uttered his fable which Shakespeare has helped to make famous. He related how the various members of the body—the hand, the eye, the ear—mutinied and refused to work any longer because it seemed to them that all the food and enjoyment for which they toiled went to another member, and not to them. It was of course easy for the accused member to clear itself of the charge of inactivity and show that the food it received was not retained for its own exclusive use, but was distributed through the rivers of the blood, and how "the strongest nerves and small inferior veins" from it received the natural competency whereby they lived.

But although this comparison of society to the body is not new, it is now being more seriously and scientifically examined and pushed to its legitimate conclusions and applications. The "real meaning of the doctrine that society is an organism is that an individual has no life except that which is social, and that he cannot realize his own purposes except in realizing the larger purposes of society." All the organs of the body by which we do our work in the world and earn our bread are themselves maintained in life and fulfil the end of their own existence by working for and maintaining the whole body; and except in the common life of the body they cannot be maintained at all. It is the same with the other organs of the body. The heart, the lungs, the digestive organs, have hard and constant work to do; but only by doing it can they fulfil the very purpose of their existence and maintain themselves in life by contributing to the life of the body in which alone they can live at all. The same principle holds good in society. It is obvious in trade and commerce; a man can only maintain himself in life by helping to maintain other people. And the ideal society is one in which each man should not only yield reluctantly to the compulsion of this natural law, but should clearly see the great ends for which mankind exists and labour zealously to promote these ends, should as eagerly seek what contributes to the good of the whole as the hand is stretched out for food or as the palate relishes what stays the appetite and nourishes the whole body.

Illustrating the relation of Christians to one another by the figure of the members of a body, Paul suggests several ideas.

1. The unity of Christians is a vital unity. The members of the body of Christ form one whole because they partake of one common life. "By one Spirit are we all baptized into one body, whether we be Jews or Gentiles, whether we be bond or free; and have been all made to drink into one Spirit." The unity of those who together form the body of Christ is not a mechanical unity, as of a pound of shot in a bag; nor is it a unity imposed by external force, as of caged wild beasts in a menagerie; nor is it a unity of mere accidental juxtaposition, as of passengers in a train or of the inhabitants of a town. But as the life of the human body maintains all the various members and nourishes them to a well-proportioned and harmonious growth, so is it in the body of Christ. Remove from the human body the life that supports it, and all the members fall away from connection with one another; but so long as the life is retained it assimilates in the most surprising way all nutriment to its own precise type and form. The lion and the tiger may eat precisely the same food, but that food nourishes in each a different form. The life that animates the human body assimilates nutriment to its own uses, imparting to each member its due proportion and maintaining all the members in their relation to one another.

The unity of Christians is a unity of this kind, a vital unity. The same spiritual life exists in all Christians, derived from the same source, supplying them with similar energy, and prompting them to the same habits and aims. They accept the Spirit of Christ, and so are formed into one body, being no more isolated, self-seeking, and each man fighting for his own hand, but banded together for the promotion of one common cause. There is no clashing between the interests of the individual and the interests of the society or kingdom to which he belongs. The member finds its only life and function in the body. It is by the freest and most deliberate exercise of his reason and his will that a man attaches himself to Christ, seeing that by so doing he enters the only path to real happiness and attainment. The individual can only utter and fulfil his best self by doing his possible for society. His devotement to public interests is no self-destroying generosity, but the dictate of duty and of reason. To quote a writer who deals with this matter from the philosophical point of view, "he who has made the welfare of the race his aim has done so, not from a generous choice, but because he regards the pursuit of this welfare as his imperative duty. The welfare of the race is his own ideal, what he must realize in order to be what he *ought* to be. The welfare of the race is his own welfare, which he must seek because he must be *himself*. Cromwell, Luther, Mahomet, were heroes, not because they did something over and above what they *ought* to have done, but because their *ideal self* was coextensive with the larger life of their world. 'I can no other' was the voice of each.... Their large purposes were what they owed to themselves just as much as to their world."[14]

Those who cannot philosophically reconcile the claims of society and the claims of the individual are yet enabled by their attachment to Christ and by their acceptance of His Spirit to merge self in the larger whole of Christ's body and find their truest life in seeking the good of others. It is by their acceptance of Christ's Spirit as the source and Guide of their own life that they enter into fellowship with the community of men.

2. Paul is careful to show that the very efficiency of the body depends upon the multiplicity and variety of the members of which it is composed: "If they were all one member, where were the body?" "If the whole body were an eye, where were the hearing? If the whole were hearing, where were the smelling?" The lowest forms of life have either no distinct organs or very few; but the higher we ascend in the scale of life the more numerous and more distinctly differentiated are the organs. In the lower forms one member discharges several functions, and the animal uses the same organ for locomotion as it uses for eating and digesting; in the higher forms each

department of life and activity is presided over by its own sense or organ. The same law holds good of society. Among tribes low down in the scale of civilisation each man is his own farmer, or shepherd, or huntsman, and his own priest, and butcher, and cook, and clothier. Each man does everything for himself. But as men become civilised the various wants of society are supplied by different individuals, and every function is specialized. The same law necessarily holds true of the body of Christ. It is highly organized, and no one organ can do the whole work of the body. Therefore one has this gift, another that. And the more nearly this body approaches perfection, the more various and distinct will these gifts be.

One important function of the Church therefore is to elicit and utilize every faculty for good which its members possess. In a society in which Christianity is but beginning to take root, it may fall to one man to do the work of the whole Christian body—to be eye, tongue, foot, hand, and heart. He must evangelise, he must teach, he must legislate, he must enforce law; he must preach, he must pray, he must lead the singing; he must plan the church and help to build it; translate the Scriptures and help to print them; teach the savages to wear a little clothing and help to make it; dissuade them from war and instruct them in the arts of peace, instilling a taste for agriculture and commerce. But when the Christian society has left this rudimentary stage behind, those various functions are discharged by different individuals; and as it advances towards a perfect condition its functions and organs become as multifarious and as distinctly differentiated as the organs of the human body. Every member of the Church is different from every other, and has a gift of his own. Some are fitted to nourish the Church herself and maintain the body of Christ in health and efficiency; some are fitted to act on the world outside: they are eyes to perceive, feet to pursue, hands to lay hold of those who are straying from the light.

Every one therefore who is drawn into the fellowship of the body of Christ has something to contribute to its good and to the work it does. He is in connection with that body because the Spirit of Christ has possessed and assimilated him to it; and that Spirit energizes in him. He may not see that anything the Church is presently engaged in is work he can undertake. He may feel out of place and awkward when he attempts to do what others are doing. He feels himself like a greyhound, compelled to run by scent and not by sight, and expected to do the work of a pointer, and not seize his quarry, or as if set to do the work of an eye with the hand. He can do it only in a groping, fumbling, imperfect manner. But this is only a hint that he is meant for other work, not for none. And it is for him to discover what his Christian instincts lead him to. The eye does not need to be told it is for seeing, or the hand that it is for grasping. The eye and the hand of the child instinctively do their office. And where there is true Christian life, it matters not what the member of Christ's body be, it will find its function, even though that function is new in the Church's experience.

The fact then that you are very different from the ordinary members of the Church is no reason for supposing you do not belong to Christ's body. The ear is very different from the eye; it can detect neither form nor colour; it cannot enjoy a landscape or welcome a friend: but "if the ear shall say, Because I am not the eye, I am not of the body; is it therefore not of the body?" Is it not, on the contrary, its very diversity from the eye that makes it a welcome addition to the body, enriching its capabilities and enlarging its usefulness? It is not by comparison with other people that we can tell whether we belong to the body of Christ, nor is our function in that body determined by anything which some other member is doing. The very difficulty we find in adjusting ourselves to others and in finding any already existing Christian work to which we can give ourselves is a hint that we have the opportunity of adding to the Church's efficiency. The Church can claim to be perfect only when she embraces the most diversely gifted individuals and allows the tastes, instincts, and aptitudes of all to be used in her work.

3. As there is to be no slothful self-disparagement in the body of Christ, so must there be no depreciation of other people. "The eye cannot say unto the hand, I have no need of thee: nor again the head to the feet, I have no need of you." When zealous people discover new methods, they forthwith despise the normal ecclesiastical system that has stood the test and is stamped with the approval of centuries. One method cannot regenerate and Christianize the world, any more than one member can do the whole work of the body. Paul goes even further, and reminds us that the "feeble" parts of the body are "the more necessary;" the heart, the brain, the lungs, and all those delicate members of the body that do its essential work entirely hidden from view are more necessary than the hand or the foot, the loss of which no doubt cripples, but does not kill. So in the Church of Christ it is the hidden souls who by their prayers and domestic godliness maintain the whole body in health and enable more conspicuously gifted members to do their part. Contempt for any member of the body of Christ is most unseemly and sinful. Yet men seem unable ever to learn how many members, and how various, it takes to complete a body, and how needful are those functions they themselves are wholly unable to discharge.

4. Lastly, Paul is careful to teach that "the manifestation of the Spirit is given to every man *to profit withal.*" It is not for the glorification of the individual that the new spiritual life manifests itself in this or that remarkable form, but for the edification of the body of Christ. However beautiful any feature of a face may be, it is hideous apart from its position among the rest and lying by itself. Morally hideous and no longer admirable is the Christian who attracts attention to himself and does not subordinate his gift to the advantage of the whole body of Christ. If in the human body any member asserts itself and is not subservient to the one central will, that is recognised as disease: St. Vitus' dance. If any member ceases to obey the central will, paralysis is indicated. And equally so is disease indicated wherever a Christian seeks his own ends or his own glorification, and not the advantage of the whole body. Simon Magus sought to make a reputation and a competence for himself by spiritual gifts. What in his case was mainly stupidity is in ours sin if we use such powers and opportunities as we have for our own purposes, and not with a view to the profit of others.

Let us then endeavour to recognise our position as members of Christ's body. Let us with seriousness accept Him as appointed by God to be our true spiritual Life and Head; let us consider what we have it in our power to do for the good of the whole body; and let us put aside all jealousy, envy, and selfishness, and with meekness honour the work done by others while humbly and hopefully doing our own.

NO GIFT LIKE LOVE

"But covet earnestly the best gifts: and yet show I unto you a more excellent way. Though I speak with the tongues of men and of angels, and have not charity, I am become as sounding brass, or a tinkling cymbal. And though I have the gift of prophecy, and understand all mysteries, and all knowledge; and though I have all faith, so that I could remove mountains, and have not charity, I am nothing. And though I bestow all my goods to feed the poor, and though I give my body to be burned, and have not charity, it profiteth me nothing. Charity suffereth long, and is kind; charity envieth not; charity vaunteth not itself, is not puffed up, doth not behave itself unseemly, seeketh not her own, is not easily provoked, thinketh no evil; rejoiceth not in iniquity, but rejoiceth in the truth; beareth all things, believeth all things, hopeth all things, endureth all things. Charity never faileth: but whether there be prophecies, they shall fail; whether there be tongues, they shall cease; whether there be knowledge, it shall vanish away. For we know in part, and we prophesy in part. But when that which is perfect is come, then that which is in part shall be done away. When I was a child, I spake as a child, I understood as a child, I thought as a child: but when I became a man, I put away childish things. For now we see through a glass, darkly; but then face to face: now I know in part; but then shall I know even as also I am known. And now abideth faith, hope, charity, these three; but the greatest of these is charity."—1 Cor. xii. 31-xiii. 13.

XIX
NO GIFT LIKE LOVE

This is one of the passages of Scripture which an expositor scruples to touch. Some of the bloom and delicacy of surface passes from the flower in the very handling which is meant to exhibit its fineness of texture. But although this eulogium of love is its own best interpreter, there are points in it which require both explanation and enforcement.

In the preceding chapter (xii.) Paul has striven to suppress the envy, vanity, and discord which had resulted from the abuse of the spiritual gifts with which the Corinthian Church was endowed. He has explained that these gifts were bestowed for the edification of the Church, and not for the glorification of the individual; and that therefore the individual should covet, not the most surprising, but the most profitable, of these manifestations of the Spirit. "Covet the best gifts," he says: Desire the gifts which edify, the gift of exhortation, or, as it was then called, prophecy. And yet there is a more excellent way to edify the Church than even to exercise apostolic gifts; this is the way of love, which he proceeds to celebrate.

1. Love is the ligament which binds together the several members of the body of Christ, the cement which keeps the stones of the temple together. Without love there can be no body, no temple, only isolated stones or disconnected, and therefore useless, members. The extraordinary gifts of which the Corinthians were so proud cannot compete with love. They may profit the Church, but without love they are no evidence of the ripe Christian manhood of their possessor. Suppose I speak all possible languages— languages of angels, if you please, as well as languages of men—and have not love, I am but a mere instrument played upon by another, no better than a bit of sounding brass, a trumpet or a cymbal, not enjoying, nor moved by, nor swayed by the music I make, but insensible. As Bunyan says, "Is it so much to be a fiddle?" If no man understands the language I am impelled to use, then I am but as a clanging cymbal, making a noise without significance. And even though I speak a tongue which some stranger recognises as his own, it is not I who am coming into contact with his soul through a living influence; I am but used as an instrument of brass is used by the player.

Or take even the higher gift of prophecy. Suppose I am enlightened by the Spirit so that I can explain things hitherto misunderstood; suppose I can make revelations of important truths which have been accessible to none besides; suppose even that I have all faith, faith, as the rabbis say, to remove mountains; suppose I can work miracles, heal the sick, raise the dead, set the whole world agape with astonishment, all this without love, however it may profit others, profits myself not at all, and neither brings me into closer connection with Christ nor gives assurance of my sound spiritual condition, I may be among the number of those who, after doing wonderful works in Christ's name, are repudiated by Him. For as among ourselves there are many gifts, such as learning, eloquence, sagacity, musical, and poetical, and artistic genius, which may greatly contribute to the edification of the Church, and yet reside in persons who can make little claim to sanctity, so in the early Church these extraordinary spiritual gifts seem to have carried with them no evidence of their possessors' personal religion. They had certainly begun a Christian career, but they might be deteriorating in character instead of developing and maturing.

There were, however, two Christian actions which might seem to be beyond question as evidence of a sound spiritual condition: almsgiving and martyrdom. The young man who sought guidance from Christ lacked but one thing: to sell his property and give to the poor. But, says Paul, "though I bestow all my goods to feed the poor, and have not love, it profiteth me nothing." It is only too possible to do great acts of charity from a love of display, or from an uneasy sense of duty which parts reluctantly and grudgingly with what it bestows. That is understood. Common-sense tells every one but the abjectly superstitious man himself that it is as impossible to buy spiritual health on a bed of death as it is to buy the cure of his mortal disease.

But martyrdom? Can a man give any stronger proof of his faith than to give his body to be burned? Certainly one would with great reluctance disparage the integrity of those courageous persons who in many ages of the Church's history have gone without flinching to the stake. But, in point of fact, a willingness to suffer for one's opinion or one's faith is not in every case a guarantee of the existence of a heart transformed from selfishness to love. At one period martyrdom became fashionable, and Christian teachers were compelled to remonstrate with those who fanatically rushed to the stake and the arena, just as suicide once became fashionable at Rome and evoked prohibitory legislation.

Not without reason then does Paul so emphatically warn men against looking upon such exceptional actions or such extraordinary endowments as undoubted evidence of a healthy spiritual state. Gifts and conduct which bring men prominently before the eye of the Church or the world are often no index to the character; and if they be not rooted in and guided by love, their possessor has little reason to congratulate himself. Too often it is a man's snare to judge himself by what he does rather than by what he is. It is so easy comparatively to do great things supposing certain gifts be present; it is at least always possible to human nature to make sacrifices and engage in arduous duties. The impossible thing is love. No eye to advantageous consequences or to public opinion can enable a man to love; no desire to maintain a character for piety can produce that grace. Love must be spontaneous, from the soul's self, not produced by considerations of the requirements of a position we wish to reach or to maintain. It must be the unconstrained, natural outcome of the real man. Not even the consideration of Christ's love will produce love in us if there be not a real sympathy with Christ. A sense of benefit received will not produce love where there is no similarity of sentiment. Love cannot be got up. It is the result of God entering and possessing the soul. "He that loveth is born of God." That is the only account to be given of the matter. And therefore it is that where love is absent all is absent.

And yet how the mistake of the Corinthians is perpetuated from age to age. The Church is smitten with a genuine admiration of talent, of the faculties which make the body of Christ bulk larger in the eye of the world, while too often love is neglected. After all that the Church has learned of the dangers which accompany theological controversy, and of the hollowness of much that passes for growth, intellectual gifts are frequently prized more highly than love. Do we not ourselves often become aware that the absence of this one thing needful is writing vanity and failure on all we do and on all we are? If we are not yet in the real fellowship of the body of Christ, possessed by a love that prompts us to serve the whole, with what complacency can we look on other acquirements? Do parents sufficiently impress on their children that all successes at school and in early life are as nothing compared to the more obscure but much more substantial acquisition of a thoroughly unselfish, generous, catholic spirit of service?

2. Paul having illustrated the supremacy of love by showing that without it all other gifts are profitless, proceeds (vers. 4-7) to celebrate its own positive excellence. It is possible, though unlikely, that Paul may have read the eulogium pronounced on love by the greatest of Greek writers five hundred years before: "Love is our lord, supplying kindness and banishing unkindness, giving friendship and forgiving enmity, the joy of the good, the wonder of the wise, the amazement of the gods; desired by those who have no part in him, and precious to those who have the better part in him; parent of delicacy, luxury, desire, fondness, softness, grace; careful of the good, uncareful of the evil. In every word, work, wish, fear—pilot, helper, defender, saviour; glory of gods and men, leader best and brightest;

in whose footsteps let every man follow, chanting a hymn and joining in that fair strain with which love charms the souls of gods and men." Five hundred years after Paul another eulogium was pronounced on love by Mohammed: "Every good act is charity: your smiling in your brother's face; your putting a wanderer in the right road; your giving water to the thirsty, or exhortations to others to do right. A man's true wealth hereafter is the good he has done in this world to his fellow-man. When he dies, people will ask, What property has he left behind him? but the angels will ask what good deeds he has sent before him."

Paul's eulogium is the more effective because it exhibits in detail the various ramifications of this exuberant and fruitful grace, how it runs out into all our intercourse with our fellow-men and carries with it a healing and sweetening virtue. It imbues the entire character, and contains in itself the motive of all Christian conduct. It is "the fulfilling of the Law." Its claims are paramount because it embraces all other virtues. If a man has love, there is no grace impossible to him or into which love will not on occasion develop. Love becomes courage of the most absolute kind where danger threatens its object. It begets a wisdom and a skill which put to shame technical training and experience. It brings forth self-restraint and temperance as its natural fruit; it is patient, forgiving, modest, humble, sympathizing. It is quite true that

"As every lovely hue is light,
So every grace is love."

Thomas a Kempis dwells with evident relish on the varied capacity of this all-comprehending grace. "Love," he says, "feels no burden, regards not labours, would willingly do more than it is able, pleads not impossibilities, because it feels sure that it can and may do all things. Love is swift, sincere, pious, pleasant, and delightful; strong, patient, faithful, prudent, longsuffering, manly, and never seeking itself: it is circumspect, humble, and upright; sober, chaste, steadfast, quiet, and guarded in all its senses."

Paul's description of the behaviour of love is drawn in view of the discords and vanities of the Corinthians and as a contrast to their unseemly and unbrotherly conduct. "Love suffereth long, and is kind;" it reveals itself in a magnanimous bearing of injuries and in a considerate and tender imparting of benefits. It returns good for evil; not readily provoked by slights and wrongs, it ever seeks to spend itself in kindnesses. Then there is nothing envious, vain, or selfish in love. "Love envieth not; love vaunteth not itself." It neither grudges others their gifts, nor is eager to show off its own. The pallor and bitter sneer of envy and the ridiculous swagger of the boastful are equally remote from love. "It is not puffed up, and doth not behave itself unseemly." Love saves a man from making a fool of himself by consequential conduct, and by thrusting himself into positions which betray his incompetence, and by immodest, irreverent, and eccentric actions. It balances a man and gives him sense by bringing him into right relations with his fellows and prompting him to esteem their gifts more highly than his own. Neither is love ever on the watch for its own rights, scrupulously exacting the remuneration, the recognition, the applause, the precedence, the deference, that may be due: "it seeketh not its own." "It is not easily provoked, nor does it take account of evil;" it is not fired with resentment at every little slight, and does not make a mental note and lay up in its memory the contempt shown by one, the indifference shown by another, the intention to wound betrayed by a third. Love is too little occupied with itself to feel these exhibitions of malice very keenly. It is bent on winning the battle for others, and the wounds received in the cause are made light of. Its eye is still on the advantage to be gained by the needy, and not on itself.

Another manifestation of love, and one the mention of which pricks the conscience, is that it "rejoiceth not in unrighteousness." It has no malignant pleasure in seeing reputations exploded, in discovering the sin, the hypocrisy, the mistakes, of other men. "It rejoiceth with the truth." Where truth scatters calumny and shows that suspicions were ill-founded, love rejoices. Successful wickedness, whether for or against its own interests, love has no pleasure in; but where goodness triumphs love is thrilled with a sympathetic joy. In place of rejoicing in discovered wickedness because it lowers a rival or seems to leave a more prominent position to itself, love hastens to cover the fault. "It covereth all things, believeth all things, hopeth all things." It has untiring charity, making every allowance, proposing every excuse, believing that explanations can be made, accepting greedily such as are made, slow to be persuaded that things are as bad as rumour paints, hoping against hope for the acquittal, or at any rate for the reformation, of every culprit.

3. Finally, Paul shows the superiority of love by comparing it in point of permanence, first, with the gifts of which the Corinthians were so proud, and, second, with the universal Christian graces.

"Love never faileth;" it is imperishable: it grows from less to more; there never comes a time when it gives place to some higher quality of soul, or when it is unimportant whether a man has it or no, or when it is no longer the criterion of the whole moral state. The most surprising spiritual gifts can make no such claim. "Whether there be prophecies, they shall be done away; whether there be tongues, they shall cease." These gifts were for the temporary benefit of the Church. However some might misapprehend their significance and fancy that these extraordinary manifestations were destined to characterise the Christian Church throughout its history, Paul was not so deceived. He was prepared for their disappearance. They were the scaffolding which no one thinks of or inquires after when the building is finished, the schoolbooks which become the merest rubbish when the boy is educated, the prop which the forester removes when the sapling has become a tree.

But knowledge? The knowledge of God and of Divine things in which good men delight, and which is esteemed the stamina of character—is not this permanent? No, says Paul. "Knowledge also shall be done away." And to illustrate his meaning Paul uses two figures: the figure of a child's knowledge, which is gradually lost in the knowledge of the man, and the figure of an object dimly seen through a semi-transparent medium. We shall understand the significance and the bearing of these figures if we consider that when we speak of imperfect knowledge we may mean either of two things: we may either mean that it is imperfect in amount or that it is imperfect in quality, in accuracy. When a boy begins the study of Euclid, the first proposition he learns is absolutely accurate and true; he may add to it, but he can never improve upon it. His knowledge is imperfect in amount, but so far as it goes it is absolutely reliable; he may build upon it and deduce other truths from it. But when we are walking on a misty morning and see an object at a distance, our knowledge is imperfect, but in quite another sense. It is imperfect in the sense of being dim, uncertain, inaccurate. We see that there is something before us, but whether a human being or a gatepost we cannot say. A little nearer we see it is a human being, but whether old or young, friend or no friend, we cannot say. Here the growth of our knowledge is from dimness to accuracy.

Both the figures used by Paul imply that our knowledge of Divine things is of this latter kind. They loom, as it were, through a mist. Many of their details are invisible. We have not got them under our hand to examine at leisure. Our present knowledge is as the light of a lantern by which we can pick our way, or as the starlight, for which we are thankful in the meantime; but when the sun of a wider, deeper, truer knowledge rises, what we now call knowledge shall be quite eclipsed. "When I was a child," says Paul, "I spake as a child, I understood as a child, I thought as a child: but when I became a man, I put away childish things." That is to say, Paul was distinctly aware that much of our present knowledge is provisional. We do not know the very truth, but only such approximations to the truth and such symbols of it as we are able to understand. We are at present in the state of childhood, which cherishes many notions destined to be exploded by maturer knowledge. We think of God as a Being very similar to ourselves, only very much greater; and in our present state we must be content with this imperfect knowledge, but prepared to put it away as "childish" when fuller knowledge comes. The atoning death of Christ may be spoken of as the substitutionary sacrifice of a Victim on whom our guilt is laid; but to speak thus of the death of Christ is to make large use of the language of symbol, and we must hold our minds open for the fuller knowledge which will make such language seem quite inadequate. Paul's language warns us against speaking, or thinking, or acting as if our knowledge of Divine things were perfectly accurate, and as if therefore we might freely and unhesitatingly condemn all who differ from us.

The other figure is still more precise, although there is great difference of opinion as to what Paul means by seeing now "through a glass, darkly." The word here rendered "glass" is used either for the dim metallic mirror used by the ancients, or for the semi-translucent talc which was their substitute for glass in windows. Of these two meanings it is the latter which in this passage gives the best sense. It was a common figure among the rabbis to illustrate dimness of vision. If they wished to denote direct and clear vision, they spoke of seeing a thing face to face; if they wished to denote uncertain and hazy vision, they spoke of seeing through a glass—that is, through a substance only a little more transparent than our own dimmed glass, through which you can see objects, but cannot tell exactly what they are or who the persons are who are moving. Thus they had a common saying, "All other prophets saw as through nine glasses, Moses as through one." The rabbis, too, had another saying which illustrates the second part of this twelfth verse: "Even as a king, who with common people talks through a veil, so that he sees them, but they do not see him, but when his friend comes to speak to him, he removes this veil, so that he might see him face to face, even so did God speak to Moses apparently, and not darkly."[15]

Interpreting Paul's language then by the language of his own kith and kin and of the schools in which he had been educated, his meaning is that in this life we can see Divine things only dimly and as through a veil, but hereafter we shall see them without the intervention of any obscuring medium. Here and now we can make out only the general outline of the unseen realities; but hereafter we shall know even as we are known, shall see God as directly as He now sees us. We shall not have even then the same perfect knowledge of Him that He has of us, but shall see Him as immediately and directly as He sees us. Now He wears a veil through which He can see, but through which we cannot see; hereafter He will lay aside this. Our present knowledge of God and of all things unseen is necessarily vague, not susceptible of exact definition. There are some things of which we may be quite sure, others of which we must be content to remain in uncertainty. We may be quite sure that God exists, that He loves us, that

He has sent His Son to save us; but if we attempt to run a sharp and clear outline round the truths thus dimly seen, we shall inevitably err.

It may be added that while Paul warns us against supposing that our knowledge is perfect, he does not mean to brand it as useless or delusive. On the contrary, his figures imply that it is necessary for our growth, and that unless we honestly use such knowledge as we have, we cannot win our way to knowledge that is perfect. It is the imperfect knowledge of the child which leads it on to further attainment. The fundamental doctrine of the Christian creed that there are three Persons in one God is certainly a very rough and childish expression of a truth far deeper than we can understand, but to reject this doctrine because it is evidently only an approximation to a truth which cannot be defined and stated in final terms is to refuse to submit to the conditions under which we now live and to ape a manhood which in point of fact we do not possess.

Paul's crowning testimony to the worth of love is given in the thirteenth verse: "But now abideth faith, hope, love, these three; and the greatest of these is love." He does not mean that love abides while faith becomes sight and hope fruition. Rather he indicates that faith and hope are also imperishable, and hereby distinguished from the spiritual gifts of which he has been speaking. Both in this life and in that which is to come faith, hope, and love abide. For faith and hope pass away only in one aspect of their exercise. If by faith be meant belief in things unseen, this passes away when the unseen is seen. If hope be taken as referring only to the future state in general, then when that state is reached hope passes away. But faith and hope are really permanent elements of human life, faith being the confidence we have in God, and hope the ever-renewed expectancy of future good. But while faith maintains us in connection with God, love is the enjoyment of God and the partaking of His nature; and while hope renews our energy and guides our aims, it can bring us to no better thing than love.

To see the beauty, fruitfulness, and sufficiency of love is easy, but to have it as the mainspring of our own life most difficult, indeed the greatest of all attainments. This we instinctively recognise as the true test of our condition. Have we that in us which really knits us to God and our fellow-men and prompts us to do our utmost for them? Have we in us this new affection which destroys selfishness and brings us into true and lasting relations with all we have to do with? This is the root of all good, the beginning of all blessedness, because the germ of all likeness to God, who Himself is love.

SPIRITUAL GIFTS AND PUBLIC WORSHIP

"Follow after charity, and desire spiritual gifts, but rather that ye may prophesy. For he that speaketh in an unknown tongue speaketh not unto men, but unto God: for no man understandeth him; howbeit in the Spirit he speaketh mysteries. But he that prophesieth speaketh unto men to edification, and exhortation, and comfort. He that speaketh in an unknown tongue edifieth himself; but he that prophesieth edifieth the Church. I would that ye all spake with tongues, but rather that ye prophesied: for greater is he that prophesieth than he that speaketh with tongues, except he interpret, that the Church may receive edifying. Now, brethren, if I come unto you speaking with tongues, what shall I profit you, except I shall speak to you either by revelation, or by knowledge, or by prophesying, or by doctrine? And even things without life giving sound, whether pipe or harp, except they give a distinction in the sounds, how shall it be known what is piped or harped? For if the trumpet give an uncertain sound, who shall prepare himself to the battle? So likewise ye, except ye utter by the tongue words easy to be understood, how shall it be known what is spoken? for ye shall speak into the air. There are, it may be, so many kinds of voices in the world, and none of them is without signification. Therefore if I know not the meaning of the voice, I shall be unto him that speaketh a barbarian, and he that speaketh shall be a barbarian unto me. Even so ye, forasmuch as ye are zealous of spiritual gifts, seek that ye may excel to the edifying of the Church. Wherefore let him that speaketh in an unknown tongue pray that he may interpret. For if I pray in an unknown tongue, my spirit prayeth, but my understanding is unfruitful. What is it then? I will pray with the spirit, and I will pray with the understanding also: I will sing with the spirit, and I will sing with the understanding also. Else when thou shalt bless with the spirit, how shall he that occupieth the room of the unlearned say Amen at thy giving of thanks, seeing he understandeth not what thou sayest? For thou verily givest thanks well, but the other is not edified. I thank my God, I speak with tongues more than ye all: yet in the Church I had rather speak five words with my understanding, that by my voice I might teach others also, than ten thousand words in an unknown tongue. Brethren, be not children in understanding: howbeit in malice be ye children, but in understanding be men. In the Law it is written, With men of other tongues and other lips will I speak unto this people;

and yet for all that will they not hear Me, saith the Lord. Wherefore tongues are for a sign, not to them that believe, but to them that believe not: but prophesying serveth not for them that believe not, but for them which believe. If therefore the whole Church be come together into one place, and all speak with tongues, and there come in those that are unlearned, or unbelievers, will they not say that ye are mad? But if all prophesy, and there come in one that believeth not, or one unlearned, he is convinced of all, he is judged of all: and thus are the secrets of his heart made manifest; and so falling down on his face he will worship God, and report that God is in you of a truth. How is it then, brethren? when ye come together, every one of you hath a psalm, hath a doctrine, hath a tongue, hath a revelation, hath an interpretation. Let all things be done unto edifying. If any man speak in an unknown tongue, let it be by two, or at the most by three, and that by course; and let one interpret. But if there be no interpreter, let him keep silence in the Church; and let him speak to himself, and to God. Let the prophets speak two or three, and let the other judge. If anything be revealed to another that sitteth by, let the first hold his peace. For ye may all prophesy one by one, that all may learn, and all may be comforted. And the spirits of the prophets are subject to the prophets. For God is not the Author of confusion, but of peace, as in all Churches of the saints. Let your women keep silence in the Churches: for it is not permitted unto them to speak; but they are commanded to be under obedience, as also saith the Law. And if they will learn anything, let them ask their husbands at home: for it is a shame for women to speak in the Church. What? came the word of God out from you? or came it unto you only? If any man think himself to be a prophet, or spiritual, let him acknowledge that the things that I write unto you are the commandments of the Lord. But if any man be ignorant, let him be ignorant. Wherefore, brethren, covet to prophesy, and forbid not to speak with tongues. Let all things be done decently and in order." —1 Cor. xiv. 1-40.

XX
SPIRITUAL GIFTS AND PUBLIC WORSHIP

In the first twenty-five verses of this chapter Paul gives his estimate of the comparative value of the two chief spiritual gifts: speaking with tongues and prophesying; in the latter half of the chapter he lays down certain rules which were to guide the exercise of these gifts and certain principles on which all the worship and public services of the Church should proceed.

A difficulty, however, meets us at the outset. We have no opportunity of observing these gifts in exercise, and cannot readily understand them. With prophecy indeed there need be no great difficulty. Prophesying is speaking for God, whether the utterance regards present or future matters. When Moses complained that he had no gift of utterance, God said, "Aaron shall be thy prophet;" that is, shall speak for thee, or be thy spokesman. Prediction is not necessarily any part of the prophet's function. It may be so, and often it was so, but a man might be a prophet who had no revelation of the future. In the sense in which Paul uses the word, a prophet was "an inspired teacher and exhorter who revealed to men the secrets of God's will and word and the secrets of their own hearts for the purpose of conversion and edification." The function of the prophet is indicated in the third verse: "He that prophesieth speaketh for edification, and exhortation, and comfort;" and still further in the twenty-fourth and twenty-fifth verses, where the results of prophesying are described in terms precisely such as we should use to describe the results of efficacious preaching. The hearer is "convinced," is conscious in himself that the words spoken are shedding light and carrying conviction into the recesses of his heart. The gift of prophecy, then, was the endowment which enabled a Christian to speak so as to bring the mind and spirit of the hearer into touch with God.

But the gift of tongues is involved in greater obscurity. On its first occurrence, as recorded in the book of Acts, it would seem to have been the gift of speaking in foreign languages. We are told that the strangers from Asia Minor, Parthia, the shores of the Black Sea, Africa, and Italy, when they heard the disciples speaking, recognised that they were speaking intelligible languages. One man was attracted by the sound of his native Arabic; another heard the familiar Latin; a third for the first time in Jerusalem heard a Jew speaking the language he was accustomed to hear on the banks of the Nile.

Naturally they were confounded by the circumstance, "every man hearing," as it is said, "his own language, the tongue wherein he was born." It would certainly seem probable, therefore, that, whether the gift afterwards changed its character or not, it was originally the power of speaking in a foreign language so as to be intelligible to any one who understood that language.

This gift was of course communicated, not as a permanent acquisition, to fit men to preach the Gospel in foreign countries, but merely as a temporary impulse to utter words which to themselves had no meaning. All spiritual gifts seem to have been inconstant in their influence. Paul had the gift of healing, and yet he "left Trophimus at Miletum sick;" his dear friend Epaphroditus was sick nigh unto death without Paul being able to help him; and when Timothy was unwell, he did not cure him by miracle, but by a very commonplace prescription. So, too, when a man by study and practice acquires the use of a foreign tongue, he has command of that language so long as memory lives and for all purposes; but this "gift of tongues" was only available "as the Spirit gave utterance" to each, and failed to communicate a constant and complete command of the language. It is not to be supposed therefore that this gift was bestowed in order to enable men more easily to proclaim the Gospel to all races. And at no period of the world's history was such a gift less needed, Greek and Latin being very generally understood throughout the Roman world. Perhaps more persons grew up bilingual in that day than at any other time.

If then this gift was intermittent and did not qualify its possessor to use a foreign language for the ordinary purposes of life or for preaching the Gospel, what was its use? It served the same purpose as other miracles; it made visible and called attention to the entrance of new powers into human nature. As Paul says, it was "for them that believe not, not for them that believe." It was meant to excite inquiry, not to instruct the mind of the Christian. It produced conviction that among the followers of Christ new powers were at work. The evidence of this took a shape which seemed to intimate that the religion of Christ was suitable for every race of mankind. This gift of tongues seemed to claim all nations as the object of Christ's work. The most remote and insignificant tribe was accessible to Him. He knew their language, suited Himself to their peculiarities, and claimed kindred with them.

It must, however, be said that the common opinion of scholars is that the gift of tongues did not consist in ability to speak a foreign language even temporarily, but in an exalted frame of mind which found expression in sounds or words belonging to no human language. What was thus uttered has been compared to the "merry, unmeaning shouts of boyhood, getting rid of exuberant life, uttering in sounds a joy for which manhood has no words." These ecstatic cries or exclamations were not always understood either by the person uttering them, or by any one else, so that there was always a risk of such utterances being considered either as the ravings of lunatics, or, as in the first instance, the thick and inarticulate mutterings of drunkards. But sometimes there was present a person in the same key of feeling whose spirit vibrated to the note struck by the speaker, and who was able to render his inarticulate sounds into intelligible speech. For as music can only be interpreted by one who has a feeling for music, and as the inarticulate language of tears, or sighs, or groans can be comprehended by a sympathetic soul, so the tongues could be interpreted by those whose spiritual state corresponded to that of the gifted person.

At various periods of the Church's history these manifestations have been reproduced. The Montanists of the early Church, the Camisards of France at the close of the seventeenth century, and the Irvingites of our own country claimed that they possessed similar gifts. Probably all such manifestations are due to violent nervous agitation. The early Quakers showed their wisdom in treating all physical manifestations as physical.

Comparing these two gifts, prophecy and speaking with tongues, Paul very decidedly gives the preference to the former, and this mainly on the score of its greater utility. It often happened that when one of the Christians spoke in tongues there was no one present who could interpret. However exalted the man's own spirit might be, the congregation could derive no benefit from his utterances. And if a number of persons spoke at once, as they seemed to do in Corinth, on the pretext that they could not control themselves, any unbeliever who came in and heard this Babel of sound would naturally conclude, as Paul says, that he had stumbled into a ward of lunatics. Such disorder must not be. If there were no one present who could interpret what the speakers with tongues were saying, they must be silent. Apart from interpretation speaking with tongues was mere noise, the blare of a trumpet sounded by one who did not know one call from another, and which was mere unintelligible sound. Prophesying was not liable to these abuses. All understood it, and could learn something from it.

From this preference shown by Paul for the less showy but more useful gift, we may gather that to make public worship the occasion of self-display or sensational exhibitions is to degrade it. This is a hint for the pulpit rather than for the pew. Preachers must resist the temptation to preach for effect, to make a sensation, to produce fine sermons. The desire to be recognised as able to move men, to say things smartly, to put the truth freshly, to be eloquent, or to be sensible is always striving against the simple-minded purpose of edifying Christ's people. Worshippers as well as preachers may, however, be so tempted. They may sing with a gratified sense of exhibiting a good voice. They may find greater pleasure in what is sensational in worship than in what is simple and intelligible.

Again, we here see that worship in which the understanding bears no part receives no countenance from Paul. "I will pray with the spirit; I will pray with the understanding also." Where the prayers of the Church are in an unknown tongue, such as Latin, the worshipper may indeed pray with the spirit, and may be edified thereby, but his worship would be better did he pray with the understanding also. Music unaccompanied by words induces in some temperaments an impressible condition which has an appearance of devoutness and probably something of the reality; but such devoutness is apt to be either hazy or sentimental or both, unless by the help of accompanying words the understanding goes hand in hand with feeling.

No countenance can be found in this chapter to the idea that worship should exclude preaching and become the sole purpose of the assembling together of Christian people. Some temperaments incline towards worship, but resent being preached to or instructed. The reverential and serious feelings which are quickened into life by devotional forms of prayer may be scattered by the buffoonery or ineptitudes of the preacher. Exasperation, unbelief, contempt, in the mind of the hearer may be the only results achieved by some sermons. It may occasionally occur to us that the Christian world would be very much the better of some years of silence, and that results which have not been reached by floods of preaching might be attained if these floods were allowed to ebb and a period of quiet and repose succeed. Unquestionably there is a danger at present of leading men to suppose that religion is a thing which must be ceaselessly talked about, and which perhaps chiefly consists of talk, so that if one only hears enough, and has the right opinions, he may accept himself as a religious person. But it is one thing to say that there is at present too much preaching or too careless and unequal a distribution of preaching, and quite another thing to say there should be none.

Having given expression to his preference for prophesying, Paul goes on to indicate the manner in which the public services should be conducted. The picture he draws is one which finds no counterpart in the greater modern Churches. The chief distinction between the services of the Corinthian Church and those we are now familiar with is the much greater freedom with which in those days the membership of the Church took part in the service. "When ye come together, every one of you hath a psalm, hath a doctrine, hath a tongue, hath a revelation, hath an interpretation." Each member of the congregation had something to contribute for the edification of the Church. The experience, the thought, the gifts, of the individual were made available for the benefit of all. One with a natural aptitude for poetry threw his devotional feeling into a metrical form, and furnished the Church with her earliest hymns. Another with innate exactness of thought set some important aspect of Christian truth so clearly before the mind of the congregation that it at once took its place as an article of faith. Another, fresh from contact with the world and intercourse with unbelieving and dissolute men, who had felt his own feet sliding and renewed his grasp on Christ, entered the meeting with the glow of conflict on his face, and had eager words of exhortation to utter. And so passed the hours of meeting, without any fixed order, without any appointed ministry, without any uniformity of service. And certainly the freshness, fulness, and variety of such services were greatly to be desired if possibly they could be attained. We lose much of what would interest and much that would edify by enjoining silence upon the membership of the Church.

And yet, as Paul observes, there was much to be desired in those Corinthian services. Had there been some authorized official presiding over them, the abuses of which this letter speaks could not have arisen. To appeal to this chapter or to any part of this letter in proof that there should be no distinction between clergy and laity would be very bad policy. It is indeed obvious that at this time there were neither elders nor deacons, bishops nor rulers of any kind, in the Church of Corinth; but then it is quite as obvious that there was great need of them, and that the want of them had given rise to some scandalous abuses and to much disorder. The ideal condition would be one in which authority should be lodged in certain elected office-bearers, while the faculty and gift of each member in some way contributed to the good of the whole Church. In most Churches of our own day, efforts are made to utilize the Christian energies of their membership in those various charitable works which are so necessary and so abundant. But probably we should all be the better of a much freer ventilation of opinion within the Church and of listening to men who have not been educated in any particular school of theology and hold their minds closely to the realities of experience.

We cannot but ask in passing, What has become of all those inspired utterances with which the Corinthian Church from week to week resounded? Doubtless they entered into the life of that generation and fostered the Christian character which so often shone out on the heathen world with surprising purity. Doubtless, too, the unknown teachers of those primitive Churches did much both in the way of suggesting aspects of truth to Paul and of confirming, and expounding, and illustrating his somewhat condensed and difficult teaching. Had their utterances been recorded, many obscurities of Scripture might have been removed, much light must have been reflected on the whole circle of Christian truth, and we should have been able to define more clearly the actual condition of the Christian Church. Shorthand was in common use at that time in the Roman courts, and by its means we are in possession of relics of that age of much less value than the report of one or two of these Christian meetings might have been. No such report, however, is forthcoming.

While Paul abstains from appointing office-bearers to preside at their meetings, he is careful to lay down two principles which should regulate their procedure. First, "let everything be done decently and in order." This advice was greatly needed in a Church in which the public services were sometimes turned into tumultuous exhibitions of rival gifts, each man trying to make himself heard above the din of voices, one speaking with tongues, another singing a hymn, a third loudly addressing the congregation, so that any stranger who might be attracted by the noise and step into the house could think this Christian meeting nothing else than Bedlam broke loose. Above all things, then, says Paul, conduct your meetings in a seemly fashion. Observe the rules of common decency and order. I do not prescribe any particular forms you must observe nor any special order you must follow in your services. I do not pronounce what portion of time should be devoted to prayer nor what to praise or exhortation; nor do I require that you should in all cases begin your service in the same stereotyped manner and carry it through in the same routine. Your services must vary both in form and in substance from week to week according to the equipment of the individual members of your Church; sometimes there may be many who wish to exhort, sometimes there may be none. But in all this freedom and variety, spontaneity must not run into obtrusiveness, and variety must be saved from disorder.

The other general principle Paul lays down in the words, "Let all things be done unto edifying." Let each use his gift for the good of the congregation. Keep the great end of your meetings in view, and you need no formal rubrics. If extempore prayer is found inspiring, use it; if the old liturgy of the synagogue is preferred, retain its service; if both have advantages, employ both. Judge your methods by their bearing on the spiritual life of your members. Make no boast of your æsthetic worship, your irreproachable liturgy, your melting music, if these things do not result in a more loyal service of Christ. Do not pique yourselves on your puritanic simplicity of worship and the absence of all that is not spiritual if this bareness and simplicity do not bring you more directly into the presence of your Lord. It matters little what we eat or in what shape it is served if we are the better for our food and are maintained in health and vigour. It matters little whether the vehicle in which we travel be highly decorated or plain so long as it brings us safely to our destination. Are we the better for our services? Is it our chief aim in them to receive and promote an earnest religious spirit and a sincere service of Christ?

It might be difficult to say whether the somewhat selfish ambition of those Corinthians to secure the surprising gifts of the Spirit or our own torpid indifference and lack of expectation is less to be commended. Certainly every one who attaches himself to Christ ought to indulge in great expectations. Through Christ lies the way out from the poverty and futility that oppress our spiritual history. From Him we may, however falsely modest we are, expect at least His own Spirit. And in this "least" there is promise of all. They who sincerely attach themselves to Christ cannot fail to end by being like Him. But lack of expectation is fatal to the Christian. If we expect nothing or very little from Christ, we might as well not be Christians. If He does not become to us a second conscience, ever present in us to warn against sin and offer opposing inducements, we might as well call ourselves by any other name. His power is exerted now not to excite to unwonted exhibitions of abnormal faculties, but to promote in us all that is most stable and substantial in character. And the fact is that they who hunger after righteousness are filled. They who expect that Christ will help them to become like Himself do become like Him. All grace is attainable. Nothing but unbelief shuts us out from it. Do not be content until you find in Christ more abundant life, until you have as clear evidence as these Corinthians had that a new spirit of power dwells within you. He Himself encourages you to expect this. It is to receive this He calls us to Him; and if we are not expecting this spirit of life, it is because we do not understand or do not believe Him. He has come to give us the best God has to give, and the best is likeness to Himself. He has come to save our life from being a folly and a failure, and He saves it by filling it with His own Spirit. All fulness resides in Him; in Him Divine resource is made available for human needs: but the distribution is moral, not mechanical; that is to say, it depends on your willingness to receive, on your expectation of good, on your true personal attachment to Christ in spirit and in will.

THE RESURRECTION OF CHRIST

"Moreover, brethren, I declare unto you the Gospel which I preached unto you, which also ye have received, and wherein ye stand; by which also ye are saved, if ye keep in memory what I preached unto you, unless ye have believed in vain. For I delivered unto you first of all that which I also received, how that Christ died for our sins according to the Scriptures; and that He was buried, and that He rose again the third day according to the Scriptures: and that He was seen of Cephas, then of the twelve: after that, He was seen of above five hundred brethren at once; of whom the greater part remain unto this present, but some are fallen asleep. After that He was seen of James; then of all the Apostles. And last of all He was seen of me also, as of one born out of due time. For I am the least of the Apostles, that am not meet to be called an apostle, because I persecuted the Church of God. But by the grace of God I am what I am: and His grace which was bestowed upon me was not in vain; but I laboured more abundantly than they all: yet not I, but the grace of God which was with me. Therefore whether it were I or they, so we preach, and so ye believed. Now if Christ be preached that He rose from the dead, how say some among you that there is no resurrection of the dead? But if there be no resurrection of the dead, then is Christ not risen: and if Christ be not risen, then is our preaching vain, and your faith is also vain. Yea, and we are found false witnesses of God; because we have testified of God that He raised up Christ: whom He raised not up, if so be that the dead rise not. For if the dead rise not, then is not Christ raised: and if Christ be not raised, your faith is vain; ye are yet in your sins." — 1 Cor. xv. 1-17.

XXI
THE RESURRECTION OF CHRIST

I. Its Place in the Christian Creed

Paul having now settled the minor questions of order in public worship, marriage, intercourse with the heathen, and the other various difficulties which were distracting the Corinthian Church, turns at last to a matter of prime importance and perennial interest: the resurrection of the body. This great subject he handles not in the abstract, but with a view to the particular attitude and beliefs of the Corinthians. Some of them said broadly, "There is no resurrection of the dead," although apparently they had no intention of denying that Christ had risen. Accordingly Paul proceeds to show them that the resurrection of Christ and that of His followers hang together, that the resurrection of Christ is essential to the Christian creed, that it is amply attested, and that although great difficulties surround the subject, making it impossible to conceive what the risen body will be, yet the resurrection of the body is to be looked forward to with confident hope.

It will be most convenient to consider first the place which the resurrection of Christ holds in the Christian creed; but that we may follow Paul's argument and appreciate its force, it will be necessary to make clear to our own mind what he meant by the resurrection of Christ and what position the Corinthians sought to maintain.

First, by the resurrection of Christ Paul meant His rising from the grave with a body glorified or made fit for the new and heavenly life He had entered. Paul did not believe that the body he saw on the road to Damascus was the very body which had hung upon the cross, made of the same material, subject to the same conditions. He affirms in this chapter that flesh and blood, a natural body, cannot enter upon the heavenly life. It must pass through a process which entirely alters its material. Paul had seen bodies consumed to ashes, and he knew that the substance of these bodies could not be recovered. He was aware that the material of the human body is dissolved, and is by the processes of nature used for the constructing of the bodies of fishes, wild beasts, birds; that as the body was sustained in life by the produce of the earth, so in death it is mingled with the earth again, giving back to earth what it had received. The arguments therefore commonly urged against the Resurrection had no relevancy against that in which Paul believed, for it was not that very thing which was buried which he expected would rise again, but a body different in kind, in material, and in capacity.

But yet Paul always speaks as if there were some connection between the present and the future, the natural and the spiritual, body. He speaks, too, of the body of Christ as the type or specimen into the likeness of which the bodies of His people are to be transformed. Now if we conceive, or try to conceive, what passed in that closed sepulchre in the garden of Joseph, we can only suppose that the body of flesh and blood which was taken down from the cross and laid there was transformed into a spiritual body by a process which may be called miraculous, but which differed from the process which is to operate in ourselves only by its rapidity. We do not understand the process; but is that the only thing we do not understand? All along the line which marks off this world from the spiritual world mystery broods; and the fact that we do not understand how the body Christ had worn on earth passed into a body fit for another kind of life ought not to prevent our believing that such a transmutation can take place. There are in nature many forces of which we know nothing, and it may one day appear to us most natural that the spirit should clothe itself with a spiritual body. The connection between the two bodies is the persistent and identical spirit which animates both. As the life that is in the body now assimilates material and forms the body to its particular mould, so may the spirit hereafter, when ejected from its present dwelling, have power to clothe itself with a body suited to its needs. Paul refuses to recognise any insuperable difficulty here. The transmutation of the earthly body of Christ into a glorified body will be repeated in the case of many of His followers, for, as he says, "we shall not all sleep, but we shall all be changed *in a moment, in the twinkling of an eye.*"

Secondly, we must understand the position occupied by those whom Paul addressed in this chapter. They doubted the Resurrection; but in that day, as in our own, the Resurrection was denied from two opposite points of view. Materialists, such as the Sadducees, believing that mental and spiritual life are only manifestations of physical life and dependent upon it, necessarily concluded that with the death of the body the whole life of the individual terminates. And it would rather appear as if the Corinthians were tainted with materialism. "Let us eat and drink, for to-morrow we die," can only be the suggestion of the materialist, who believes in no future life of any kind.

But many who opposed materialism held that the resurrection of the body, if not impossible, was at all events undesirable. It was the fashion to speak contemptuously of the body. It was branded as the source and seat of sin, as the untamed bullock which dragged its yokefellow, the soul, out of the straight path. Philosophers gave thanks to God that He had not tied their spirit to an immortal body, and refused to allow their portrait to be taken, lest they should be remembered and honoured by means of their material part. When Paul's teaching was accepted by such persons, they laid great stress on his inculcation of the mystical or spiritual dying with Christ and rising again, until they persuaded themselves this was all he meant by resurrection. They declared that the Resurrection was past already, and that all believing men were already risen in Christ. To be free from all connection with matter was an essential element in their idea of salvation, and to promise them the resurrection of the body was to offer them a very doubtful blessing indeed.

In our own day the resurrection of Christ is denied both from the materialist and from the spiritualist or idealist point of view. It is said that the resurrection of Christ is an undoubted fact if by the resurrection it be meant that His spirit survived death and now lives in us. But the bodily resurrection is a thing of no account. Not from the risen body flows the power that has altered human history, but from the teachings and life of Christ and from His devotement of Himself even unto death to the interests of men. Christ lay in His grave, and the elements of His body have passed into the bosom of nature, as ours will before long; but His spirit was not imprisoned in the grave: it lives, perhaps in us. Statements to this effect you may hear or read frequently in our day. And either of two very different beliefs may be expressed in such language. It may, on the one hand, mean that the person Jesus is individually extinct, and that although virtue still flows from His life, as from that of every good man, He is Himself unconscious of this and of everything else, and can exert no new and fresh influence, such as emanates from a person presently alive and aware of the exigencies appealing to His interference. This is plainly a form of belief entirely different from that of the Apostles, who acted for a living Lord, to whom they appealed and by whom they were guided. Belief in a dead Christ, who cannot hear prayer and is unconscious of our service, may indeed help a man who has nothing better to help him; but it is not the belief of the Apostles.

On the other hand, it may be meant that although the body of Christ remained in the tomb, His spirit survived death, and lives a disembodied but conscious and powerful life. One of the profoundest German critics, Keim, has expressed himself to this effect. The Apostles, he thinks, did not see the actual risen body of the Lord; their visions of a glorified Jesus were not, however, delusive; the appearances were not the creations of their own excitement, but were intentionally produced by the Lord Himself. Jesus, it is believed, had actually passed into a higher life, and was as full of consciousness and of power as He had been on earth; and of this glorified life in which He was He gave the Apostles assurance by these appearances. The body of the Lord remained in the tomb; but these appearances were intended, to use the critic's own words, as a kind of telegram, to assure them He was alive. Had such a sign of His continued and glorified life not been given, their belief in Him as the Messiah could not have survived the death on the cross.

This view, although erroneous, can do little harm to experimental or practical Christianity. The difference between a disembodied spirit and a spiritual body is really unappreciable to our present knowledge. And if any one finds it impossible to believe in the bodily resurrection of Christ, but easy to believe in His present life and power, it would only be mischievous to require of him a faith he cannot give in addition to a faith which brings him into real fellowship with Christ. The main purpose of Christ's appearances was to give to His disciples assurance of His continued life and power. If that assurance already exists, then belief in Christ as alive and supreme supersedes the use of the usual stepping-stone towards that belief.

At the same time, it must be maintained that not only did the Apostles believe they saw the body of Christ, by which indeed they first of all identified Him, but also they were distinctly assured that the body they saw was not a ghost or a telegram, but a veritable body that could stand handling, and whose lips and throat could utter sound. Besides, it is not in reason to suppose that when they saw this appearance, whatever it was, they should not at once go to the sepulchre and see what was there. And if there they saw the body while in various other places they saw what seemed to be the body, what a world of incomprehensible and mystifying jugglery must they have felt themselves to be involved in!

It is a fact then that those who knew most both about the body and about the spirit of Jesus believed they saw the body and were encouraged so to believe. Besides, if we accept the view that though Christ is alive, His body remained in the grave, we are at once confronted with the difficulty that Christ's glorification is not yet complete. If Christ's body did not partake in His conquest over the grave, then that conquest is partial and incomplete. Human nature both in this life and in the life to come is composed of body and spirit; and if Christ now sits at God's right hand in perfected human nature, it is not as a disembodied spirit, but as a complete person in a glorified body, we must conceive of Him. No doubt it is a spiritual influence which Christ now exerts upon His followers, and their belief in His risen life may be independent of any statements made by the disciples concerning His body; at the same time, to suppose that Christ is now without a body is to suppose that He is imperfect: and it must also be remembered that the primitive faith and restored confidence in Christ, to which the very existence of the Church is due, were created by the sight of the empty tomb and the glorified body.

In the face of such chapters as this and other passages equally explicit, modern believers in a merely spiritual resurrection have found some difficulty in reconciling their views with the statements of Paul. Mr. Matthew Arnold undertakes to show us how this may be done. "Not for a moment," he says, "do we deny that in Paul's earlier theology, and notably in the Epistles to the Thessalonians and Corinthians, the physical and miraculous aspect of the Resurrection, both Christ's and the believer's, is primary and predominant. Not for a moment do we deny that to the very end of his life, after the Epistle to the Romans, after the Epistle to the Philippians, if he had been asked whether he held the doctrine of the Resurrection in the physical and miraculous sense as well as in his own spiritual and mystical sense, he would have replied with entire conviction that he did. Very likely it would have been impossible to him to imagine his theology without it. But—

> 'Below the surface stream, shallow and light,
> Of what we *say* we feel—below the stream,
> As light, of what we *think* we feel, there flows
> With noiseless current strong, obscure and deep,
> The central stream of what we feel indeed;'

and by this alone are we truly characterised." This, however, is not to interpret an author, but to make him a mere nose of wax that can be worked into any convenient shape. Probably Paul understood his own theology quite as well as Mr. Arnold; and, as his critic says, he considered the physical resurrection of Christ and the believer an essential part of it.

Considering the place which our Lord's risen body had in Paul's conversion, it could not be otherwise. At the very moment when Paul's whole system of thought was in a state of fusion the risen Lord was pre-eminently impressed upon it. It was through his conviction of the resurrection of Christ that both Paul's theology and his character were once for all radically altered. The idea of a crucified Messiah had been abhorrent to him, and his life was dedicated to the extirpation of this vile heresy that sprang from the Cross. But from the moment when with his own eyes he saw the risen Lord he understood, with the rest of the disciples, that death was the Messiah's appointed path to supreme spiritual headship. As truly in Paul's case as in that of the other disciples faith sprang from the sight of the glorified Christ; and to none could it be so inevitable as to him to say, "If Christ be not risen, then is our preaching vain, and your faith is also vain."

From the first Paul had put the resurrection of Christ forward as an essential and fundamental part of the Gospel he had received, and which he was accustomed to deliver.

And, generally speaking, this place is assigned to it both by believers and by unbelievers. It is recognised that it was the belief in the Resurrection which first revived the hopes of Christ's followers and drew them together to wait for the promise of His Spirit. It is recognised that whether the Resurrection be a fact or no, the Church of Christ was founded on the belief that it had taken place, so that if that had been removed the Church could not have been. This is affirmed as decisively by unbelievers as by believers. The great leader of modern unbelief (Strauss) declares that the Resurrection is "the centre of the centre, the real heart of Christianity as it has been until now;" while one of his ablest opponents says, "The Resurrection created the Church, the risen Christ made Christianity; and even now the Christian faith stands or falls with Him.... If it be true that no living Christ ever issued from the tomb of Joseph, then that tomb becomes the grave, not of a man, but of a religion, with all the hopes built on it and all the splendid enthusiasms it has inspired" (Fairbairn).

It is not difficult to perceive what it was in the resurrection of Christ which gave it this importance.

1. First, it was the convincing proof that Christ's words were true, and that He was what He had claimed to be. He Himself had on more occasions than one hinted that such proof was to be given, "Destroy this temple," He said, "and in three days I will raise it again." The sign which was to be given, notwithstanding His habitual refusal to yield to the Jewish craving for miracle, was the sign of the prophet Jonah. As he had been thrown out and lost for three days and nights, but had thereby only been forwarded in his mission, so our Lord was to be thrown out as endangering the ship, but was to rise again to fuller and more perfect efficiency. In order that His claim to be the Messiah might be understood, it was necessary that He should die; but in order that it might be believed, it was needful that He should rise. Had He not died, His followers would have continued to expect a reign of earthly power; His death showed them no such reign could be, and convinced them His spiritual power sprang out of apparent weakness. But had He not risen again, all their hopes would have been blighted. All who had believed in Him would have joined with the Emmaus disciples in their hopeless cry, "We thought that this had been He who should have redeemed Israel."

It was the resurrection of our Lord, then, which convinced His disciples that His words had been true, that He was what He had claimed to be, and that He was not mistaken regarding His own person, His work, His relation to the Father, the prospects of Himself and His people. This was the answer given by God to the doubts, and calumnies, and accusations of men. Jesus at the last had stood alone, unsupported by one favouring voice. His own disciples forsook Him, and in their bewilderment knew not what to think. Those who considered Him a dangerous and seditious person or at best a crazed enthusiast found themselves backed by the voice of the people and urged to extreme measures, with none to remonstrate save the heathen judge, none to pity save a few women. This delusion, they congratulated themselves, was stamped out. And stamped out it would have been but for the Resurrection. "Then it was seen that while the world had scorned the Son of God, the Father had been watching over Him with unceasing love; that while the world had placed Him at its bar as a malefactor and blasphemer, the Father had been making ready for Him a seat at His own right hand; that while the world nailed Him to the cross, the Father had been preparing for Him 'many crowns' and a name that is above every name; that while the world had gone to the grave in the garden, setting a watch and sealing the stone, and had then returned to its feasting and merriment, because the Preacher of righteousness was no longer there to trouble it, the Father had waited for the third morning in order to bring Him forth in triumph from the grave."[16]

This contrast between the treatment Christ received at the hands of men and His justification by the Father in the Resurrection fills and colours all the addresses delivered by the Apostles to the people in the immediately succeeding days. They evidently accepted the Resurrection as God's great attestation to the person and work of Christ. It changed their own thoughts about Him, and they expected it would change the thoughts of other men. They saw now that His death was one of the necessary steps in His career, one of the essential parts of the work He had come to do. Had Christ not been raised, they would have thought Him weak and mistaken as other men. The beauty and promise of His words which had so attracted them would now have seemed delusive and unbearable. But in the light of the Resurrection they saw that the Christ "ought to have suffered these things and so to enter His glory." They could now confidently say, "He died for our sins, and was raised again for our justification."

2. Secondly, the resurrection of Christ occupies a fundamental place in the Christian creed, because by it there is disclosed a real and close

connection between this world and the unseen, eternal world. There is no need now of argument to prove a life beyond; here is one who is in it. For the resurrection of Christ was not a return to this life, to its wants, to its limitations, to its inevitable close; but it was a resurrection to a life for ever beyond death. Neither was it a discarding of humanity on Christ's part, a cessation of His acceptance of human conditions, a rising to some kind of existence to which man has no access. On the contrary, it was because He continued truly human that in human body and with human soul He rose to veritable human life beyond the grave. If Jesus rose from the dead, then the world into which He is gone is a real world, in which men can live more fully than they live here. If He rose from the dead, then there is an unseen Spirit mightier than the strongest material powers, a God who is seeking to bring us out of all evil into an eternally happy condition. Quite reasonably is death invested with a certain majesty, if not terror, as the mightiest of physical things. There may be greater evils; but they do not affect all men, but only some, or they debar men from certain enjoyments and a certain kind of life, but not from all. But death shuts men out from everything with which they have here to do, and launches them into a condition of which they know absolutely nothing. Any one who conquers death and scatters its mystery, who shows in his own person that it is innocuous, and that it actually betters our condition, brings us light that reaches us from no other quarter. And He who shows this superiority over death in virtue of a moral superiority, and uses it for the furtherance of the highest spiritual ends, shows a command over the whole affairs of men which makes it easy to believe He can guide us into a condition like His own. As Peter affirms, it is "by the resurrection of Jesus Christ from the dead we are begotten again unto a lively hope."

3. For, lastly, it is in the resurrection of Christ we see at once the norm or type of our life here and of our destiny hereafter. Holiness and immortality are two aspects, two manifestations, of the Divine life we receive from Christ. They are inseparable the one from the other. His Spirit is the source of both. "If the Spirit that raised up the Lord Jesus from the dead dwelleth in you, He that raised up Christ Jesus from the dead shall also quicken your mortal bodies through His Spirit that dwelleth in you." If we have now the one evidence of His indwelling in us, we shall one day have the other. The hope that should uplift and purify every part of the Christian's character is a hope which is shadowy, unreal, inoperative, in those who merely know about Christ and His work; it becomes a living hope, full of immortality, in all who are now actually drawing their life from Christ, who have their life

truly hid with Christ in God, who are in heart and will one with the Most High, in whom is all life.

Therefore does Paul so continually hold up to us the risen life of Christ as that to which we are to be conformed. We are to rise with Him to newness of life. As Christ has done with death, having died to sin once, so must His people be dead to sin and live to God with Him. Sometimes in weariness or dejection one feels as if he had seen the best of everything experienced all he can experience, and must now simply endure life; he sees no prospect of anything fresh, or attractive, or reviving. But this is not because he has exhausted life, but because he has not begun it. To the "children of the Resurrection," who have followed Christ in His path to life by renouncing sin, and conquering self, and giving themselves to God, there is a springing life in their own soul that renews hope and energy.

XXII
THE RESURRECTION OF CHRIST (continued)

II. Its Proof

Paul, having affirmed that the resurrection of Christ is an essential element of the Gospel, proceeds to sketch the evidence for the fact. That evidence mainly consists in the attestation of those who at various times and in various places and circumstances had seen the Lord after His death. Other evidence there is, as Paul indicates. In certain unspecified passages of the Old Testament he thinks a discerning reader might have found sufficient intimation that when the Messiah came He would both die and rise again. But as he himself had not at first recognised these intimations in the Old Testament, he does not press them upon others, but appeals to the simple fact that many of those who had been familiar with the appearance of Christ while He lived saw Him after death alive.

As a preliminary to the positive evidence here adduced by Paul, it may be remarked that we have no record of any contemporary denial of the fact, save only the story put in the mouths of the soldiers by the chief priests. Matthew tells us that it was currently reported that the soldiers who had been on guard at the sepulchre were bribed by the priests and elders to say that the disciples had come in the night and stolen the body. But whatever temporary purpose they fancied this might serve, the great purpose it now serves is to prove the truth of the Resurrection, for the main point is admitted, the tomb was empty. As for the story itself, its falsehood must have been apparent; and probably no one in Jerusalem was so simple as to be taken in by it. For, in point of fact, the authorities had taken steps to prevent this very thing. They were resolved there should be no tampering with the grave, and accordingly had set their official seal upon it and placed a guard to watch.

The evidence thus unintentionally furnished by the authorities is important. Their action after the Resurrection proves that the tomb was empty; while their action previous to the Resurrection proves that it was emptied by no ordinary interposition, but by the actual rising of Jesus from the dead. So beyond doubt was this that when Peter stood before the Sanhedrim and affirmed it no one was hardy enough to contradict him. Had they been able to persuade themselves that the disciples had tampered with the guard, or overpowered them, or terrified them in the night by strange appearances, why did they not prosecute the disciples for breaking the official seal? Could they have had a more plausible pretext for exploding the Christian faith and stamping out the nascent heresy? They were perplexed and alarmed at the growth of the Church; what hindered them from bringing proof that there had been no resurrection? They had every inducement to do so, yet they did not. If the body was still in the grave, nothing was easier than to produce it; if the grave was empty, as they affirmed, because the disciples had stolen the body, no more welcome handle against them could have been furnished to the authorities. But they could not in open court pretend any such thing. They knew that what their guard reported was true. In short, there was no object the Sanhedrim would more gladly have compassed than to explode the belief in the resurrection of Christ; if that belief was false, they had ample means of showing it to be so: and yet they did absolutely nothing that had any weight with the public mind. It is apparent that not only the disciples, but the authorities, were compelled to admit the fact of the Resurrection.

The idea that there was only a pretended resurrection, vamped up by the disciples, may therefore be dismissed; and indeed no well-informed person nowadays would venture to affirm such a thing. It is admitted by those who deny the Resurrection as explicitly as by those who affirm it that the disciples had a *bonâ fide* belief that Jesus had risen from the dead and was alive. The only question is, How was that belief produced? And to this question there are three answers: (1) that the disciples saw our Lord alive after the Crucifixion, but He had never been dead; (2) that they only thought they saw Him; and (3) that they did actually see Him alive after being dead and buried.

1. The first answer is plainly inadequate. We are asked to account for the Christian Church, for the belief in a risen Lord which animated the first disciples with a faith, a hope, a courage, whose power is felt to this day; we ask for an explanation of this singular circumstance that a number of men arrived at the conclusion that they had an almighty Friend, One who had all power in heaven and on earth; and we are told, in explanation of this, that they had seen their Master barely rescued from crucifixion, creeping about the earth, scarcely able to move, all stained with blood, soiled from the tomb, pale, weak, helpless, and this object caused them to believe He was almighty. As one of the most sceptical of critics himself says, "one who had thus crept forth half dead from the grave and crawled about a sickly patient, needing medical and surgical assistance, nursing and strengthening, and who finally succumbed to his sufferings, could never have given his

followers the impression that he was the Conqueror over death and the grave, the Prince of life. Such a recovery could only have weakened or at best given a pathetic tinge to the impression which he had made upon them by his life and death; it could not possibly have changed their sorrow into ecstasy, and raised their reverence into worship."

This explanation then may be dismissed. It is neither in harmony with the facts, nor is it adequate as an explanation.

It is not in harmony with the facts, because the fact of His death was certified by the surest authority. There was in the world at that time, and there is in the world now, nothing more punctiliously accurate than a soldier trained under the old Roman discipline. The punctilious exactness of this discipline is seen in the conduct both of the soldiers at the cross and of Pilate. Though the soldiers see that Jesus is dead, they make sure of His death by a spear-thrust, a handbreadth wide, sufficient of itself, as they very well knew, to cause death. And when Pilate is applied to for the body, he will not give it up until he has received from the centurion on duty the necessary certificate that the sentence of death has actually been executed.

Neither is the supposition that Jesus survived the Crucifixion and appeared to His disciples in this rescued condition any explanation of their faith in Him as a risen, glorious, almighty Lord. The Person they saw and afterwards believed in was not a bleeding, crushed, defeated man, who had death still to look forward to, but a Person who had passed through and conquered death, and was now alive for evermore, opening for Himself and to them the gates of a glorious and deathless life.

2. The belief of the disciples is explained with greater appearance of insight by those who say that they imagined they saw the risen Lord, although in reality they did not. There are, it is pointed out, several ways in which the disciples may have been deceived. For example, some clever and scheming person may have personated Jesus. Such personations have been made, but never with such results. When Postumus Agrippa was killed, one of his slaves secreted or dispersed the ashes of the murdered man, to destroy the evidence of his death, and retired for a time till his hair and beard were grown, to favour a certain likeness which he actually bore him. Meanwhile, taking a few intimates into his confidence, he spread a report, which found ready listeners, that Agrippa still lived. He glided from town to town, showing himself in the dusk for a few minutes only at a time to men prepared for the sudden apparition, until it came to be noised abroad that the gods had saved the grandson of Agrippa from the fate intended for him, and that he was about to visit the city and claim his rightful inheritance. But no sooner did the vulgar imposture take this

practical shape and come into contact with the realities of life than the whole trick exploded. Imposture, in fact, does not fit the case before us at all; and the more we consider the combination of qualities required in any one who could undertake to personate the risen Lord, the more we shall be persuaded that the right explanation of the belief in the Resurrection is not to be sought in this direction.

Again, one of the most reasonable and influential of our contemporaries ascribes "the great myth of Christ's bodily revival to the belief on the part of the disciples that such a soul could not become extinct. In a lesser way the grave of a beloved friend has been to many a man the birthplace of his faith; and it is obvious that in the case of Christ every condition was fulfilled which would raise such sudden conviction to the height of passionate fervour. The first words of the disciples to one another on that Easter morn may well have been 'He is not dead. His spirit is this day in paradise among the sons of God.'" Quite so; they of course believed that His spirit was in paradise, and for that very reason fully expected to find His body in the tomb. No ordinary visit to a grave, nor any ordinary results flowing from such a visit, throw light on the case before us, because in ordinary circumstances sane men do not believe that their friends are restored to them, and are standing in bodily palpable shape before them. There is no likelihood whatever that their belief in the continued existence of their Master's spirit should have given rise to the conviction that they had seen Him. It might have given rise to such expressions as that He would be with them to the end of the world, but not to the conviction that they had seen Him in the body.

Here, again, is Rénan's account of the growth of this belief: "To Jesus was to happen the same fortune which is the lot of all men who have riveted the attention of their fellow-men. The world, accustomed to attribute to them superhuman virtues, cannot admit that they have submitted to the unjust, revolting, iniquitous law of the death common to all. At the moment in which Mahomet expired Omar rushed from the tent, sword in hand, and declared that he would hew down any one who should dare to say that the prophet was no more.... Heroes do not die. What is true existence but the recollection of us which survives in the hearts of those who love us? For some years this adored Master had filled the little world by which He was surrounded with joy and hope; could they consent to allow Him to the decay of the tomb? No; He had lived so entirely in those who surrounded Him, that they could but affirm that after His death He was still living." M. Rénan is careful not to remind us that the uproar occasioned by Omar's announcement was stilled by the calm voice of Abu Bekr, who also came forth from the deathbed of Mahomet with the memorable words, "Whoso hath worshipped Mahomet, let him know that Mahomet is dead, but whoso hath worshipped God that the Lord liveth and doth not die." The great critic omits also to notice that none of the Apostles said, like Omar, that their Master was not dead; they admitted and felt His death keenly; and it is vain to attempt to confound things essentially distinct, the assertion of a matter of fact, viz., that the Lord had risen again, with the sentimental or regretful resuscitation of a man's image in the hearts of his surviving friends.

Besides, it should be observed that all these hypotheses which explain the belief in the Resurrection by supposing that the disciples imagined they had seen Christ, or persuaded themselves that He still lived, omit altogether to explain how they disposed of the tomb of our Lord, in which, according to this hypothesis, His body was still quietly reposing. One or two persons in a peculiarly excitable state might suppose they had seen a figure resembling a person about whom they were concerned; but how the belief that the tomb was empty could take any hold on them or on the thousands who must have visited it in the succeeding weeks is not explained, nor is any attempt made to explain it.

Is there then no possibility of the disciples having been deceived? May they not have been mistaken? May they not have seen what they wished to see, as other men have sometimes done? Men of vivid fancy or of a boastful spirit sometimes come really to believe they have done and said things they never did or said. Is it out of the question to imagine that the disciples may have been similarly misled? Had the belief in the Resurrection depended on the report of one man, had there been only one or a few eyewitnesses of the matter, their evidence might have been explained away on this ground. It is possible, of course, that one or two persons who were anxiously looking for the resurrection of Jesus might have persuaded themselves they saw Him, might persuade themselves that some distant figure or some gleam of morning sunshine among the trees of the garden was the looked-for person. It requires no profound psychological knowledge to teach us that occasionally visions are seen. But what we have here to explain is how not one but several persons, not together but in different places and at different times, not all in one mood of mind but in various moods, came to believe they had seen the risen Lord. He was recognised, not by persons who expected to see Him alive, but by women who went to anoint Him dead; not by credulous, excitable persons, but by men who would not believe till they had gone to and into the sepulchre; not by persons so enthusiastic and creative of their own belief as to mistake any passing stranger or even a gleam of light for Him they sought, but so slow to believe, so scornfully incredulous of resurrection, so resolutely sceptical and so keenly alive to the possibility of delusion, that they vowed nothing would satisfy them but the test of touch and sight. It was a belief produced, not by one extraordinary and doubtful appearance, but by repeated and prolonged appearances to persons in various places and of various temperaments.

This supposition, therefore, that the disciples were prepared to believe in the Resurrection and wished to believe it, and that what they wished to see they thought they saw, must be given up. It has never been shown that the disciples *had* such a belief; it formed no part of the Jewish creed regarding the Messiah: and the idea that they actually were in this expectant state of mind is thoroughly contradicted by the narrative. So far from being hopeful, they were sad and gloomy, as witness the melancholy, resigned despair of the two friends on the road to Emmaus.

> "It is a woe 'too deep for tears' when all
> Is reft at once, when some surpassing spirit,
> Whose light adorned the world around it, leaves
> Those who remain behind, not sobs or groans,
> But pale despair and cold tranquillity."

Such was the state of mind of the bereft disciples. They thought all was over. The women who went with their spices to anoint the dead—*they* certainly were not expecting to find their Lord risen. The men to whom they announced what they had seen were sceptical; some of them laughed at the women, and called their report "idle tales," and would not believe. Mary Magdalene was so little expecting to see her Lord alive again that when He did appear to her she thought He was the gardener, the *only* person she dreamt of seeing going about at that hour in the garden. Thomas, with all the resolute distrust of others which a modern sceptic could show, vows he will believe such a wild imagination on no man's word, and unless he sees the Lord with his own eyes and is allowed to test the reality of the figure by touch as well, he will not be convinced. To the disciples on the way to Emmaus, though they had never heard such conversation before as that of the Person who joined them, it never once occurred that this could be the Lord. In short, there was not one person to whom our Lord appeared who was not taken wholly by surprise. So far were they from depicting the Resurrection in their hopes and fancies with such vividness as to make it seem to take outward shape and reality, that even when it did actually take place they could scarcely believe it on the strongest evidence. We are compelled, therefore, to dismiss the idea that the first disciples believed in the resurrection because they wished to do so and were prepared to do so.

3. There remains, therefore, only the third explanation of the disciples' belief in the Resurrection: they did see Him alive after He had been dead and buried. Plainly it was no phantom, or ghost, or imaginary appearance which could personate their lost Master and rouse them from the despondency,

and inaction, and timidity of disappointed hopes to the calmest consistency of plan and the firmest courage. It was no vision created by their own imagination which could at once and for ever alter the idea of the Messiah which the disciples, in common with all their countrymen, held. It was no phantom who could imitate the impressive individuality of the Lord and continue His identity into new scenes, who could inspire the disciples with unity of purpose, and who could lead them forward to the most splendid victories men have ever won. No; nothing will explain the faith of the Apostles and of the rest but the fact of their really seeing the Lord after His death clothed in power. The men who said they had seen Him were men of probity; they were men who showed themselves worthy of being witnesses to so great an event; men animated by no paltry spirit of vainglory, but by seriousness, even sublimity, of mind; men whose lives and conduct require an explanation, and which are explained by their having been brought in contact with the spiritual world in this surprising and solemnizing manner.

The testimony of Paul himself is in some respects more convincing than that of those who saw the Lord immediately after the Resurrection. Certainly he was neither anxious to believe nor likely to be ignorant of the facts. He had devoted himself to the extermination of the new faith; all his hopes as a Pharisee and as a Jew were banded against it. He had the best means of ascertaining the truth, living on terms of friendship with the leading men in Jerusalem. It is simply inconceivable that he should have abandoned all his prospects and entered on a wholly different life without carefully investigating the chief fact which influenced him in making this change. It is of course said that Paul was a nervous, excitable creature, probably epileptic, and certainly liable to see visions. It is insinuated that his conversion was due to the combined influence of epilepsy and a thunderstorm—of all the unlucky suggestions of modern scepticism perhaps the unluckiest. Were it true, one could only wish epilepsy commoner than it is. We have to account not only for Paul's conversion, but for his abiding by the convictions at first produced in him. It is out of the question to suppose that he did not spend much of the immediately succeeding years in examining the grounds of the Christian faith and in questioning himself as to his own belief. Paul was no doubt eager and enthusiastic, but no man was ever better fitted to move among the realities of life or to ascertain what these realities are. Englishmen regard Paley as one of the best representatives of the combined acuteness and sense, penetration and solidity of judgment, by which English judges are supposed to be characterized; and Paley says of Paul, "His letters furnish evidence of the soundness and sobriety of his judgment, and his morality is everywhere calm, pure, and rational; adapted to the condition, the activity, and the business of social life and of its various relations; free from the overscrupulousness and austerities of superstition, and from what was more perhaps to be apprehended, the abstractions of quietism and the soarings and extravagances of fanaticism." But really no person of ordinary capacity needs certificates of Paul's sanity. No saner or more commanding intellect ever headed a complex and difficult movement. There is no one of that generation whose testimony to the Resurrection is more worth having, and we have it in the most emphatic form of a life based upon it.

No one, so far as I know, who has taken a serious interest in the evidence adduced for this event, has denied that it would be quite sufficient to authenticate any ordinary historical event. In point of fact, the majority of the events of past history are accepted on much slenderer evidence than that which we have for the Resurrection. The evidence we have for it is of precisely the same kind as that on which we accept ordinary events; it is the testimony of the persons concerned, the simple statements of eyewitnesses and of those who were acquainted with eyewitnesses. It is not a prophetical, or poetical, or symbolical, or supernatural statement, but the plain and unvarnished testimony of ordinary men. The accounts vary in many particulars, but as to the central fact that the Lord rose and was seen over and over again there is no variation, and such variations as there are are merely such as exist in all similar accounts by different individuals of one and the same event. In short, the evidence can be refused only on the ground that no evidence, however strong, could prove such an incredible event. It is admitted that the evidence would be accepted in any other case, but this reported event is in itself incredible. The idea of any interference with the physical laws which rule the world, no matter how important an end is to be served by the interference, is rejected as out of the question. This seems to me quite an illogical method of dealing with the subject. The supernatural is rejected as a preliminary, so as to bar any consideration of the most appropriate evidences of the supernatural. Before looking at that which, if not the most effective proof of the supernatural, is at least among those arguments which chiefly deserve attention, the mind is made up to reject all evidence of the supernatural.

The first business of scientific men is to look at facts. Many facts which at first sight seemed to contradict previously ascertained laws were ultimately found to indicate the presence of a higher law. Why are men of science so terrified by the word "miracle"? This event may, like the visit of a comet, have occurred only once in the world's history; but it need not on that account be irreducible to law or to reason. The resurrection of Christ is unique, because He is unique. Find another Person bearing the same relation to the race and living the same life, and you will find a similar resurrection. To say that it is unusual or unprecedented is to say nothing at all to the purpose.

Besides, those who reject the resurrection of Christ as impossible are compelled to accept an equally astounding moral miracle—the miracle, I mean, that those who had the best means of ascertaining the truth and every possible inducement to ascertain it should all have been deceived, and that this deception should have been the most fruitful source of good, not only to them, but to the whole world.

We are brought then to the conclusion that the disciples believed in the resurrection of Christ because it had actually taken place. No other account of their belief has ever been given which commends itself to the common understanding which accepts what appeals to it. No account of the belief has been given which is at all likely to gain currency or which is more credible than that which it seeks to supplant. The belief in the Resurrection which so suddenly and effectively possessed the first disciples remains unexplained by any other supposition than the simple one that the Lord did rise again.

CONSEQUENCES OF DENYING RESURRECTION

"Now if Christ be preached that He rose from the dead, how say some among you that there is no resurrection of the dead? But if there be no resurrection of the dead, then is Christ not risen: and if Christ be not risen, then is our preaching vain, and your faith is also vain. Yea, and we are found false witnesses of God; because we have testified of God that He raised up Christ: whom He raised not up, if so be that the dead rise not. For if the dead rise not, then is not Christ raised: and if Christ be not raised, your faith is vain; ye are yet in your sins. Then they also which are fallen asleep in Christ are perished. If in this life only we have hope in Christ, we are of all men most miserable. But now is Christ risen from the dead, and become the firstfruits of them that slept. For since by man came death, by man came also the resurrection of the dead. For as in Adam all die, even so in Christ shall all be made alive. But every man in his own order: Christ the firstfruits; afterward they that are Christ's at His coming. Then cometh the end, when He shall have delivered up the kingdom to God, even the Father; when He shall have put down all rule and all authority and power. For He must reign, till He hath put all enemies under His feet. The last enemy that shall be destroyed is death. For He hath put all things under His feet. But when He saith, all things are put under Him, it is manifest that He is excepted, which did put all things under Him. And when all things shall be subdued unto Him, then shall the Son also Himself be subject unto Him that put all things under Him, that God may be all in all. Else what shall they do which are baptized for the dead, if the dead rise not at all? why are they then baptized for the dead? And why stand we in jeopardy every hour? I protest by your rejoicing which I have in Christ Jesus our Lord, I die daily. If after the manner of men I have fought with beasts at Ephesus, what advantageth it me, if the dead rise not? let us eat and drink; for to-morrow we die. Be not deceived: evil communications corrupt good manners. Awake to righteousness, and sin not; for some have not the knowledge of God: I speak this to your shame." — 1 Cor. xv. 12-34.

XXIII
CONSEQUENCES OF DENYING RESURRECTION

In endeavouring to restore among the Corinthians the belief in the resurrection of the body, Paul shows the fundamental place occupied in the Christian creed by the resurrection of Christ, and what attestation His resurrection had received. He further exhibits certain consequences which flow from denial of the resurrection. These consequences are (1) that if there is no resurrection of the body, then Christ is not risen, and that, therefore, (2) the Apostles who witnessed to that resurrection are false witnesses; (3) that those who had already died believing in Christ, had perished, and that our hope in Christ must be confined to this life; (4) that baptism for the dead is a vain folly if the dead rise not. To the statement and discussion of these consequences Paul devotes a large part of this chapter, from verse 12 to verse 34. Let us take the least important consequence first.

1. "If the dead rise not at all, what shall they do who are baptized for the dead?" (ver. 29)—an enquiry of which the Corinthians no doubt felt the full force, but which is rather lost upon us because we do not know what it means. Some have thought that as baptism is sometimes used in Scripture as equivalent to immersion in a sea of troubles, Paul means to ask, "What shall they do, what hope have they, who are plunged in grief for the friends they have lost?" Some think it refers to those who have been baptized with Christ's baptism, that is to say, have suffered martyrdom and so entered into the Church of the dead. Others again think, that to be baptized "for the dead" means no more than ordinary baptism, in which the believer looks forward to the resurrection from the dead. The primitive form of baptism brought death and the resurrection vividly before the believer's mind, and confirmed his hope in the resurrection, which hope was vain if there is no resurrection.

The plain meaning of the words, however, seems to point to a vicarious baptism, in which a living friend received baptism as a proxy for a person who had died without baptism. Of such a custom there is historical trace. Even before the Christian era, among the Jews when a man died in a state of ceremonial defilement it was customary for a friend of the deceased to perform in his stead the washings and other rites which the dead man would have performed had he recovered. A similar practice prevailed to some small extent among the primitive Christians, although it was never admitted as a valid rite by the Church Catholic. Then, as now, it sometimes happened that on the approach of death the thoughts of unbelieving persons were strongly turned towards the Christian faith, but before baptism could be administered death cut down the intending Christian. Baptism was generally postponed until youth or even middle life was passed, in order that a large number of sins might be washed away in baptism, or that fewer might stain the soul after it. But naturally miscalculations sometimes occurred, and sudden death anticipated a long-delayed baptism. In such cases the friends of the deceased derived consolation from vicarious baptism. Some one who was persuaded of the faith of the departed answered for him and was baptized in his stead.

If Paul meant to say, On the supposition that death ends all, what is the use of any one being baptized as proxy for a dead friend? he could not have used words more expressive of his meaning than when he says, "If the dead rise not at all, why are they then baptized for the dead?" The only difficulty is, that Paul might thus seem to draw an argument for a fundamental doctrine of Christianity from a foolish and unjustifiable practice. Is it possible that a man of such sagacity can have sanctioned or countenanced so absurd a superstition? But his alluding to this custom in the way he here does, scarcely implies that he approved of it. He rather differentiates himself from those who practised the rite. "What shall *they* do who are baptized for the dead?"—referring, probably, to some of the Corinthians themselves. In any case, the point of the argument is obvious. To be baptized for those who had died without baptism, and whose future was supposed thereby to be jeopardized, had at least a show of friendliness and reason; to be baptized for those who had already passed out of existence was of course, on the face of it, absurd.

2. The second consequence which flows from the denial of the resurrection is, that Paul's own life is a mistake. "Why stand we in jeopardy every hour? What advantageth it me to risk death daily, and to suffer daily, if the dead rise not?" If there is no resurrection, he says, my whole life is a folly. No day passes but I am in danger of death at the hands either of an infuriated mob or a mistaken magistrate. I am in constant jeopardy, in perils by land and sea, in perils of robbers, in nakedness, in fasting; all these dangers I gladly encounter because I believe in the resurrection. But "if in this life only we have hope in Christ, then we are of all men most miserable." We lose both this life and that which we thought was to come.

Paul's meaning is plain. By the hope of a life beyond, he had been induced to undergo the greatest privations in this life. He had been exposed to countless dangers and indignities. Although a Roman citizen, he had been cast into the arena to contend with wild beasts: there was no risk he had not run, no hardship he had not endured. But in all he was sustained by the assurance that there remained for him a rest and an inheritance in a future life. Remove this assurance and you remove the assumption on which his conduct is wholly built. If there is no future life either to win or to lose, then the Epicurean motto may take the place of Christ's promises, "Let us eat and drink, for to-morrow we die."

It may indeed be said that even if there be no life to come, this life is best spent in the service of man, however full of hazard and hardship that service be. That is quite true; and had Paul believed this life was all, he might still have chosen to spend it, not on sensual indulgence, but in striving to win men to something better. But in that case there would have been no deception and no disappointment. In point of fact, however, Paul believed in a life to come, and it was because he believed in that life he gave himself to the work of winning men to Christ regardless of his own pains and losses. And what he says is that if he is mistaken, then all these pains and losses have been gratuitous, and that his whole life has proceeded on a mistake. The life to which he sought to win and for which he sought to prepare men does not exist.

Besides, it must be acknowledged that the mass of men do sink to a merely sensual or earthly life if the hope of immortality is removed, and that Paul did not require to be very guarded in his statement of this truth. In fact, the words "Let us eat and drink, for to-morrow we die" were taken from the history of his own nation. When Jerusalem was besieged by the Babylonians and no escape seemed possible, the people gave themselves up to recklessness and despair and sensual indulgence, saying, "Let us eat and drink, for to-morrow we die." Similar instances of the recklessness produced by the near approach of death may very readily be culled from the history of shipwrecks, of pestilences, and of besieged cities. In the old Jewish book, the Book of Wisdom, it finds a very beautiful expression, the following words being put into the mouth of those who knew not that man is immortal: "Our life is short and tedious, and in the death of man is no remedy; neither was any man ever known to return from the grave: for we are all born at an adventure, and shall be afterwards as though we had never been; for the breath of our nostrils is as smoke, and a little spark is the moving of our heart, which, being extinguished, our bodies will be burnt to ashes, and our spirit vanish as the soft air: and our name shall be forgotten in time, and no man shall hold our works in remembrance, and our life shall pass away like the trace of a cloud, and shall be dispersed as a mist that is driven away with the beams of the sun, and overcome with the heat thereof.... Come on therefore, let us enjoy the good things that are present, and let us speedily use the creatures like as in youth, Let us fill ourselves with costly wine and ointments, and let no flower of the spring pass by us; let us crown ourselves with rosebuds before they be withered; let none of us go without his share of voluptuousness; let us leave tokens of our joyfulness in every place, for this is our portion and our lot is this."

It is obvious therefore that this is the conclusion which the mass of mankind draw from a disbelief in immortality. Convince men that this life is all, that death is final extinction, and they will eagerly drain this life of all the pleasure it can yield. We may say that there are some men to whom virtue is the greatest pleasure: we may say that to all the denial of appetite and self-indulgence is a more genuine pleasure than the gratification of it: we may say that virtue is its own reward, and that irrespective of the future it is right to live now spiritually and not sensually, for God and not for self: we may say that the judgments of conscience are pronounced without any regard to future consequences, and that the highest and best life for man is a life in conformity to conscience and in fellowship with God, whether such life is to be long or short, temporal or eternal. And this is true, but how are we to get men to accept it? Teach men to believe in a future life and you strengthen every moral sentiment and every Godward aspiration by revealing the true dignity of human nature. Make men feel that they are immortal beings, that this life, so far from being all, is the mere entrance and first step to existence; make men feel that there is open to them an endless moral progress, and you give them some encouragement to lay the foundations of this progress in a self-denying and virtuous life in this world. Take away this belief, encourage men to think of themselves as worthless little creatures that come into being for a few years and are blotted out again for ever, and you destroy one mainspring of right action in men. It is not that men do noble deeds for the sake of reward: the hope of reward is scarcely a perceptible influence in the best of men, or indeed in any men; but in all men trained as we are, there is an indefinite consciousness that, being immortal creatures, we are made for higher ends than those of this life, and have prospects of enjoyments which should make us independent of the grosser pleasures of the present bodily condition.

Apparently the Corinthians themselves had argued that morality was quite independent of a belief in immortality. For Paul goes on: "Be not deceived:" you cannot, however much you may think so, you *cannot* hear such theories without having your moral convictions undermined and your tone lowered. This he conveys to them in a common quotation from a heathen poet—"Evil communications corrupt good manners;" that is to say, false opinions have a natural tendency to produce unsatisfactory and immoral conduct. To keep company with those whose conversation is frivolous or cynical, or charged with dangerous or false views of things, has a natural tendency to lead us to a style of conduct we should not otherwise have fallen into. Men do not always recognise this; they need the warning, "Be not deceived." The beginnings of conduct are so hidden from our observation, our lives are formed by influences so imperceptible, what we hear sinks so insidiously into the mind and mingles so insensibly with our motives, that we can never say *what* we have heard without moral contamination. No doubt it is possible to hold the most erroneous opinions and yet to keep the life pure; but they are strong and guileless spirits who can preserve a high moral tone while they have lost faith in those truths which mainly nourish the moral nature of the mass of men. And many have found to their surprise and grief that opinions which they fancied they might very well hold and yet live a high and holy life, have somehow sapped their moral defences against temptation and paved the way for shameful falls. We cannot always prevent doubts, even about the most fundamental truths, from entering our minds, but we can always refuse to welcome such doubts, or to be proud of them; we can always be resolved to treat sacred things in a reverent and not in a flippant spirit, and we can always aim at least at an honest and eager seeking for the truth.

3. But the most serious consequence which results if there be no resurrection of the dead, is that in that case Christ is not risen. "If there be no resurrection of the dead, then is Christ not risen." For Paul refused to consider the resurrection of Christ as a miracle in the sense of its being exceptional and aside from the usual experience of man. On the contrary, he accepts it as the type to which every man is to be conformed. Precedent in time, exceptional possibly in some of its accidental accompaniments, the resurrection of Christ may be, but nevertheless as truly in the line of human development as birth, and growth, and death. Christ being man must submit to the conditions and experience of men in all essentials, in all that characterises man as human. And, therefore, if resurrection be not a normal human experience, Christ has not risen. The time at which resurrection takes place, and the interval elapsing between death and resurrection, Paul makes nothing of. A child may live but three days, but it is not on that account any the less human than if he had lived his threescore years and ten. Similarly the fact of Christ's resurrection identifies Him with the human race, while the shortness of the interval elapsing between death and resurrection does not separate Him from man, for in point of fact the interval will be less in the case of many.

Both here and elsewhere Paul looks upon Christ as the representative man, the one in whom we can see the ideal of manhood. If any of our own friends should veritably die, and after death should appear to us alive, and should prove his identity by remaining with us for a time, by showing an interest in the very things which had previously occupied his thought, and by taking practical steps to secure the fulfilment of his purposes, a strong probability that we too should live through death would inevitably be impressed on our mind. But when Christ rises from the dead this probability becomes a certainty, because He is the type of humanity, the representative person. As Paul here says, "He is the firstfruits of them that sleep." His resurrection is the sample and pledge of ours. When the farmer pulls the first ripe ears of wheat and carries them home, it is not for their own sake he values them, but because they are a specimen and sample of the whole crop; and when God raised Christ from the dead, the glory of the event consisted in its being a pledge and specimen of the triumph of mankind over death. "If we believe that Jesus died and rose again, even so them also which sleep in Jesus will God bring with Him."

And yet while Paul distinctly holds that resurrection is a normal human experience, he also implies that but for the interposition of Christ that experience might have been lost to men. It is in Christ that men are made alive after and through death. As Adam is the source of physical life that ends in death, so Christ is the source of spiritual life that never dies. "By man came death, by man came also the resurrection of the dead." Adam's severance from God and preference of what was physical, brought man under the powers of the physical world: Christ by perfect adhesion to God, and constant conquest of all physical allurements, won life eternal for Himself and for those who have His Spirit. As a man of genius and wisdom will by his occupation of a throne enlarge men's ideas of what a king is, and bring many blessings to his subjects, so Christ by living a human life enlarged it to its utmost dimensions, compelling it to express His ideas of life, and winning for those who follow Him entrance into a larger and higher condition. Resurrection is here represented, not as an experience which men would have enjoyed had Christ never appeared on earth, nor as an experience opened to men by God's sovereign goodwill, but as an experience in some way brought by Christ within human reach. "By man came death, by man came also the resurrection of the dead. For as in Adam all die, even so in Christ shall all be made alive." That is to say, all who are by physical derivation truly united to Adam, incur the death which by sinning he introduced into human experience; and similarly all who by spiritual affinity are in Christ, enjoy the new life which triumphs over death, and which He won. Adam was not the only man who died, but the firstfruits of a rich harvest; and so, Christ is not alone in resurrection, but is become the firstfruits of them that sleep. According to Paul's theology, the conduct of a man, the sin of Adam, carried in it disastrous consequences to all connected with him: but equally fruitful in consequences was the human life, death, and resurrection of Christ. The death of Adam was the first stroke of that funeral knell that has ceaselessly sounded through all generations: but the resurrection of Christ was equally the pledge and earnest that the same experience would be enjoyed by all "that are Christ's."

Paul is carried on from the thought of the resurrection of "them that are Christ's," to the thought of the consummation of all things which this great event introduces and signalizes. This exhibition of the triumph over death is the signal that all other enemies are now defeated. "The last enemy that shall be destroyed is death;" and this being destroyed, all Christ's followers being now gathered in and having entered on their eternal condition, the work of Christ so far as this world is concerned is over. Having reunited men to God, His work is done. The provisional government administered by Him having accomplished its work of bringing men into perfect harmony with the Supreme Will, it gives place to the immediate and direct government of God. What is implied in this it is impossible to say. A condition in which sin shall have no place and in which there shall be no need of means of reconciliation, a condition in which the work of Christ shall be no longer needed and in which God shall be all in all, pervading with His presence every soul and as welcome and natural as the air or the sunlight,—that is a condition not easy to be imagined. Neither can we readily imagine what Christ Himself shall be and do when the term of His mediatorial administration is finished and God is all in all.

One idea conspicuous in this brief and pregnant passage is that Christ came to subdue all the enemies of mankind, and that He will continue His work until His purpose is accomplished. He alone has taken a perfectly comprehensive view of the obstacles to human happiness and progress, and He has set Himself to remove these. He alone has penetrated to the root of all human evil and misery, and has given Himself to the task of emancipating men from all evil, of restoring men to their true life, and of abolishing for ever the miseries which have so largely characterised man's history. Slowly indeed, and unseen, does His work proceed; slowly, because the work is for eternity, and because only gradually can moral and spiritual evils be removed. "It is by no breath, turn of eye, wave of hand, salvation joins issue with death," but by actual and sustained moral conflict, by real sacrifice and persistent choice of good, by long trial and development of individual character, by the slow growth of nations and the interaction of social and religious influences, by the leavening of all that is human with the spirit of Christ, that is, with self-devotement in practical life to the good of men. All this is too great and too real to be other than slow. The tide of moral progress in the world has often seemed to turn. Even now, when the leaven has been working for so long, how doubtful often seems the issue, how concerned even Christian people are about the merest superficialities and how little labouring to put down in Christ's name the common enemies. Can any one who looks at things as they are find it easy to believe in the final extinction of evil? Whither tend the prevalent vices, the empty-souled love of pleasure and demand for excitement, the unyielding, brazen-faced selfishness of the principles of business if not of the men who engage in it, the diligent propagation of error, the oppression of the rich and the greed and sensuality that poverty induces? One needs to be reminded that these things are the enemies, not only of good men, but of Christ, and that by God's will He is to defeat them. One needs to be reminded also that to see this victory accomplished and to have had no share in it will be the sorest humiliation and the most painful reflection to every generous mind. However slight be our power, let us strike such blow as we can at the common enemies which must be destroyed ere the great consummation is reached.

THE SPIRITUAL BODY

"But some man will say, How are the dead raised up? and with what body do they come? Thou fool, that which thou sowest is not quickened, except it die: and that which thou sowest, thou sowest not that body that shall be, but bare grain, it may chance of wheat, or of some other grain: but God giveth it a body as it hath pleased Him, and to every seed his own body. All flesh is not the same flesh: but there is one kind of flesh of men, another flesh of beasts, another of fishes, and another of birds. There are also celestial bodies, and bodies terrestrial: but the glory of the celestial is one, and the glory of the terrestrial is another. There is one glory of the sun, and another glory of the moon, and another glory of the stars: for one star differeth from another star in glory. So also is the resurrection of the dead. It is sown in corruption; it is raised in incorruption: it is sown in dishonour; it is raised in glory; it is sown in weakness; it is raised in power: it is sown a natural body; it is raised a spiritual body. There is a natural body, and there is a spiritual body. And so it is written, The first man Adam was made a living soul; the last Adam was made a quickening spirit. Howbeit that was not first which is spiritual, but that which is natural; and afterward that which is spiritual. The first man is of the earth, earthy: the second man is the Lord from heaven. As is the earthy, such are they also that are earthy: and as is the heavenly, such are they also that are heavenly. And as we have borne the image of the earthy, we shall also bear the image of the heavenly. Now this I say, brethren, that flesh and blood cannot inherit the kingdom of God; neither doth corruption inherit incorruption. Behold, I show you a mystery; We shall not all sleep, but we shall all be changed, in a moment, in the twinkling of an eye, at the last trump: for the trumpet shall sound, and the dead shall be raised incorruptible, and we shall be changed. For this corruptible must put on incorruption, and this mortal must put on immortality. So when this corruptible shall have put on incorruption, and this mortal shall have put on immortality, then shall be brought to pass the saying that is written, Death is swallowed up in victory. O death, where is thy sting? O grave, where is thy victory? The sting of death is sin; and the strength of sin is the law. But thanks be to God, which giveth us the victory through our Lord Jesus Christ. Therefore, my beloved brethren, be ye steadfast, unmovable, always abounding in the work of the Lord, forasmuch as ye know that your labour is not in vain in the Lord."—1 Cor. xv. 35-58.

XXIV
THE SPIRITUAL BODY

The proofs of the Resurrection which Paul has adduced are satisfactory. So long as they are clearly before the mind, we find it possible to believe in that great experience which will finally give us possession of the life to come. But after all proof rises doubt irrepressible, owing to the difficulty of understanding the process through which the body passes and the nature of the body that is to be. "Some man will say, How are the dead raised up? and with what body do they come?" Not always in an unbelieving or scoffing spirit, often in mere perplexity and justifiable inquisitiveness, will men ask these questions.

Paul answers both inquiries by referring to analogies in the natural world. Only by death, he says, does seed reach its designed development; and the body or form in which seed rises is very different in appearance from that in which it is sown. These analogies have their place and their use in removing objections and difficulties. They are not intended or supposed to establish the fact of the Resurrection, but only to remove difficulties as to its mode. By analogy you can show that a certain process or result is not impossible, you may even create a presumption in its favour, but you cannot establish it as an actuality. Analogy is a powerful instrument for removing objections, but utterly weak for establishing positive truth. Seed lives again after burial, but it does not follow that our bodies will do so. Seed when it rots away beneath the soil gives birth to a better thing than that which was sown, but this is no proof that the same result will follow when our bodies pass through a similar treatment. But if a man says, as Paul here supposes he may, "Such a thing as this resurrection you speak of is an unnatural, unheard-of, and impossible thing," the best reply is to point him to some analogous process in nature, in which this apparent impossibility or something very similar is actually brought to pass.

Even outside the circle of Christian thought these analogies in nature have always been felt to remove some of the presumptions against the Resurrection and to make room for listening to evidence in its favour. The transformation of the seed into the plant and the development of the seed to a fuller life through apparent extinction, the transformation of the grub into the brilliant and powerful dragon-fly through a process which terminates the life of the grub—these and other natural facts show that one life may be continued through various phases, and that the termination of one form of life does not always mean the termination of all life in a creature. We need not, these analogies tell us, at once conclude that death ends all, for in some visible instances death is only a birth to a higher and freer life. Neither need we point to the dissolution of the natural body and conclude that no more perfect body can be connected with such a process, because in many cases we see a more efficient body disengaged from the original and dissolving body. Thus far the analogies carry us. It is doubtful whether they should be pushed further, although they might seem to indicate that the new body is not to be a new creation, but is to be produced by virtue of what is already in existence. The new body is not to be irrespective of what has gone before, but is to be the natural result of causes already working. What these causes are, or how the spirit is to impress its character on the body, we do not know.

It is not impossible, then, nor even quite improbable, that the death of our present body may set free a new and far more perfectly equipped body. The fact that we cannot conceive the nature of this body need not trouble us. Who without previous observation could imagine what would spring from an acorn or a seed of wheat? To each God gives its own body. We cannot imagine what our future body, subject to no waste or decay, can be; but we need not on that account reject as childish all expectation that such a body shall exist. "All flesh is not the same flesh." The kind of flesh you now wear may be unfit for everlasting life, but there may await you as suitable and congenial a body as your present familiar tenement. Consider the inexhaustible fertility of God, the endless varieties already existing in nature. The bird has a body which fits it for life in the air; the fish lives with comfort in its own element. And the variety already existing does not exhaust God's resources. We read at present but one chapter in the history of life, and what future chapters are to unfold who can imagine? A fertile and inventive man knows no bound to his progress; will God stand still? Are we not but at the beginning of His works? May we not reasonably suppose that a truly infinite expansion and development await God's works? Is it not entirely unreasonable to suppose that what we see and know is the measure of God's resources?

Paul does not attempt to describe the future body, but contents himself with pointing out one or two of its characteristics by which it is distinguished from the body we now wear. "It is sown in corruption; it is raised in incorruption: it is sown in dishonour; it is raised in glory: it is sown in weakness; it is raised in power: it is sown a natural body; it is raised a spiritual body." In this body there is decay, humiliation, weakness, a life that is merely temporary; in the body that is to be decay gives place to incorruptibility, humiliation to glory, weakness to power, animal life to spiritual.

The present body is subject to decay. Not only is it easily injured by accident and often rendered permanently useless, but it is so constituted that all activity wastes it; and this waste needs constant repair. That we may constantly seek this repair, we are endowed with strong appetites, which sometimes overbear everything else in us and both defeat their own ends and hinder the growth of the spirit. The organs by which the waste is repaired themselves wear out, so that by no care or nourishment can a man make out to live as long as a tree. But the very decay of this body makes way for one in which there shall be no waste, no need of physical nourishment, and therefore no need of strong and overbearing physical appetites. Instead of impeding the spirit by clamouring to have its wants attended to, it will be the spirit's instrument. A great part of the temptations of this present life arise from the conditions in which we necessarily exist as dependent for our comfort in great measure on the body. And one can scarcely conceive the feeling of emancipation and superiority which will possess those who have no anxiety about a livelihood, no fear of death, no distraction of appetite.

The present body is for similar reasons characterized by "weakness." We cannot be where we would, nor do what we would. A man may work his twelve hours, but he must then acknowledge he has a body which needs rest and sleep. Many persons are disqualified by bodily weakness from certain forms of usefulness and enjoyment. Many persons also, though able to do a certain amount of work, do it with labour; their vitality is habitually low, and they never have the full use of their powers, but need continually to be on their guard, and go through life burdened with a lassitude and discomfort more difficult to bear than passing attacks of pain. In contradistinction to this and to every form of weakness, the resurrection body will be full of power, able to accomplish the behests of the will, and fit for all that is required of it.

But the most comprehensive contrast between the two bodies is expressed in the words, "It is sown a natural body; it is raised a spiritual body." A natural body is that which is animated by a human life and is fitted for this world. "The first man Adam was made a living soul," or, as we should more naturally say, an animal. He was made with a capacity for living; and because he was to live upon earth, he had a body in which this life or soul was lodged. The natural body is the body we receive at birth, and which is suited for its own requirements of maintaining itself in life in this world into which we are born. The soul, or animal life, of man is higher than that of the other animals, it has richer endowments and capacities, but it is also in many respects similar. Many men are quite content with the merely animal life which this world upholds and furnishes. They find enough to satisfy them in its pleasures, its work, its affairs, its friendships; and for all these the natural body is sufficient. The thoughtful man cannot indeed but look forward and ask himself what is to become of this body. If he turns to Scripture for light, he will probably be struck with the fact that it sheds no light whatever on the future of the natural body. Those who are in Christ enter into possession of a spiritual body, but there is no hint of any more perfect body being prepared for those who are not in Christ.

The spiritual body, which is reserved for spiritual men, is a body in which the upholding life is spiritual. The natural life of man both forms to a human shape and upholds the natural body; the spiritual body is similarly maintained by what is spiritual in man. It is the soul, or natural life, of man which gives the body its appetites and maintains it in efficiency; remove this soul, and the body is mere dead matter. In like manner it is the spirit which maintains the spiritual body; and by the spirit is meant that in man which can delight in God and in goodness. The body we now have is miserable and useless or happy and serviceable in proportion to its animal vitality, in proportion to its power to assimilate to itself the nutriment this physical world supplies. The spiritual body will be healthy or sickly in proportion to the spiritual vitality that animates it; that is to say, in proportion to the power of the individual spirit to delight in God and find its life in Him and in what He lives for.

We have already seen that Paul refuses to consider the resurrection of Christ as miraculous in the sense of its being unique or abnormal; on the contrary, he considers resurrection to be an essential step in normal human development, and therefore experienced by Christ. And now he enunciates the great principle or law which governs not only this fact of resurrection, but the whole evolution of God's works: "first that which is natural, afterward that which is spiritual." It is this law which we see ruling the history of creation and the history of man. The spiritual is the culminating point towards which all the processes of nature tend. The gradual development of what is spiritual, of will, of love, of moral excellence—this, so far as man can see, is the end towards which all nature constantly and steadily is working.

Sometimes, however, it occurs to one to question the law "first that which is natural, afterward that which is spiritual." If the present body hinders rather than helps the growth of the spirit, if at last all Christians are to have a spiritual body, why might we not have had this body to begin with? What need of this mysterious process of passing from life to life and from body to body? If it is true that we are here only for a few years and in the future life for ever, why should we be here at all? Why might we not at birth have been ushered into our eternal state? The answer is obvious. We are not at once introduced into our eternal condition because we are moral creatures, free to choose for ourselves, and who cannot enter an eternal state save by choice of our own: first that which is natural, first that which is animal, first a life in which we have abundant opportunity to test what appears good and are free to make our choice; then that which is spiritual, because the spiritual can only be a thing of choice, a thing of the will. There is no spiritual life or spiritual birth save by the will. Men can become spiritual only by choosing to be so. Involuntary, compulsory, necessitated, natural spirituality is, so far as man is concerned, a contradiction in terms.

Human nature is a thing of immense possibilities and range. On the one side it is akin to the lower animals, to the physical world and all that is in it, high and low; on the other side it is akin to the highest of all spiritual existences, even to God Himself. At present we are in a world admirably adapted for our probation and discipline, a world in which, in point of fact, every man does attach himself to the lower or to the higher, to the present or to the eternal, to the natural or to the spiritual. And although the results of this may not be apparent in average cases, yet in extreme cases the results of human choice are obtrusively apparent. Let a man give himself unrestrainedly and exclusively to animal life in its grosser forms, and the body itself soon begins to suffer. You can see the process of physical deterioration going on, deepening in misery, until death comes. But what follows death? Can one promise himself or another a future body which shall be exempt from the pains which unrepented sin has introduced? Are those who have by their vice committed a slow suicide to be clothed hereafter in an incorruptible and efficient body? It seems wholly contrary to reason to suppose so. And how can their probation be continued if the very circumstance which makes this life so thorough a probation to us all— the circumstance of our being clothed with a body—is absent? The truth is, there is no subject on which more darkness hangs or on which Scripture preserves so ominous a silence as the future of the body of those who in this life have not chosen God and things spiritual as their life.

On the other hand, if we consider instances in which the spiritual life has been resolutely and unreservedly chosen, we see anticipations here also of the future destiny of those who have so chosen. They may be crushed by diseases as painful and as fatal as the most flagrant of sinners endure, but these diseases frequently have the result only of making the true spiritual life shine more brightly. In extreme cases, you would almost say, the transmutation of the tortured and worn body into a glorified body is begun. The spirit seems dominant; and as you stand by and watch, you begin to feel that death has no relation to the emotions, and hopes, and intercourse you detect in that spirit. These, which seem, and are, the very life of the spirit, cannot be thought of as terminated by a merely physical change. They do not spring from, nor do they depend upon, what is physical; and it is reasonable to suppose that they will not be destroyed by it. Looking at Christ Himself and allowing due impression to be made upon us by His concernment about the highest, and best, and most lasting things, by His recognition of God and harmony with Him, by His living in God, and by His superiority to earthly considerations, we cannot but feel it to be most unlikely that such a spirit should be extinguished by bodily death.

This spiritual body we receive through the intervention of Christ. As from the first man we receive animal life, from the second we receive spiritual life. "The first man Adam was made a living soul, the last Adam a quickening spirit. And as we have borne the image of the earthy, we shall also bear the image of the heavenly." The image of the first man we have by our natural and physical derivation from him, the image of the second by spiritual derivation; that is to say, by our choosing Christ as our ideal and by our allowing His Spirit to form us. This Spirit is life-giving; this Spirit is indeed God, communicating to us a life which is at once holy and eternal.

The mode of Christ's intervention is more fully described in the words, "The sting of death is sin; and the strength of sin is the law. But thanks be to God, which giveth us the victory through our Lord Jesus Christ." Everywhere Paul teaches that it was sin which brought death upon man; that man would have broken through the law of death which reigns in the physical world had he not by sin brought himself under the power of things physical. And this poisonous fang was pressed in by the Law. The strength of sin is the Law. It is positive disobedience, the preference of known evil to known good, the violation of law whether written in the conscience or in spoken commandments, which gives sin its moral character. The choice of the evil in presence of the good — it is that which constitutes sin.

The words are no doubt susceptible of another meaning. They could be used by one who wished to say that sin is that which makes death painful, which adds terror of future judgment and gloomy forebodings to the natural pain of death. But it must be owned that this is not so much in keeping with Paul's usual way of looking at the connection between death and sin.

Christ's victory over death is thus explained by Godet: "Christ's victory over death has two aspects, the one relating to Himself, the other concerning men. He first of all conquered *sin* in relation to Himself by denying to it the right of existence in Him, condemning it to non-existence in His flesh, similar though it was to our sinful flesh (Rom. viii. 3); and thereby He disarmed *the Law* so far as it concerned Himself. His life being the Law in living realization, He had it for Him, and not against Him. This twofold personal victory was the foundation of His own resurrection. Thereafter He continued to act that this victory might extend to us. And first He freed us from the burden of condemnation which *the Law* laid on us, and whereby it was ever interposing between us and communion with God. He recognised in our name the right of God over the sinner; He consented to satisfy it to the utmost in His own person. Whoever appropriates this death as undergone in his room and stead and for himself, sees the door of reconciliation to God open before him, as if he had himself expiated all his sins. The separation established by the Law no longer exists; the Law is disarmed. By that very fact *sin* also is vanquished. Reconciled to God, the believer receives Christ's Spirit, who works in him an absolute breach of will with sin and complete devotion to God. The yoke of sin is at an end; the dominion of God is restored in the heart. The two foundations of the reign of death are thus destroyed. Let Christ appear, and this reign will crumble in the dust for ever."

It is then with joy and triumph Paul contemplates death. Naturally we shrink from and fear it. We know it only from one side: only from seeing it in the persons of other men, and not from our own experience. And what we see in others is necessarily only the darker side of death, the cessation of bodily life and of all intercourse with the warm and lively interests of the world. It is a condition exciting tears, and moaning, and grief in those that remain in life; and though these tears arise chiefly from our own sense of loss, yet insensibly we think of the condition of the dead as a state to be bewailed. We see the sowing in weakness, in dishonour, in corruption, as Paul says; and we do not see the glory, and strength, and incorruption of the spiritual body. The dead may be in bright regions and be living a keener life than ever; but of this we see nothing: and all we do see is sad, depressing, humiliating.

But to "faith's foreseeing eye" the other side of death becomes also apparent. The grave becomes the robing room for life eternal. Stripped of "this muddy vesture of decay," we are there to be clothed with a spiritual body. Death is enlisted in the service of Christ's people; and by destroying flesh and blood, it enables this mortal to put on immortality. The blow which threatens to crush and annihilate all life breaks but the shell and lets the imprisoned spirit free to a larger life. Death is swallowed up in victory, and itself ministers to the final triumph of man. Our instincts tell us that death is critical and has a determining power on our destinies. We cannot evade it; we may depreciate or neglect, but we cannot diminish, its importance. It has its place and its function, and it will operate in each one of us according to what it finds in us, destroying what is merely animal, emancipating what is truly spiritual. We cannot as yet stand on the further side of death, and look back on it, and recognise its kindly work in us; but we can understand Paul's burst of anticipated triumph, and with him we can forecast the joy of having passed all doubtful struggle and anxious foreboding, and of finally experiencing that all the evils of humanity have been overcome. With a triumph so complete in view, we can also listen to his exhortation, "Therefore, my beloved brethren, be ye steadfast, unmovable, always abounding in the work of the Lord, forasmuch as ye know that your labour is not in vain in the Lord."

But if we have any fit conception of the magnitude of the triumph, we shall also cherish some worthy idea of the reality of the conflict. Those who have felt the terror of death know that it can be counterbalanced only by something more than a surmise, a hope, a longing, only indeed by a fact as solid as itself. And if to them the resurrection of Christ approves itself as such a fact, and if they can listen to His voice saying, "Because I live, ye shall live also," they do feel themselves armed against the graver terrors of death, and cannot but look forward with some confident hope to a life into which the ills they have here experienced cannot follow them. But at the same time, and in proportion as the reality of the future life quickens hope within them, it must also reveal to them the reality of the conflict through which that life is reached. By no mere idle naming of the name of Christ or resultless faith in Him can men pass from what is natural to what is spiritual. We are summoned to believe in Christ, but for a purpose; and that purpose is that, believing in Him as the revelation of God to us, we may be able to choose Him as our pattern and live His life. It is only what is truly spiritual in ourselves that can put us in possession of a spiritual body. From Christ we can receive what is spiritual; and if our belief in Him prompts us to become like Him, then we may count upon sharing in His destiny.

This is the permanent incentive of the Christian life. This present experience of ours leads to a larger, more satisfying experience. Beyond our horizon there awaits us an endlessly enlarging world. Death, which seems to bound our view, is really but our real birth to a fuller, and eternal, and true life. "Therefore be ye steadfast, unmovable, always abounding in the work of the Lord." The promptings of conscience do not delude you; your instinctive hopes will not be put to shame; your faith is reasonable; there is a life beyond. And no effort you now put forth will prove vain; no prayer, no earnest desire, no struggle towards what is spiritual, will fail of its effect. All that is spiritual is destined to live; it belongs to the eternal world: and all that you do in the Spirit, all mastery of self, and the world, and the flesh, all devoted fellowship with God—all is giving you a surer place and a more abundant entrance into the spiritual world, for "your labour is not in vain in the Lord."

"Now concerning the collection for the saints, as I have given order to the Churches of Galatia, even so do ye. Upon the first day of the week let every one of you lay by him in store, as God hath prospered him, that there be no gatherings when I come. And when I come, whomsoever ye shall approve by your letters, them will I send to bring your liberality unto Jerusalem. And if it be meet that I go also, they shall go with me. Now I will come unto you, when I shall pass through Macedonia: for I do pass through Macedonia. And it may be that I will abide, yea, and winter with you, that ye may bring me on my journey whithersoever I go. For I will not see you now by the way; but I trust to tarry a while with you, if the Lord permit. But I will tarry at Ephesus until Pentecost. For a great door and effectual is opened unto me, and there are many adversaries. Now if Timotheus come, see that he may be with you without fear: for he worketh the work of the Lord, as I also do. Let no man therefore despise him: but conduct him forth in peace, that he may come unto me: for I look for him with the brethren. As touching our brother Apollos, I greatly desired him to come unto you with the brethren: but his will was not at all to come at this time; but he will come when he shall have convenient time. Watch ye, stand fast in the faith, quit you like men, be strong. Let all your things be done with charity. I beseech you, brethren, (ye know the house of Stephanas, that it is the first-fruits of Achaia, and that they have addicted themselves to the ministry of the saints,) that ye submit yourselves unto such, and to every one that helpeth with us, and laboureth. I am glad of the coming of Stephanas and Fortunatus and Achaicus: for that which was lacking on your part they have supplied. For they have refreshed my spirit and yours: therefore acknowledge ye them that are such. The Churches of Asia salute you. Aquila and Priscilla salute you much in the Lord, with the Church that is in their house. All the brethren greet you. Greet ye one another with an holy kiss. The salutation of me Paul with mine own hand. If any man love not the Lord Jesus Christ, let him be Anathema Maranatha. The grace of our Lord Jesus Christ be with you. My love be with you all in Christ Jesus, Amen."—1 Cor. xvi.

XXV
THE POOR

In closing his letter to the Corinthians, Paul, as usual, explains his own movements, and adds a number of miscellaneous directions and salutations. These for the most part relate to matters of merely temporary interest, and call for no comment. Interest of a more permanent kind unfortunately attaches to the collection for the poor Christians of Jerusalem which Paul invites the Corinthians to make. Several causes had contributed to this poverty; and, among others, it is not improbable that the persecution promoted by Paul himself had an important place. Many Christians were driven from their homes, and many more must have lost their means of earning a livelihood. But it is likely that Paul was anxious to relieve this poverty, not so much because it had been partly caused by himself as because he saw in it an opportunity for bringing more closely together the two great parties in the Church. In his Epistle to the Galatians Paul tells us that the three leaders of the Jewish Christian Church—James, Peter, and John—when they had assured themselves that this new Apostle was trustworthy, gave him the right hand of fellowship, on the understanding that he should minister to the Gentiles, "only," he adds—"only they would that we should remember the poor, the same which I also was forward to do." Accordingly we find him seeking to interest the Gentile Churches in their Jewish brethren, and of such importance did he consider the relief that was to be sent to Jerusalem that he himself felt it an honour to be the bearer of it. He saw that no doctrinal explanations were likely to be so fruitful in kindly feeling and true unity as this simple expression of brotherly kindness.

In our own day poverty has assumed a much more serious aspect. It is not the poverty which results from accident, nor even that which results from wrong-doing or indolence, which presses for consideration. Such poverty could easily be met by individual charity or national institutions. But the poverty we are now confronted with is a poverty which necessarily results from the principle of competition which is the mainspring of all trade and business. It is the poverty which results from the constant effort of every man to secure custom by offering a cheaper article, and to secure employment by selling his labour at a cheaper rate than his neighbour. So overstocked is the labour-market that the employer can name his own terms. Where he wants one man, a hundred offer their services; and he who can live most cheaply secures the place. So that necessarily wages are pressed down by competition to the very lowest figure; and wherever any trade is not strong enough to combine and resist this constant pressure, the results are appalling. No slaves were ever so hunger-bitten, no lives were ever more crushed under perpetual and hopeless toil, than are thousands of our fellow-countrymen and countrywomen in our own time. It is the fact that in all our large cities there are thousands of persons who by working sixteen hours a day earn only what suffices to maintain the most wretched existence. Every day hundreds of children are being born to a life of hopeless toil and misery, unrelieved by any of the comforts or joys of the well-to-do.

The most painful and alarming feature of this condition of things is, as every one knows, that it seems the inevitable result of the principles on which our entire social fabric is built. Every invention, every new method of facilitating business, every contrivance or improvement in machinery, makes life more difficult to the mass of men. The very advances made by civilised nations in the rapid production of needful articles increase the breach between rich and poor, throwing larger resources into the hands of the few, but making the lot of the many still darker and more poverty-stricken. Every year makes the darkness deeper, the distress more urgent. Here individual charity is unavailing. It is not the relief of one here or there that is needed; it is the alteration of a system of things which inevitably produces such results. Individual charity is here a mere mop in the face of the tide. What is wanted is not larger workhouses where the aged poor may be sheltered, but such a system as will enable the working man to provide for himself against old age. What is wanted is not that the charitable should eke out by voluntary contributions the earnings of the labouring classes, but that these earnings should be such as to amply cover all ordinary human wants. "Money given in aid of wages relieves the employer, not the employed; reduces wages, not misery." What is wanted is a social system which tends to bring within the reach of all the comforts and the joys of life which men legitimately desire, and which does not tend, as our present social system does, to overload a small number of men with more wealth than they need, or desire, or can use, while the millions are crushed with toil and pinched with semi-starvation. What the working classes at present demand is, not charity, but justice. They do not wish to seem to be indebted to others for support which they feel they have toiled for and earned. They require a social system, in which the honest toil of a lifetime shall be sufficient to secure the toiler and his family from the dangers and degradation of utter poverty.

That a change is desirable no one who has spent two thoughts on the subject can doubt. The only question is, What change is desirable and possible? Is there any organization or social system which could check the evils resulting from the present competitive system, and secure that every one who is willing to work should be furnished with remunerative employment? Socialists are quite convinced that the whole problem would be solved were private capital to be converted into co-operative or public capital. Socialism demands that society shall be the only capitalist, and that all private captains of industry and capital be abolished. No return is possible to the state of things in which every man worked by himself with his own hands and at his own risk, producing his one or two webs, tilling his one or two acres. It is recognised that far more and better products can be produced when manufactures are carried on in large factories. But on the socialistic principle these factories must be owned, not by private capitalists, but by the State, or at any rate by co-operative societies of some kind. This is the essence of the demand of Socialism: that "whereas industry is at present carried on by private capitalists served by wage-labour, it must in the future be conducted by associated or co-operating workmen jointly owning the means of production."

The difficulty in pronouncing judgment on such a demand arises from the fact that very few men indeed have sufficient imagination and sufficient knowledge of our complicated social system to be able to forecast the results of so great a change. In the present stage of human progress personal interest is undoubtedly one of the strongest incentives to industry, and to this motive the present system of competition appeals. And although Socialists declare that their system would not exclude competition, it is difficult to see what field it would have or at what point it would find its opportunity. Certain departments of industry are already in the hands of the State or of co-operative societies, but the organization of all industries and the management and remuneration of all labour demand a machinery so colossal that it is feared it would fall to pieces by its own weight. Still it is possible that ways and means of working a socialistic scheme may be devised; and it is quite certain that if any system could be devised which is really workable, and which should at once save us from the disastrous results of competition and yet evoke all the energy which competition evokes, that system would forthwith be adopted in every civilised country.

As yet, however, no such social system has been elaborated. General principles, ruling ideas, theories, paper plans, have been enunciated by the score; but, in point of fact, there is no system yet devised which appeals either to the common-sense and instincts of the masses, or which stands the criticism of experts. And some of those who have given greatest attention to social subjects, and have made the greatest personal sacrifices in behalf of the poor and down-trodden, are inclined to believe that no such system can be devised, and that deliverance from the present wretched state of matters is to be found, not in compulsory enactment, nor even in the sudden adoption of a different social system, but in the application of Christian principles to the working of the present competitive system. That is to say, they believe that true progress here, as elsewhere, begins in character, not in outward organization, or, as it has been put, that "the soul of improvement is the improvement of the soul." They consider that the present system rests on unchangeable laws of human nature, but that if men worked that system with consideration, unworldliness, and brotherly kindness, the present evil results would be avoided. Or they believe that it is at any rate useless to alter the present system violently by mere legislative enactment or by revolution, but that if it is to be altered, it can effectually, and permanently, and beneficially be so only under the pressure and at the dictation of an improved public opinion.

Appeal is confidently made to the mind of Christ by both parties, both by those who trust to the enforcement of a socialistic scheme, and by those who believe only in the social improvement which results from the improvement of the individual. By the one party it is confidently affirmed that were Jesus Christ now on earth He would be a communist, would aim at equalizing all classes and at commuting private property into a public fund. Communism has been tried to some extent in the Church. In monastic societies private property is surrendered for the good of the community, and this practice professes to find its sanction in the communism of the primitive Church. But the account we have of that communism shows that it was neither compulsory nor permanent. It was not compulsory, for Peter reminds Ananias that his property was his own, and that even after he had sold it he was at liberty to do what he pleased with the proceeds. And it was not permanent nor universal, for here we find that Paul had to ask contributions for the relief of the poor Christians of Jerusalem; while we see that there were rich and poor in the same congregations, and that such duties as almsgiving and hospitality, which could not be practised without private means, were enjoined upon Christians. It is also obvious that many of the duties inculcated in the Epistles of Paul could not be discharged in a society in which all classes were levelled.

It is perhaps of more importance to observe that in probably the most critical period of the world's history our Lord took no part in any political movement; nay, He counted it a temptation of the devil when He saw how much inducement there was to head some popular party and compete with kings or statesmen. He was no agitator, although He lived in an age abounding in abuses. And this limitation of His work was due to no superficial view of social movements nor to any mere shrinking from the rougher work of life, but to His perception that His own task was to touch what was deepest in man, and to lodge in human nature forces which ultimately would achieve all that was desirable. The cry of the poor against the oppressor was never louder than in His lifetime; slavery was universal: no country on earth enjoyed a free government. Yet our Lord most carefully abstained from following in the steps of a Judas the Gaulanite, and from intermeddling with social or State affairs. He came to found a kingdom, and that kingdom was to exist on earth, and was to be the ideal condition of mankind; but He trusted to move and mould society by regenerating the individual and by teaching men to seek in the first place not what "the Gentiles seek"—happy outward conditions—but the kingdom of God, the rule of God's Spirit in the heart, and the righteousness that comes of that. It was by the regeneration of individuals society was to be regenerated. The leaven which contact with Him imparted to the individual would touch and purify the whole social fabric.

In any case the duty of individual Christians is plain. Whether needless and unjust poverty is to be relieved by social revolution or by the happier and surer, if slower, method of leavening society with the spirit of Christ, it is the part of every Christian man to inform himself of the state of his fellow-citizens and to bring himself in some practically helpful way into connection with the wretchedness in the midst of which we are living. To shut our eyes to the squalor, and vice, and hopelessness which poverty too often brings, to seclude ourselves in our own comfortable homes and shut out all sounds and signs of misery, to "abhor the affliction of the afflicted," and practically to deny that it is better to visit the house of mourning than the house of feasting—this is simply to furnish proof that we know nothing of the spirit of Christ. We may find ourselves quite unable to rectify abuses on a large scale or to discern how poverty can be absolutely prevented, but we can do something to brighten some lives; we can consider those whose hard and bare lives make our comforts cheap; we can ask ourselves whether we are quite free from blood-guiltiness in using articles which are cheap to us because wrung out of underpaid and starving hands. It is true that anything we can do may be but a scratching of the surface, the lifting of a bucketful out of an overflowing flood which should be stopped at the source; still we must do what we can, and all knowledge of social facts and kindly feeling and action towards the oppressed are helpful, and on the way to a final settlement of our social condition. Let every Christian give his conscience fair play, let him ask himself what Christ would do in his circumstances, and this final settlement will not be long postponed. But so long as selfishness rules, so long as the world of men is like a pit full of loathsome creatures, each struggling to the top over the heads and crushed bodies of the rest, no scheme will alter or even disguise our infamy.

The method of collecting which Paul recommends was in all probability that which he himself practised. "Upon the first day of the week let every one of you lay by him in store, as God hath prospered him, that there be no gatherings when I come." This verse has sometimes been quoted as evidence that the Christians met for worship on Sundays as we do. Manifestly it shows nothing of the kind. It is proof that the first day of the week had a significance, *probably* as the day of our Lord's resurrection, possibly only for some trade reasons now unknown. It is expressly said that each was to lay up "by him"—that is, not in a public fund, but at home in his own purse—what he wished to give. But what is chiefly to be noticed is that Paul, who ordinarily is so free from preciseness and form, here enjoins the precise method in which the collection might best be made. That is to say, he believed in methodical giving. He knew the value of steady accumulation. He laid it on each man's conscience deliberately to say how much he would give. He wished no one to give in the dark. He did not carry out in the letter, even if he knew, the precept, "Let not thy right hand know what thy left hand doeth." He knew how men seem to themselves to be giving much more than they are if they do not keep an exact account of what they give, how some men shrink from knowing definitely the proportion they give away. And therefore he presents it as a duty we have each to discharge to determine what proportion we can give away, and if God prospers us and increases our incomes, to what extent we should increase our personal expenditure and to what extent use for charitable objects the additional gain.

The Epistle concludes with an overflowing expression of affection from Paul and his friends to the Church of Corinth; but suddenly in the midst of this there occur the startling words, "If any man love not the Lord Jesus Christ, let him be Anathema." "Anathema" means accursed. What induced Paul to insert these words just here, it is difficult to see. He had taken the manuscript out of the hand of Sosthenes and written the salutation with his own hand, and apparently still with his own hand adds this startling sentence. Probably his feeling was that all his lessons of charity and every other lesson he had been inculcating would be in vain without love to the Lord Jesus. All his own love for the Corinthians had sprung from this source; and he knew that their love for the Jews would prove hollow unless it too was animated by this same principle, They are serious words for us all—serious because our own hearts tell us they are just. If we do not love the Lord Jesus, what good thing can we love? If we do not love Him who is simply and only good, must there not be something accidental, superficial, unsafe, about our love for anything or any one besides? If we have not learned by loving Him to love all that is worthy, may we not justly fear that we are yet in danger of losing what life is meant to teach and to give? Trying to reach the truth about ourselves, do we find that we have attained to see and to love what is worthy? Can we say with something of Paul's conviction and joy, "Maranatha"—"The Lord is at hand"? Is it the true stay of our spirit that Christ rules, and will in His own time reconcile all things by His own spirit?

FOOTNOTES:

[1]   Comp. F. W. Robertson's *Lectures on Corinthians.*

[2]   Evans.

[3]   Godet.

[4]   Some account of the Jewish and other forms of excommunication is given in the *Encycl. Brit.*, art. Excommunication. Milman's *History of the Jews*, Book XIX., should also be consulted, and the *Pontificale Romanum.*

[5]   Godet.

[6]   See Mill's *Liberty*, p. 21.

[7]   See Landels' *True Glory of Woman.*

[8]   The experience of the Society of Friends throws light on this matter.

[9]   For a highly coloured description of the love-feasts see Renan's *St. Paul*, pp. 261-270.

[10] Möhler's *Symbolism*, i., 351.

[11] Waterland, *Works*, iv., p. 781.

[12]

"You stick a garden-plot with ordered twigs
To show inside lie germs of herbs unborn,
And check the careless step would spoil their birth;
But when herbs wave, the guardian twigs may go,
Since should ye doubt of virtues, question kinds.
It is no longer for old twigs ye look,
Which proved once underneath lay store of seed,
But to the herb's self, by what light ye boast,
For what fruit's signs are. This book's fruit is plain,
Nor miracles need prove it any more.
Doth the fruit show? Then miracles bade 'ware

At first of root and stem, saved both till now
From trampling ox, rough boar, and wanton goat."

[13] Godet.

[14] Professor Jones in *Essays in Philosophical Criticism.*

[15] See the passages in Wets ein and Schöttgen.

[16] Milligan, *The Resurrection of our Lord,* p. 150.